THE
Westminster Pulpit

VOLUME X

THE
Westminster
Pulpit

VOLUME X

The Preaching of
G. CAMPBELL MORGAN

WIPF & STOCK · Eugene, Oregon

Wipf and Stock Publishers
199 W 8th Ave, Suite 3
Eugene, OR 97401

The Westminster Pulpit vol. X
The Preaching of G. Campbell Morgan
By Morgan, G. Campbell
Copyright©1954 by Morgan, G. Campbell
ISBN 13: 978-1-60899-319-2
Publication date 1/15/2012
Previously published by Fleming H. Revell, Co., 1954

G. Campbell Morgan Reprint Series

Foreword

IF IT is true that the measure of a person's greatness is their influence, not only on his own time but on future generations, G. Campbell Morgan must be regarded as a great person. His greatness is seen not only in the wide impact of his ministry on both sides of the Atlantic, but in the fact that his books are still read and studied sixty-five years after his death. Named one of the ten greatest preachers of the twentieth-century by the contributing board of *Preaching* magazine, Morgan made the Bible a new and living book not only to the congregations who listened to him, but the vast multitude of persons who read his books.

Fox sixty-seven years Morgan preached and taught the Scriptures and served churches in England and the United States. What is remarkable is that his commentaries and expositions of the Bible still speak to persons of a new millennium. There have been many changes in the world since he faithfully preached and taught the Scriptures, but the wide appeal of his books testify to the timelessness of his message.

Although he held pastorates in the Congregational and Presbyterian denominations, he had an ecumenical appeal to persons of all denominations and traditions. The mystic

Thomas á Kempis once wrote, "He to whom the eternal word speaks is delivered from many opinions." In one of his sermons, he referred to the words of Amos that there would be a famine for hearing the word of God (Amos 8:11). The timeless work of G. Campbell Morgan addresses that hunger, as his books enable his readers to get beyond opinions to the living Word.

Wipf and Stock Publishers have rendered a great gift to the religious world in reprinting dozens of Morgan's books. This growing collection makes his books more available, so that readers have an option other than searching the internet for used, and often expensive, copies. Among this collection is the classic *The Great Physician* and commentaries on the Gospel of Matthew and John. Persons seeking a living faith and a meaningful encounter with God would profit from reading any of these Morgan books.

Near the end of his ministry, in a sermon entitled "But One Thing," Morgan commented on how Portugal changed the words of a coin after Christopher Columbus discovered America. No longer did the inscription say, *Ne Plus Ultra* (nothing more beyond) but *Plus Ultra* (more beyond). It is the hope of the G. Campbell Morgan Trust that the reprinting of these books will bring readers to the "more beyond," and an even deeper encounter with the Word in Scripture.

THE MORGAN TRUST
Richard L. Morgan
Howard C. Morgan
John C. Morgan

CONTENTS

CHAPTER		PAGE
I	Short Beds and Narrow Coverings	9
II	Wisdom: The False and the True	23
III	Conscience	37
IV	How Can a Man Walk with God?	49
V	How God Has Made Possible What He Requires	63
VI	Our Hope and Inheritance	77
VII	Individuality in Religion	91
VIII	How the Wall Is Built	103
IX	Regeneration	115
X	The Ethic and Evangel of Jesus	127
XI	The Conditions of Coming to God	139
XII	The Opportunity of Calamity	151
XIII	Preparing the Highway	163
XIV	Manifestations of the Risen Lord	175
XV	Led Out—Led In	188
XVI	The Fourfold Glory of the Church	201
XVII	We Have the Mind of Christ	213
XVIII	The Church's Debt to the World	226
XIX	Faith's Outlook	238
XX	The Fixed Heart in the Day of Frightfulness	250
XXI	"As an Eagle . . . the Lord . . . Did Lead."	263

CHAPTER		PAGE
XXII	THE ACCOMPLISHED MYSTERY	275
XXIII	THE WELL-DOING THAT BRINGS HARVEST	287
XXIV	THE SPELL WHICH JESUS CASTS ON MEN	298
XXV	THE SHOCK WHICH THE SPELL OF JESUS BRINGS TO THE SOUL	310
XXVI	THE FAITH THAT CANCELS FEAR	322
	TOPICAL INDEX	335
	TEXTUAL INDEX	347

THE
Westminster Pulpit

VOLUME X

CHAPTER I

SHORT BEDS AND NARROW COVERINGS

For the bed is shorter than that a man can stretch himself on it; and the covering narrower than that he can wrap himself in it.

ISAIAH 28:20.

THIS IS THE LANGUAGE OF A FINE SATIRE. AT THIS POINT THE prophet, burning in anger, indulged in sarcasm. It was caustic and severe, but behind it throbbed the great heart of the man who was carrying the burden of his people's sin and attempting to lead them from the folly of their unbelief and rebellion back again to allegiance to God.

To understand this text in its final application and in its perpetual meaning, we must consider the context. The prophet was addressing a people who had been created as a people by God, a people who had been familiar from childhood with the law and with the testimony. He was addressing a people, moreover, who owed all their material prosperity to Him. Yet, he was speaking to a people whose life in its underlying impulses and its perpetual mode was the life of godlessness. The greatest difficulty confronting the prophet as he delivered his message was not the mere fact of the godlessness of the people, but that of the form this godlessness had taken. It was that of self-satisfied contempt for all that he had to say concerning the claim of God and God's methods in judgment. Intellectually, these men had not abandoned belief in God, but, practically, they had abandoned the truth concerning God. They still believed in Him, but they did not believe in His immediate government.

The whole story of the prophet Isaiah, as it is revealed to us in this one book, is that of a man who spoke to an inattentive age or to an age which, if attentive, mocked him and refused to obey his message, until, as the prophetic period drew to a close, he inquired in anguish, "Who hath believed our report? and to whom hath the arm of the Lord been revealed?"

In this twenty-eighth chapter we have a tremendous and terrific utterance concerning the judgment of God; and as we read it carefully, we discover the interruptions of the mocking rulers. We hear the contemptuous speech of the men who listened to him but declined to believe the things he said. The prophetic message is always that of the government of God. Occasionally this man—who was a man of heart and a man of tears, a man who understood the suffering of the Divine heart, and foretold more perfectly than any other prophet of the old economy how, in the fulness of time, the suffering of the Divine heart would have its expression in the suffering Servant of God—occasionally this man broke out into denunciation, fierce and terrible; announced that God is not only the God of mercy, but also a God of judgment, in the sense of vengeance and punishment of sin. Every now and then, this man of tears became a man of thunder; this man—whose heartbeat seems as though it reverberated through the centuries until it found its perfect harmony with the heartbeat and the heartbreak of the Son of God—declared another side of the Divine nature; told men of God's "strange act" of judgment. Judgment as punishment is contrary to the Divine wish, but nevertheless part of the Divine will, that which God would never do, if man did not compel Him to the doing.

The answer of the men of that time is clearly brought out in the particular chapter in which our text occurs. These men taunted the prophet. A careful reading of the chapter shows that he repeated what they said. These are the words of the men who had heard his message, words uttered in regard to him, Isaiah; words that reveal their contempt for him: "*Whom will he teach knowledge? and whom will he make to understand the message? them that are weaned from the milk, and drawn from the breasts?*"

Then follows a revelation of what they objected to in his message, and the voice of their scorn is heard. They said, "*For it is precept upon precept, precept upon precept; line upon line, line upon line; here a little, there a little.*"

If I may interpret the attitude of these men by the language of our own days, they said, "This kind of preaching is out of date! Whom is he trying to teach knowledge? Let him talk to children! This halting method, of precept upon precept, of line upon line, of here a little and there a little, is of no use."

"Whom will he teach knowledge?" says the advanced age! "Whom does he imagine he can convince?" says the intellectual giant, who may be a moral leper. So the men of his day contemned the prophet. Then he told them of judgment. He thundered of the Divine government. They said, "We are not afraid! We have made a covenant with death! We have entered into a covenant with hell." Then the passion of the prophet blazed, and he said to them, ". . . Behold, I lay in Zion for a foundation a stone, a tried stone, a precious corner stone, a sure foundation: he that believeth shall not make haste." There shall be no fever, no fret, no fear, for that man! But beyond that, what? The scourge is also coming; the hail shall beat, the whirling flood shall sweep across, and "your covenant with death shall be disannulled, and your agreement with hell shall not stand; . . ."

Then it was that he said: "*For the bed is shorter than that a man can stretch himself on it; and the covering narrower than that he can wrap himself in it.*" In other words, I have told you of Divine government, I have announced the Divine judgment. You try to find rest by declaring that you have made an agreement with death, a covenant with hell. The bed is too short for you. You have never rested on it yet. The cold and biting windstorm will sweep upon you, and the covering will not keep you warm. You cannot rest on the beds you are making. You cannot hide in the covers in which you are attempting to wrap yourselves.

We are thus brought face to face with the principle that underlies the text. This age is very much like that age, but I am not proposing to make any wide application of this great message. I bring it down to its individual application, and I want to say two things, the first with all brevity, the second at greater length, and close with a return to the first.

The first thing I want to say is this: "Behold," said God through Isaiah, and says God to us today, "Behold, I lay in Zion for a foundation a stone, a tried stone, a precious corner stone, a sure foundation: he that believeth shall not make haste." That is the first thing. I say it briefly now. I will return to it in conclusion. The prophecy has become history. The prophetic foretelling has had its gracious and glorious fulfilment. Whereas the prophet spoke in the abstract of principles, at last in the fulness of time the abstract message was wrought out into concrete history, and there came to men God's Stone, a tried Stone, an elect, a precious Stone. We know the connection between the New Testament and this message. We know how in the New Testament we read of that Stone, as He Himself spoke to men, "He that falleth on this stone shall be broken to pieces; but on whomsoever it shall fall, it will scatter him as dust." The message of the prophet has become the fact of history, and there is rest for the heart of man in Him Whom God set forth to be a Propitiation for our sin, and not for our sins only, but for the sins of the whole world. Wherever a man is weary of sin, weary of sorrow, weary of self; wherever a man is feeling the pressure of life, and attempting to realize his manhood and failing, thank God for the Stone laid in Zion, elect and precious. You need not wait for an after-meeting. Believe as I preach. Before I get to the end of my sermon, if some tired broken man or woman will but fall on that stone, it will break him, but break to remake, and he will find God's rest, God's covering; presently, when the storms break and judgment begins,

> Bold shall he stand in that great day,
> For who aught to his charge shall lay?
> While by His blood absolved he is
> From sin's tremendous curse and shame.

But now, if we are not resting there, where are we resting? Of all other rests than that I say, "The bed is shorter than that a man can stretch himself on it; and the covering narrower than that he can wrap himself in it." Unless we have found rest for our souls in Jesus, we have found no rest. Unless we have taken refuge in Him, we have no covering that hides us. The first half of the figure refers to a present experience. The second half of the figure refers to an experience that must come to every soul of us—the final day, the day of assize, the day of inquisition, the day of wrath. The rest is that which men are seeking now. The refuge is that which they will need when the hailstorm sweeps, and the Divine judgments are abroad. In Jesus we may have rest today, and refuge forever. Out of Him there is no rest today, and there will be no refuge in the great and awful day of God.

Let us take the first of these matters. There is no rest for any man save on that cornerstone built in Zion, and yet men seem to be resting. What do we mean by rest? In the underlying deeps of our consciousness we know that this life is not all. I am not now going to argue with the man who doubts that assertion. I pray for him, for probably no argument of mine can convince him. I speak now to the rank and file, to the great mass of human souls. We know that this life is not all. We are also profoundly conscious that whatever else we may do, we cannot stay the moving wheels of time. You may smile at my folly when I tell you that once as a boy I remember wanting an hour longer for recreation. Seeking to obtain it, I stopped the clock! God help you to see that you smile at the folly of every man who imagines he can put back or delay the turning wheels of time. They bear us onward to a consummation. If we have fear in thinking of the end, then there is something wrong in our life. If, when a man speaks of death, you object, shall I tell you why? It is because sin is unforgiven. Christian men and women in the frailty of the flesh sometimes at the end shrink from death because of its mystery. Yet they look into the face of the rider on the pale horse, and with the dignity of an assured victory they say, "O death, where is thy victory? O death, where is thy sting?"

"The sting of death is sin." If we do not like the preacher to speak of death, it is because sin is not dealt with in our experience. We ought to look on toward the last day. Let us honestly face it. Presently these turning wheels will bring us to the end, to the margin of life, where burdens are laid down; will bring us to the confines, crossing over which, we go out into what has been spoken of as "that bourne from which no traveler returns." In view of that day, and in view of the fact of the spiritual nature of man, how are we resting? On what have we attempted to lay down our humanity, our soul, our personality, so that we are not affrighted when we think of the close?

I talk to men individually, and I find their answers to these questions are very different. One man says, I have no fear of God, or of the end, or the future, because my life has always been a moral life. That man is making a bed for himself of his own morality.

Another man says, I have no fear of the future, because I am a Christian by all the rites and ceremonies of Christianity, by all religious observances on the part of my parents, and on my own part. That man is making a bed of external religious observance.

I find another man who says, Well, ten years ago, fifteen years ago, twenty years ago, I yielded myself to Jesus Christ, and it is all right. That man is making a bed of worn-out experience.

I come to yet another man, and he says, I have no fear; God is a God of love, and God will never punish me, or let me suffer for my sin. That man is making a bed of a false doctrine of God, utterly unwarranted by the revelation which He has made of Himself to men.

Another man puts me aside when I attempt to speak to him, saying, Oh, don't talk to me. I know these things are important, but I have no time for them yet. That man is resting his soul on the unspoken conviction that there is time yet to be, when business will not press, and pleasure will not allure, and he will have inclination to deal with the things spiritual and eternal, and with God.

These are but samples. I say to you in the presence of every one of them, and of all similar ones, first, "The bed is shorter than that a man can stretch himself on it"; and, second, "The covering is narrower than that he can wrap himself in it." In other words, none of these things brings perfect rest to the soul of man; none of these things will be sufficient to enwrap and hide him in that awful day of wrath which must break forth against all wilful disobedience and rebellion and sin.

I say, in the first place, these things do not constitute beds on which men can rest. Take the man who says that he has no fear of God and of the future, because he has been a moral man. What is morality? Morality demands a standard. What is your standard? It would be ludicrous, if it were not tragic, to hear the answers that human beings will give to that inquiry. One man says, I have always paid my way; I have never defrauded anyone, or harmed anyone. These things are advanced as though they were of the essence of morality. We see at once what is the standard of that man's morality. It is the policeman. Here is a man in the image of God, with the very stamp and likeness of Divinity on his brow; and yet he talks as though everything that the universe can ask of him, and God Almighty demand of him, is that he escape the clutch of a human policeman, and that is supposed to be morality. Morality must have a standard, and the standard of true morality must come as a revelation from Him Who is God. He has given us a standard of morality. I do not choose for the moment to find it in the words of Jesus, simple and sublime and all inclusive as they are; I go back rather to the ten words written by the finger of God long ago for the government of human life, and I ask, Does our morality bear the test of that high standard? When men consent to measure their morality by that standard, they too often begin among the things of secondary importance. What is the first word, the fundamental word of morality. "Thou shalt have no other gods before Me." "Thou shalt love the Lord thy God with all thy heart, and with all thy soul, and with all thy mind." That is morality. The man who is simply moral enough to escape imprisonment, moral enough to maintain the respect of the crowd of people that live around him, because he never harmed them, is immoral—unless his life is crowned with worship, unless he realizes the highest thing in his being as his soul goes out in love and adoration to the God of all.

And we know it. There are moments when the consciousness surges upon us. There are moments when the whispering of the other world rings through our souls, when an infinite light such as never was on land or sea flashes on our consciousness; somewhere in the silence of the night, in the loneliness of the mountain; somewhere amid the more tragic loneliness of the crowded city, God breaks in upon our souls, and we think of the infinite distances, and spaces, and eternities, and tremble! Yes, the bed is too short for us to stretch on, and our souls find no rest on any morality in which we have made our boast.

Some there are who trust in religious observances. I find persons who say, I was baptized in my infancy; I was confirmed when I came to a certain age; I have regularly attended the sacrament; therefore I am a Christian. By no means therefore. To begin with, spiritual life is never generated by material action; the life of God is not communicated by the sprinkling of water, nor could be. It is a lie, of all lies the most dastardly, that tells a child that in baptism it was made the child of God and inheritor of the kingdom of heaven. We dare not, even at the risk of uttering things that sound controversial, consent to say nothing about that lie; for thousands of souls are being deluded by it; they are led to think of themselves as Christians, and yet the Christ-life has never touched them, and they are devoid of the love of God. The warrant of my assertion is not any formulated creed, but the Scriptures of truth, the revelation of God, in which it is said to men, not, Ye must be baptized into life by water, either more or less; but, "Ye must be born again." Any man who puts his trust in any ceremony such as this finds a bed on which he cannot stretch all his manhood, and finds, therefore, no perfect and positive rest.

I have known men and women who most surely on the day of confirmation were born again. Let us consider this. What did you promise on the day of confirmation? You took upon yourself vows that others, alas in their folly, had taken upon themselves for you long ago, and never fulfilled. You say that is a drastic statement. I challenge you to find me any godparent who ever fulfilled his vows. It cannot be done. I cannot do it for my own children, let alone the children of other people. But there came a day when you took these vows. What did you promise? You promised three things, in what you believed to be the presence of God's minister: you promised to renounce the world, the flesh, and the devil. Did you mean it? Did you do it? If so, that was repentance; and if in the doing of it, you yielded to Christ, then and there you were born again. But did you do it? Did you renounce the world? Did you renounce the flesh? Did you renounce the devil? If not, your bed is too short to stretch on. You cannot rest on a broken vow, can you? Instead of renouncing the flesh you have pampered and ministered to its constant, clamant cry. Instead of renouncing the devil, you have allowed the devil to lead you and drive you at his will. And yet you are a Christian, forsooth! No, a thousand times no! "For the bed is shorter than that a man can stretch himself on it." In the honest integrity of conviction, you know that on such a bed there is no rest; on such a false assumption there is no place for the soul's security.

But someone else will say, Ten years ago—fifteen, twenty—I gave myself to Christ, and I am all right. By no means necessarily so. The fact that Jesus saved me yesterday is in itself no use now. Unless I am able to link on to my past tense a present tense, then woe is me, for I am undone. The great apostle, writing his own biography in rapid sentences in the Philippian epistle, said, ". . . I count all things but loss . . ." That is what happened on the way to Damascus. Suppose that, having counted all things but dross, he had gone back and picked them up again and said they were precious; suppose sin had triumphed because he had gone back to the world and forsaken the things of Christ; suppose he had turned his back on the Christ and crucified Him afresh, and had counted the blood of the covenant an unholy thing, and done despite unto the spirit of grace, what then? Then, I tell you, his cleansing long years before would have been of no avail. But in that great chapter he said something else. "Yea, verily, and I count all things but loss . . ." The past is the present also. The attitude taken up long ago is maintained today. Jesus saved me on the Damascene road; Jesus saves me now.

I am afraid the Church of Jesus Christ is full of men and women who are living on a past experience; and they sing at rare or regular intervals, as their choice may be:

> Where is the blessedness I had
> When first I found the Lord?

Men and women sing that as though it were a sign of saintship. It is a sign that they have lost their saintship. The blessedness I had when first I found the Lord is with me yet;

but it is greater, mightier, and flows as a river instead of a rivulet. That should be the language of the soul. The bed is shorter than that a man can stretch himself on it. There is no rest in a past profession that is not merged into a perpetual possession.

Once again. Here is the man who tells me that he is trusting God, that he is casting himself on God, that God is too good to punish him. Oh, man, *God is too good to let you go unpunished!* There are men who if they passed into heaven as they are would turn it into hell. God writes on the portal of His home, "There shall in no wise enter into it anything unclean, or he that maketh an abomination and a lie." God is so good that He will not let anything that works abomination into His dwelling-place and home. If we will not accept the conditions of His heaven, in love to heaven, in love to truth, in love to the well-being of multitudes, He must shut us out, He must visit on us the vials of His wrath, the punishment we have positively and deliberately chosen.

If you can persuade me that God will allow a man to sin until character becomes sin, and then let him, the impure, into the land of light, then you will persuade me that God is unkind with an unkindness that is tragic and awful. His wrath flames in the passion of His love. The punishment that He visits on the sinner is the necessary outcome of the infinite compassion of His heart. "Be not deceived; God is not mocked; for whatsoever a man soweth, that shall he also reap."

Let me turn to the last illustration I used. A man tells me that there is time enough yet, that he has no time yet, that he is postponing these things to a more convenient season, that business presses and pleasures allure, but that some day, in a little while, he will attend to his religion. Oh, how often the messengers of the Cross have had to speak of the fatuous folly of this position. Long before the Christian light had fallen on men, the philosopher said to his students, "Gentlemen, the supreme thing is that we be ready to die." One of their number said, "That is true, and I propose to be ready." Asked the teacher, "When do you propose to prepare?" "Just before I die," came the flippant answer. Then the old man said, "And now, sir, have you fixed the date of your dying? Do you know when it will be? Seeing that you may die within a moment, this is the time to prepare for dying."

I grant you that the soul cast on God in the last extremity is mercifully saved for Jesus' sake; but when is the hour of your last extremity? Moreover, how do you know that when the passing comes, all the intellect will not have lost its power to think? God's time is the perpetual Now! Now is the accepted time, now is the day of salvation! There is not a man really at rest who is postponing the decision of infinite and eternal and important things. The bed is shorter than that a man can stretch himself on it.

Let us remember that the thing on which we are trying to rest we shall need as a refuge in the day that is coming. How will our morality hide us from the searching eyes of Him Who judges, not the external action, but the internal character? How will our religious observance cover us if it have not produced in us religious life? Will a profession of the long ago hide us from the eyes of Him if it have not continued, and if our life have not harmonized with it in all its process? How will our affirmation of the love of God stand us as refuge when, in love, to save others from the contamination of our pollution, He hurls us into the darkling void? How will our excuse as to time avail us when He will remind us that the one supreme and first business of life is the adjustment of the soul to Himself?

But thank God for the message of the prophet, who, ere he satirized the men who thought they had made an agreement with death, uttered these words: "Behold, I lay in Zion for a foundation a stone, a tried stone, a precious corner stone of sure foundation: he that believeth shall not make haste." He who rests there shall have no restlessness. He who takes refuge there shall know nothing of the fitful fever of the man who attempts to wrap himself in a narrow covering. That resting place is long enough, and broad enough, and strong enough, to rest the weary soul and give it perfect peace.

> Bold shall I stand in that great day

if I am arrayed in the robe that He brings to me, that righteousness of which Paul writes, which has been set forth as at the disposal of men by faith and unto faith.

Turn from your false rest, and come to the true; and you will find in God all that your soul is needing now, and all that it will need in the last unutterable day.

CHAPTER II

WISDOM: THE FALSE AND THE TRUE

But of Him are ye in Christ Jesus, Who was made unto us wisdom from God, and righteousness and sanctification, and redemption.
                                    I CORINTHIANS 1:30.

Christ Jesus, Who was made unto us wisdom from God, both righteousness and sanctification and redemption.
                                    A.V.

THIS LETTER OF PAUL WAS ADDRESSED TO "THE ECCLESIA OF God which is at Corinth." There can be no full or final interpretation of it, save as we understand the significance of that introductory description. I do not feel that the opening verse is so arresting to us as it must have been to those who dwelt in Corinth. The Greek citizen would have said: What does this mean? I know what the *ecclesia* of Corinth is; but I know nothing about the *ecclesia of God* in Corinth.

It is that distinction which is important. The ecclesia in Corinth was the municipal authority. Every Greek city had its ecclesia. The ecclesia—I hardly like to put it this way, and yet the modern phrase will certainly help us—was the town council. The ecclesia, moreover, was composed of free men. No slave could become a member thereof. It was a called-out company, governing the life of the city.

Now let us come back to the epistle itself. Paul here made use of a term which our Lord Himself had employed, the explanation of which was the peculiar stewardship especially committed to him. He was pre-eminently the apostle of the Church. His Gospel was supremely that of the Church. Wherever he went he planted churches. As men believed in Christ he gathered them into fellowship, and thus constituted an ecclesia. The ecclesia of God in Corinth, then, was God's authoritative fellowship in Corinth, the fellowship of souls in Christ gathered together in order that God's voice might be heard, God's authority be found, and God's will be made known. When Paul wrote to the Church at Corinth he was not at all anxious about ecclesiastical order merely for the sake of ecclesiastical order. He was anxious about ecclesiastical order and life for the sake of Corinth. It was in order that the city might be reached, that the city might have a true light, and a true love, and a true life; he was anxious that God's fellowship of governing souls therein might be in such right relationship with God that their testimony might be a testimony of truth, and a testimony of power.

The city of Corinth at that time was noted principally for its schools of philosophy, for its luxury, and for its lasciviousness. It was the day of decadent philosophy in the Greek life. Intellectually, in Corinth it was the hour of debates, discussions, divisions, disputes. Men ranged themselves around emphases into sects, and parties, and schools.

Moreover, at the time this letter came to it, Corinth was morally depraved. The standard of morality was at the very lowest. It was degenerate, wallowing in bestiality.

And, once again, Corinth at this time was religiously materialistic. Men had fastened their faith on the idols they had erected. Men were living in the atmosphere of a Sadducean philosophy, a rationalistic philosophy; and religion was devitalized because it had become materialistic.

Now, when we take up this letter to the Corinthians, we discover that all these things in Corinth had invaded the Church of God in Corinth. The Church, which had been placed in Corinth in order to interpret to Corinth the will of God, had been affected, influenced, demoralized by the forces of Corinth. The Church that should have invaded Corinth, strong in her own essential life and light and love, had been invaded by Corinth, and her testimony had been weakened. The Church was affected by the spirit of the times, and was weakened in her influence.

Our text occurs in that section of the letter which is devoted to the intellectual condition of the church, resulting from the fact that she had fallen under the influence of the intellectual condition of the city. Throughout this section the apostle puts two things in contrast: the "wisdom of words," and "the Word of the Cross." Corinth was the center of the wisdom of words. The philosophical discussions were discussions around words. This spirit had come into the church. Men had listened to the different emphases of Christian teachers, and, disputing around these, some had said: We are of Paul; others, We are of Apollos; and yet others, We go back to the true foundation; we are of Peter. Lastly, there were those who said—it is wonderful how these things continue through the centuries—You are all wrong if you name these names; we are of Christ only. Here we find the spirit of disputation invading the church, and Paul dealing with this wisdom of words, proclaimed anew the Logos of the Cross. In the course of his argument he claimed that this is the true wisdom; it is the wisdom of God.

To the Hebrew, the Cross was a stumbling-block, something across the pathway of Hebrew progress. That is what all the Hebrew disciples had felt—Peter, James, and John—when they had protested against the Cross.

To the Greek the Cross was unutterable foolishness, characterized by a lack of intellectuality. A cross, a Roman gibbet, and a crucified man, and some empty talk about resurrection—unutterable foolishness!

All this Paul admitted; but, continuing, he declared that to us who are being saved, to those who having heard the evangel, have yielded themselves to it; to those who are determined to test the evangel, not by their own inability to understand it, as the Greek, not by their own prejudices as to a Divine economy, as the Hebrew, but by yielding to its claims and seeing what result it produces in the lives of others—to such it is the power of God and the wisdom of God.

In that connection Paul made this great declaration: "Christ Jesus. Who was made unto us wisdom from God, both righteousness and sanctification, and redemption." The text is the summarized word concerning Christian wisdom made by this Christian apostle in a Greek city. He admits that it is foolishness to the Greek mind, but he emphatically claims that it is wisdom.

We observe, further, that the text falls between two passages which constitute a contrast. The apostle first declared that we are not to glory in the things in which the world glories. He finally declared that we are to glory in the Lord. Between the two declarations he utters this word of wisdom, and declares that Christ Jesus is the Wisdom, and therefore as men know Him and come into living relationship with Him they have, on the foundation of the profoundest philosophy and the most perfect wisdom, the true cause for glorying. Such is the argument of the apostle.

For a moment let us glance at our text quite technically. There is a difference of opinion among expositors as to whether the apostle here refers to four values when he says, "Of Him are ye in Christ Jesus, Who was made unto us wisdom from God; righteousness, sanctification, redemption"; or whether he names one, Wisdom, and then gives the qualities of that wisdom, Righteousness, Sanctification, Redemption. I am not going into any discussion on the point; but immediately assume the latter view, which I believe to be the true one, and that in our Revised Version we have a more illuminative translation than in the Authorized in this particular passage. But even this translation might be amended, so that the text should read: "Of Him are ye in Christ Jesus, Who was made unto us wisdom from God; *both* righteousness *and* sanctification *and* redemption." The apostle had said everything when he had written *wisdom*. What, then, is this wisdom? He immediately gives an analysis of it; *righteousness, sanctification, redemption.*

Now carefully observe—for this is most pertinent to our meditation—that if we take the text in this way, Wisdom as the one, Righteousness, Sanctification, and Redemption as the three in the one, we have matters that stand in immediate contrast to things already referred to.

God chose the *foolish* things of this world. What are they? The things of wisdom, that is, things of Christian wisdom, the foolish things of the world. God's wisdom is the Cross whereby Righteousness is made possible. God hath chosen the foolish things that He might put to shame the things that are wise, all the philosophies of men, which had not prevented Corinth becoming unutterably corrupt.

God hath chosen the *weak* things of the world. What are they? The things of righteousness, the things which in Corinth were held in supreme contempt as being weak: the things that men did not believe in, the things that men there did not take into account when arranging municipal or national affairs. Righteousness was at a discount, it was a weak thing. God hath chosen the weak things, that He might put to shame the things that are strong. All the things in which men had trusted for the realization of human life individually, and socially, and nationally God will put to shame by the way of the things the world counts weak, which is righteousness.

Yet again, "the *base* things of the world, and the things that are *despised*." What are they? The things of sanctification, the things of holiness, the things of separation to God, the things of the spirit life, which the world looks on as despised things, base things, things not to be taken into account. God has chosen them.

Finally, "and the things that *are not*." What are they? The things of redemption, as the word redemption is used in my text. The particular Greek word here used is one that signifies the ultimate in redemption: resurrection, the renewal of humanity, and the realization of full spiritual life in a realm beyond the material. The world says, These things are not. There is no life beyond. There is no resurrection. There is no spirituality which will ultimately triumph so that life shall be renewed in larger meaning, and for fuller purpose. The things that are not, God has chosen these.

Christ has come into the world to make known God's wisdom to men, and to carry out its purposes for men. God's wisdom is expressed in righteousness, in sanctification, and in the ultimate redemption and realization of human life. The foundation is righteousness, the process is sanctification, the ultimate goal is that of full and perfect redemption. The wisdom of God is a wisdom that deals with humanity in such a way as to be able to save it from corruption, to realize it, and to remake and glorify it. Therefore we will not glory in the philosophy of Corinth, which looks on the Cross of Jesus as foolishness; but we will glory in the Lord, through Whom God's wisdom is thus made manifest.

Let us pass over the text again in another way, taking the great words one by one. The word "wisdom" was the common word of Greek speech; but it is to be very carefully noted by the diligent student of Holy Scripture that this word is therein used only of God, or of good men, except where the sense is most evidently ironical. It is a word that stands for the highest thought in wisdom. It has reference to a clear intelligence, rather than to capacity for intelligence. It has reference to that insight and understanding which are essential and final wisdom. It is what the Greeks were seeking in all their discussions in the schools of Corinth. All their philosophies were attempts to be wise, to come to an ultimate knowledge of truth, to see things as they really are, and understand the deepest and profoundest secrets of life. Paul said that ultimate wisdom is not in man, it is in God; and he claimed that while men were disputing over the wisdom of words and looked on the Gospel as foolishness, while they looked in contempt on the Cross—in Christ and in his Cross the ultimate, final, clear, essential wisdom of God had found speech.

The test of Wisdom is that of the results produced; and the results produced by this Divine Wisdom may be expressed in these very words.

Righteousness. The word signifies in the New Testament, and from the pen of this Christian writer, perfect conformity to the Divine standard. Christ was that in Himself. He appeared in human history, One Whose whole human life was conformed to a Divine standard, to a Divine pattern; One, the keynote of Whose life had been struck in boyhood's years when He had stood in the courts of the Temple at

Jerusalem and said, "I must be in the things of My Father." From that moment to the last the music of His life had been true to that chord of the dominant; it was a life adjusted to God; it was righteous life. And yet righteousness meant far more than that in the case of Jesus, and in the case of all Christian writers. We may illuminate its meaning by going back again to the New Testament story, and listening to the second of the recorded words of Jesus. As He came up out of the waters of baptism, baptized by the last of the Hebrew prophets, the Spirit descended upon Him. As He passed into the waters He said to John, "Suffer it now: for thus it becometh us to fulfil all righteousness." That is one of the profoundest words, I reverently affirm, that ever passed His lips, a word not declaring that He was obeying a prophet, or keeping the law, but that He was fulfilling righteousness. How was He fulfilling righteousness? In that mystic baptism the Sinless was identifying Himself with sinning men and unveiling forevermore to the sons of men the fact that God's righteousness is not merely purity, integrity, but a passion of love that must find a way by which unrighteous souls may be made righteous. God's righteousness cannot be fully satisfied by the ninety and nine that need no repentance. It must go out after the one that is lost, and bring that one back again. God's righteousness can never find its ultimate expression in the vessels that were never marred in the hand of the potter; it can find its fulfilment only as it goes into the potter's field and gathers up the waste and broken materials, and makes them again conformable to Himself. Righteousness when we see it in Christ is far more than hard, cold, ethical accuracy; it is fire, passion, sacrifice to make failure a success, to uplift the fallen. There is ransom in it, redemption in it. Righteousness is not a pattern merely, but a potentiality; and a potentiality at the disposal of man through the infinite mystery of a passion and death that no man yet has fathomed.

The foolishness of all this to the Greek, and the foolishness of all this to the philosophy of the twentieth century, is self-evident. I am afraid that the philosophy of the twentieth century has so invaded the Church that there are people in the Church a little questioning, and inclined to think that it is all very foolish. Yet, I pray you, mark the wisdom of it in the long years. Admit all the failure of the centuries, recognize the sad fact that the Church of God has never yet come to the fulfilment of her own life, or of God's ideal for her; recognize it all, I say, and yet mark this fact, that through that Man of Nazareth, that central Person in human history, there has been flowing down the centuries, among all sorts and conditions of men, a new river of energy, which touching men, has made to live those who had been dead, remade those who had been ruined. Righteousness has been realized as the result of the work of the Christ.

This surely is "wisdom from God." That is not wisdom which merely erects its standard of life, and speaks of a high ideal, and gathers all who realize it into some select circle, while the flotsam and the jetsam are swept away to the sea of ruin. That is wisdom which fastens on the ruined and the spoiled, and remakes, remolds, revives, and gives back to humanity its lost sons and daughters, enabling them anew for life. Righteousness, then, is the first note of the Divine wisdom as an ideal and a dynamic.

Immediately following it, and expressing a process, we have the word *sanctification*, a word that signifies purification by separation to the will and service of God, a word that indicates the life as entirely at the disposal of God and harmonizing with God in His purity. This is the second fact in the mission of Christ. He was Himself sanctified, as He Himself did say; and He, taking hold of men, sanctifies them by putting them into that fellowship with God wherein they walk after Him and with Him, and rise into His life and into His light and into His love. Oh, soul of mine, the process is slow; I know it, not by observing others, but by living with myself! But however slow the process is, this also I know, that the passion for it is within the heart, and the aspiration of it is ever with the soul; and slowly, stumblingly, and, ah, me, shamefully, unworthily, we are yet growing up into Him Who is the Head, even Christ.

Redemption is the great word, a word signifying the final loosing of the life from everything which destroys it, the final loosing of humanity from all the things that break up and spoil. This word occurs only ten times in the New Testament. It is always used in connection with the thought of the ultimate victory. There is a sense in which a man is redeemed in the moment when he yields to Christ. There is a sense in which he will not find his full redemption until the work of God be perfected within him. That is the ultimate value. Given the righteousness which is in Christ, and the sanctification which is through Christ, the redemption by Christ is assured.

Let us take the thoughts and make them personal, particular, individual. What is righteousness? It is Christ imputed to me. No, my brethren, we cannot get away from that word! It is a great word, one that our fathers more often used than we do; but it is not the final word of Christian experience. When a man, not merely a sinner racially, but a sinner polluted and weakened by his own sin—such a man as knows sin in his own heart—when that man trusts himself to Christ he is not immediately conscious of the fulness of strength, for the habits of the Christian life have to be formed, just as evil habits had to be formed. Do not forget that. Here is a young man who gives himself to Christ, or a man far on in life, and he talks of the difficulty of being a Christian. Let such men remember that they have to form habits of Christian living as surely as they formed the habits that spoiled them. There is a growth into habit, and we must be patient in the process. Nevertheless, in the moment in which a soul casts itself on the unutterable mercy of God, in that moment Christ is imputed to that soul, and the spirit is immediately readmitted to fellowship with God. That is righteousness, Christ imputed to a man for the salvation of his spirit.

When, then, is sanctification? Not Christ imputed, but Christ imparted to the soul. Now we touch the realm of process and of development and of growth, the growing up in all things to Him Who is the Head, the growing in the grace and the knowledge of our Lord and Saviour Jesus Christ, the process of separation by which Christ is imparted to the life. This is the realm of slowness. This is the place where we mourn. It need not be so slow as it too often is. Do not let us excuse our slowness. I came across something in my reading recently, just a conversation between two people. One man said to his friend: "Well, you know, thank God, He knoweth our frame, He remembers that we are dust." "Yes," was the reply, "but we need not be any dustier than is necessary." We often quote a text like that, and then stay in the dust when we need not. But there is a necessary slowness in this process of sanctification as Christ is imparted. But slowness is not failure. The growth into Him is continuous. If we are Christian men and women we are growing more like Jesus—I will take the old, dear, sweet, ineffable name of the Nazarene—we are growing more like Him. Are we? There is no person more evangelical or orthodox in the universe than the devil! He holds no heresy, he knows all the truth. A man may know all the truth, and yet not be like his Lord. The thing that matters is that we should be actually growing up to Him in all things, that He should be imparted to us, that we look with His eyes, and become like Him, love-mastered, and light-illuminated souls. That is wisdom surely, God's wisdom in Christ, bringing men into conformity with Him Who was perfectly conformed to God; and so having them realize their own humanity.

Then shall come the hour, the final hour. How shall I speak of it, that final experience when Christ shall be not merely imputed as righteousness, or imparted as sanctification, but implanted as redemption? That is the hour to which the seer looked forward when he said: "Beloved, now are we children of God, and it is not yet made manifest what we shall be. We know that, if He shall be manifested, we shall be like Him." That is the hour to which the psalmist of the old economy looked forward, not so intelligently perhaps, but with equal glory of expression, when he said: "I shall be satisfied, when I awake, with Thy likeness." Perfect redemption!

The Greek philosophers were unequal to producing these effects in human lives; and there came into Corinth an apostle of the Gospel, and he preached, and a few souls believed, and the process commenced. In their Church fellowship these souls became the new regenerative center for Corinth, if Corinth would but hear and obey. This is wisdom on the highest level, because it is not the wisdom of an idea that vaporizes, it is the wisdom of a truth that energizes, and, touching life, heals it and helps it.

We do not wonder that the apostle said: "He that glorieth, let him glory in the Lord." Christ is the Wisdom of God, and all earthly wisdom is but foolishness. The philosophies of men are vain when we come into the presence of corruption and sin, and the undoing of humanity! But when He comes, lo! the desert blossoms as the rose, the marred vessel is made again, and I, even I, withered, paralyzed, darkened in the mind, groveling in the dust, even I begin to breathe, live, hope, aspire, and climb. We glory in the Lord!

Christ is the Righteousness of God. All earthly strength and power will pass and perish. Man is unequal to the maintenance of himself, or of those relationships which make for permanence. This righteousness will take hold on the individual man, and will remake him as within himself, setting back into true proportion and balance his complex nature of spirit, mind, and body, until at last he himself shall be a veritable kingdom of God. By the multiplying of the number of such grows the Kingdom of God. We glory in the Lord!

Christ is the Sanctification of God. All earthly values fail, the things that the world counts of worth. The honored and the noble things of men are base and mean. It is true that the honored and the noble things of God are base and mean in the view of the worldly philosopher; but yet we know that at last purity will abide. We glory in the Lord!

Christ is the Redemption of God. All earthly hopes are doomed. The goals of men are but mirage. The final realization of the spiritual purpose, and the beatification of humanity in the Kingdom of God, this is the hope that burneth like a beacon and flasheth in perpetual glory. It is in the presence of this that we lift up the heart, and are assured. We glory in the Lord!

Our glorying in the Lord is vain save as we are abandoned to Him in will, and so co-operate with Him in power. Our position is sure. Our promise is certain. If we have believed in Him we are responsible only for the process. We shall demonstrate to our intellectual satisfaction the wisdom of the Gospel of the Cross only as we yield ourselves to its claim. In proportion as we do that it will produce in us the effects that demonstrate its infinite and abiding wisdom.

Let us, then, submit ourselves to that indwelling Spirit Who carried forward the process, and go forth, for our own lives, and for all our social outlook, and our racial hope, to glory in the Lord, Who is the Wisdom of God, "both righteousness and sanctification and redemption."

CHAPTER III

CONSCIENCE

TO-NIGHT I HAVE NO TEXT. IF ANYONE IS SUFFICIENTLY UNDER the power of tradition to feel that a text is necessary, then either of the twenty-nine verses in the New Testament in which the word "conscience" is found will serve, for conscience is my theme.

Conscience is that at which some men mock, and if we could but know the truth, while they mock they feel the power of it in their own souls. Conscience is that in deference to which some men to-day in England are suffering imprisonment rather than disobey the dictates for which they are prepared to die.

The power of conscience has been recognized by philosophers, poets, prophets, and all great leaders of human thought. Shakespeare expresses it in the words of Hamlet:

> ... the dread of something after death,
> The undiscover'd country, from whose bourne
> No traveller returns, puzzles the will
> And makes us rather bear those ills we have
> Than fly to others that we know not of.
> Thus conscience does make cowards of us all;
> And thus the native hue of resolution
> Is sicklied o'er with the pale cast of thought

Crabbe, in his *Struggles of Conscience*, has these lines:

> Oh Conscience! Conscience, man's most faithful friend,
>   Him canst thou comfort, ease, relieve, defend;
> But if he will thy friendly checks forego,
>   Thou art, Oh! woe for me, his deadliest foe!

Sterne, in *Tristam Shandy*, says:

> Trust that man in nothing who has not a conscience in everything.

George Washington, in his *Moral Maxims*, wrote:

> Labor to keep alive in your breast that little spark of celestial fire, called conscience.

Or once again, and perhaps in the whole realm of literature nothing is found more remarkable than the words of Byron:

> Yet still there whispers the small voice within,
>   Heard through gain's silence, and o'er glory's din;
> Whatever creed be taught, or land be trod,
>   Man's conscience is the oracle of God.

What, then, is conscience? What is its value? What part does it play in life? How much heed ought we to pay to it? These and many other related questions are being forced upon us in this strange hour in which many things we have held as sacred are being postponed to a more convenient season. It goes without saying that in this pulpit, if we discuss the theme, it is in order that we may seek the Biblical light thereupon; and to that I may add that our discussion will be concerned with the truth itself rather than with any application thereof.

As to the Biblical light, I shall begin by making some general statements. First, the word "conscience" is not found in the Old Testament; but the literature is full of the story of the operations of conscience in the human soul. Every record of a moral heroism is the answer of man to the call of his conscience. Every manifestation of immoral anger is produced by the activity of conscience. All the sobs of the penitent, and all the songs of the forgiven, are inspired by the working of conscience.

The word is found in the New Testament. Presently we shall discuss it. For the moment let us note some general things concerning its use there. According to the New Testament, conscience "bears witness," "gives testimony," produces action, for things are done "for conscience' sake." In the New Testament conscience is described as "good," as "void of offense," as "pure," as "toward God." But conscience is also described in the New Testament as "weak," as "seared," or, more literally, branded with a hot iron; as "defiled," as "evil." Finally, the New Testament declares that conscience can be "cleansed."

There is no clear-cut definition of conscience in the Bible. Perhaps the passages which come nearest to definition are two. The first is to be found in the Old Testament: "The spirit of man is the lamp of the Lord searching all the inward parts of the belly." In the New Testament the passage which always seems to me to come nearest to a definition of conscience occurs in the prologue to the Gospel of John: "The true light, . . . which lighteth every man." The spirit of man has many qualities, many quantities, many capacities, many activities. Among the rest it is in itself the lamp of the Lord. A light shines in every man.

Let us, then, consider, first, conscience in itself; second, conscience as to its place and power in personality; third and finally, conscience as to its place and power in society.

Our word "conscience" is almost a transliteration of the Latin word from which it is derived, *conscientia*, which means simply, knowledge with.

That definition, which is perfectly accurate, and perfectly justified, and beyond which, in some senses, we shall not be able to go, leaves us asking questions. The suggestion of the word is evidently agreement. Necessarily, the next question is, Knowledge with whom or with what? Recently, a writer on conscience said: "The original connotation of the word implies a common agreement, a social idea shared by the community." Is that so? I think not. There is absolutely nothing in the history of the word to warrant the impression that conscience means a social idea shared by the community, and there is certainly nothing in Biblical use to warrant it. Conscience is ever referred to in a peculiarly individualistic sense; it is personal, it is lonely.

Therefore we ask again, What is the suggestion of the word? If it be individual, if it be personal, if it be lonely, how can it be knowledge or conviction *with?* The answer is that the agreement suggested is agreement between a man's understanding and the fact that he understands. Certain standards are postulated, use what terms you will to describe them. Speak with the old philosophers of the reason, the idea, the essential and eternal truth; or speak in the language of religion, of the law, of ethics, of truth—conscience is the sense of the soul that apprehends those things. The knowledge is true, whether I apprehend it or not; but when I apprehend it, that is conscience.

In process of time the word has been reserved for the moral realm, so that to-day almost invariably we draw a distinction between conscience and consciousness. Conscience is the recognition of good and bad, the distinction between right and wrong, a distinction created, not by laws written outside the man which govern his life, but by the inherent sense of his soul in the presence of these things.

But conscience in the Biblical sense is far more than that.

Normally, conscience is always a warning against the bad and an urging toward the good. Conscience is that activity of the human soul which recognizes the difference between goodness and badness, which makes the distinction quite clearly to the soul itself, and which then inevitably urges the soul toward goodness, and warns the soul from badness.

Of the actual New Testament word, our word "conscience" is in every sense so trustworthy and accurate a translation that I need simply stay to remind you what that word is, and of the slight difference, which finally is no difference at all. It means seeing with; that is co-perception. Again, we have the supposition of agreement, and it always has a moral value, and the moral value is exactly the same as that to which we have been referring. So much for the words themselves as to their meaning and their use.

Now as to the fact. Conscience is an activity of the human spirit in the moral realm, and normally it is wholly beneficent. Conscience is that within the soul of man which reveals goodness as goodness, which reveals badness as badness. Conscience is that which calls things by their right name, refuses to allow any evil thing to be rebaptized by a name that robs it of its real meaning and significance. Conscience will call a lie a lie, and will not allow a man to escape by applying to it the high sounding name of hyperbole. Conscience cannot prevent a man saying the untrue thing, but it will trouble him. It cannot prevent him saying it, but it does prevent him thinking it. No liar escapes that voice. He can become so accustomed to it as to laugh at it. That is the ultimate tragedy. Nevertheless, conscience persists. It is always unveiling the truth, always unmasking a lie, forever warning the soul against the wrong of wrong and the peril of wrong. That is the terror of conscience. But it is always luring the soul toward the high and the noble and the true, always inspiring the soul to follow the light, to follow the gleam, to obey the truth. That is the hope of conscience.

Conscience is an activity inherent in man by Divine creation, and active under Divine activity. This is the Biblical teaching from first to last, in both the Old Testament, in which the word is never found, though the idea prevails; and in the New Testament, in which the word occurs, and the idea is even more powerful. God never leaves a man alone in this world. That may be challenged, I know. Well, then, if it be true, as some theologians have taught, that there is a line over which a man may pass in this world and leave hope behind; if it be true that a man can in this life, and before this probationary state ends, cross such a border line and be as hopelessly lost as though he had reached the darkling void where God is not; if that be true—I do not admit it—but if it be true, then remember that a man so abandoned of God has no conscience, he has no trouble about his sin, no pain of heart in the presence of it, no sense of the badness of badness. That agony of soul that is almost despair, when alone a man thinks of sin, is the touch of God in infinite mercy on the man's soul. That is conscience. Conscience is infinitely more, and I am inclined to say infinitely other than a moral sentinel threatening a man with damnation. It will do that also. But why? In order to turn a man back from the darkness toward which he is proceeding. The severer the voice of conscience, the more terrific its appeal; the more poignant the agony of soul, the surer the evidence of the unfathomable and unutterable love of God. The very agony of conscience is a call of love.

Therefore conscience is a capacity to create responsibility. Its warnings must be heeded, its promptings must be obeyed, or it will become weakened, it will not act with the readiness it once did; it will become seared as if branded with a hot iron; be insensitive to every movement in the spiritual world; it will be defiled, until, at last, it is made utterly evil. Only as men obey conscience can they escape from the perils suggested by these words of the New Testament.

Now as to the place and power of conscience in personality. All I have already been saying is pertinent at this point. Conscience exists in every human being, and originally it is good, pure, without offense, God-governed. Take a child naturally. I mean any child: that little child born in the slum, born in the East End slum, with all its squalor and its filth, where the street is the only playground; or born in the West End slum, which is all veneer and false refinement and godlessness—wherever a child is born, in that child spiritually the conscience is good, pure, without offense, God-governed.

The first exercise of conscience, of the normal conscience, is witnessing. It is that activity within the soul which is wholly personal. Yet the soul knows that, somehow, it is other than personal. Have you never sat down in the presence of some temptation, opportunity, duty, responsibility, and talked to yourself? Oh, no, I am not speaking now of that muttering aloud which is a sign of old age creeping on. I am thinking of something far profounder, of the moment when you think all by yourself, and you first say, Yes, that thing is wrong; and then you say, I do not really see that it is wrong. Then, still alone, you argue with yourself. That is conscience, it is you. Ah, but "the spirit of a man is the lamp of the Lord"; that is also God, God dealing with you. That is the first activity of conscience, witnessing to the difference between good and bad, and always urging the soul toward the right, and warning the soul from the wrong. Later on, when we have disobeyed the voice, when we have not followed the gleam, when we have refused to walk in the light, when knowing the good we have chosen the bad, then conscience still witnesses within the soul, still emphasizes the difference, but now the supreme note of conscience is the condemnation of the wrong done. That is the haunting of conscience. The fame of Jesus spread over Galilee and Judæa, and there was a man on a throne who said, It is John, whom I beheaded, risen from the dead! What was the matter with that man? He was an Idumean; he was a Sadducee; he did not believe in resurrection. Ah, did he not? Conscience never let him escape from the wrong he had done, never allowed him to dodge the truth, that in a drunken debauch, to please a wanton woman, he had violated conscience. Conscience violated, wronged, battered, kept on; and when he heard that there was another voice sounding he said, It is John whom I beheaded, risen from the dead. That is a wholly beneficent activity, that is still God in the soul; and had Herod repented, Herod had been ransomed and redeemed. Conscience is always calling men back. Consequently, the first human responsibility in the matter of conscience is obedience, immediate, utter, and at all costs.

Yet there is another phase of responsibility. It is not enough that I shall obey my conscience; I must constantly seek the correction and readjustment of my conscience. Conscience may be weakened, conscience may be seared, conscience may be defiled, conscience may have become permeated and saturated with evil. Hence the necessity for the perpetual correction and readjustment of conscience. I must seek the light which comes from God Himself, in order that I may know whether the light that is in me—to use the marvelous words of Jesus—be darkness or not. Conscience may be out of gear, may lead a man astray. Who shall correct it? Not you, not I; no human being can do it; God alone is able to do it. I well remember once crossing the Atlantic without a gleam of sunshine from the first moment to the last. As we were nearing New York the captain said to me, "We have been going by dead reckoning, and we are a little out of our course. We have had no sun, and all our mathematical precision breaks down unless the sun shines." That is the whole point. Suppose you come late to business, my dear young friend, and the person in charge of your work says, "You are late." You reply, "You will excuse me; I am not late, it wants a minute to nine." The sharp reply is, "Your watch is wrong." Ah, yes, you must readjust your watch by Big Ben. Is that enough? No, Big Ben must be readjusted from Greenwich. Is that enough? It is if you remember that Greenwich is governed by the sun. Your conscience may get out of gear, it may be wrong. This is a most solemn consideration that every man ought to face in this particular hour. Your conscience may be misleading you. It may need readjustment, correction. That readjustment is a solemn responsibility. Prejudice must be denied. Pride must be impossible. Persistently, with regularity, sincerity, and determination, conscience must be remitted to the Son, to the essential Light, to the Light beyond which there is no light, to the Authority beyond which there is no authority, to the God Who is good, and from Whom the spirit of man proceeds. That spirit which is His candle must be held in His light, that a man may know whether or not his conscience is leading him astray. That is the human responsibility for conscience.

And so, finally, what is the place and power of conscience in society? If all consciences were normal, that is, good, pure, without offense, God-governed, there would be no difficulty in the matter of conscience. The conscience of each would be the conscience of all, and life would be a perfect harmony; and that is what will be when God has finished His work with the race and completed His victory. But it is not so to-day. There are seared, defiled, evil consciences in the world. There are also weak consciences, and these are in the majority. Weak consciences are such as are not clear in their apprehension of good and evil; they are not quick to discern. Weak consciences are not keen of scent in the fear of the Lord; they are not quick of understanding in the fear of the Lord. Here is the cause of conflict and difficulty in the realm of conscience. Here is a man whose conscience says to him, I am bound to-day to enlist and fight. Here is a man who says, My understanding of the will of Jesus is that I cannot do it. Who is to judge? I declare to you that you cannot, and you have no right to do so. I declare to the man who says that his conscience forbids his fighting that he has no business to impose that conviction on the man who says that he must fight; and I declare to the man who feels the tremendous obligation of the present hour—there are multitudes of them, men whom we honor in proportion as they are true men—must respect the man who cannot share his conviction. There can be no judgment. "Judge not, that ye be not judged. For with what judgment ye judge, ye shall be judged." That is a very solemn and searching word. This whole Biblical conception of conscience teaches us, first, that there must be respect for the individual conscience; and, further, that no attempt must be made to impose the law of personal conscience on other men.

However, every man who takes his stand on conscience should, at least, have the ability to give a reason for the faith that inspires him. Even though he may not be able to persuade another, even though he have no right to try to compel another to stand where he stands, surely he should be able to give a reason for the faith that is in him. During the period of stress—I do not mean this war now, I mean all life as we know it—the period of human imperfection, the period during which the temporary and imperfect expedient of government by majority is in force, during that time, minorities are to be respected. If history teaches anything, it teaches that over and over again it has been proved that the minority was right, and not the majority. I give it you as a personal conviction that in every commission that has considered a great question, from the time when the commission sat in the days of Joshua to decide whether they should obey God or not, the minority report has been the correct one, and not the majority. The majority said, There is the land, it is a great and wonderful land, but we cannot take it; there are giants and walled cities! That was the majority report. The minority said, We see the giants, and the walled cities, but we see God. I come right down from then until the very latest Royal Commission that comes to my mind, the commission on Divorce, and it is the same story of the rightness of minorities. At least, that should give us pause. It is a great thing when the multitude is right, but I am never going to be persuaded that anything is right because the multitude says it is. There must be in the heart of men who believe in this Biblical revelation a respect for minorities.

In any such consideration, however, the conclusion must be on the individual note. For every man the last stand of life is his personal conscience, that conscience being cleansed and void of offense. If taking that stand shall bring that man into the place of suffering, then let him suffer. A man who for conscience' sake suffers and whimpers, calls in question the reality of his conscience. "For this is acceptable, if for conscience toward God a man . . . suffereth wrongfully." Let the man who suffers for conscience know that in all probability the whole conception of the Bible bearing witness, and all human experience bearing testimony, his suffering is winning a victory for the principle for which he suffers.

So whether this way or that way we may be doubtful at the moment as to what the path of duty is, one thing only matters—that every man shall be fully persuaded in his own mind as he stands before God. So may He Who cleanses human conscience give to us the conscience which is good and pure and void of offense, so that having done all things, we may stand.

CHAPTER IV

HOW CAN A MAN WALK WITH GOD?

Shall two walk together, except they have agreed?
—AMOS 3:3.

THE SERMON TONIGHT IS A SEQUEL TO THAT OF LAST SUNDAY evening, and the text is a starting point. In that sermon we considered what God requires of a man as that requirement is revealed in the message of Micah: "He hath shewed thee, O man, what is good; and what doth the Lord require of thee, but to do justly, and to love mercy, and to walk humbly with thy God?" The Divine requirement, then, is to walk humbly with God, loving mercy and doing justice.

The text this evening, taken from the prophecy of Amos, is the first of a series of seven questions which the prophet asked in order to illustrate the relation between cause and effect, each of them showing that an effect demands and demonstrates a cause. These are the questions:

Shall two walk together, except they have agreed?
Will a lion roar in the forest, when he hath no prey?
Will a young lion cry out of his den, if he have taken nothing?
Can a bird fall in a snare upon the earth, where no gin is set for him?
Shall a snare spring up from the ground, and have taken nothing at all?

Shall the trumpet be blown in a city, and the people not be afraid?

Shall evil befall a city, and the Lord hath not done it?

The force of the illustrations may thus be summarized. Communion proves agreement. If you see two people walking together you know they have agreed. The lion roaring demonstrates the prey. Do not forget that Amos was a shepherd from Tekoa, a man used to the desert and the hills, to vineyards and to sheep, living the agricultural life of the time; and almost all his illustrations have that desert background. He was accustomed to the sound of the roaring of the lion, and so he says, I know when I hear the lion roaring that the prey is in sight; the cry of the young lion proves that the prey is caught, possessed; the fall of a bird into the snare proves the setting of the gin; the spring of the snare proves that the bird is taken, the trumpet in the city proves the alarm of the city; calamity in the city proves that God is acting.

The purpose of the prophet was to vindicate the authority of his own message. He went on to declare that his prophecy proved that the Lord had spoken to him. Let me say immediately that with that application of my text I have nothing more to do. As I have said, the text is a starting point.

We begin by admitting the principle: an effect proves a cause. Two people walking together proves that they met, that they agreed ere they started. Consequently, the text is intended to show that you cannot have an effect without a cause; you cannot have two people walking together unless, in the sense of the text, they have agreed. If we change our text from the interrogatory form we may read it thus: Two who walk together must have agreed. Therefore, we may once again change its form and get at that phase of the truth that we desire now to emphasize, as we read it thus: Two must agree if they are to walk together. "He hath shewed thee, O man, what is good; and what doth the Lord require of thee, but to do justly, and to love mercy, and to walk humbly with thy God?" The Lord hath shewed thee what is good; to humbly walk with thy God. "Shall two walk together, except they have agreed?" God and a man must agree if they are to walk together.

That brings us to our special theme. Granted that God requires of a man that He should walk with Him, we inquire, How can a man walk with God? How is the necessary agreement out of which such walk proceeds to be insured?

Eliphaz, that wonderful old Easterner, gave Job the highest and best advice when he said: "Acquaint now thyself with Him, and be at peace"; but Job's answer was very pertinent, coming out of human experience: "O that I knew where I might find Him." Our business for this evening, then, is to investigate what is necessary if a man is to begin to walk with God, and to continue to walk with God.

In attempting to answer these inquiries, How can a man walk with God? How can agreement be insured? I will, first of all, consider this conception in itself a little more fully, that of walking with God; and, second, I propose to deal with the condition which is revealed in the question, agreement between God and a man if they are to walk together.

With the general conception we need not tarry for very many minutes. The thought is persistent in the Biblical literature. It emerges in that radiantly beautiful and comprehensively final biography, one of the greatest biographies in all the Old Testament literature, found in that apparently most uninteresting chapter in Genesis, the fifth chapter, the chapter of the long names, and the perpetual, monotonous tolling of the knell of death. Right in the heart of the chapter is the briefest and most inclusive biography, "Enoch walked with God; and he was not; for God took him." That is all we know about Enoch, and there is more in it than we shall discover, even if we give all the remainder of our life to careful thought on the subject. There the phrase emerges in Biblical literature. It often recurs in the apostolic writings, especially in the writings of Paul, who was constantly thinking of life as a walk with God. It finds its fullest and richest interpretation and expression in the life of Jesus of Nazareth, that being a theme with which I am not going to deal at any length; but we will come back to it, God willing, on a subsequent occasion. While we need not tarry long with the conception, there are some of the fundamental suggestions of the phrase of which we do well to remind ourselves. Let us first take the words *walk together*, and consider them. The word walk is perfectly simple, yet it is full of suggestiveness. Walking implicates life, volition, effort, direction. Apart from life, there is no walking, and there can be no walking which is not preceded by volition. We have never walked anywhere without willing so to do. Although we may not wish to go, we will ere we do so. Walking is the simplest exercise; there seems to be nothing in it—until we have ceased to do it for three months and then try again, when we find there is much in it! Walking implies effort. It always means direction. We walk toward somewhere. Even if you walk in a circle, you are ever going round toward the starting point. These are simple things, but they are fundamental to our meditation.

The word "together" is a more arresting word, quite simple, quite common, yet here almost startling. Literally, it means, as a unit. I might read my text like this: How shall two walk as a unit, except they have agreed? That is the root meaning, and the use of the word shows that it suggests a walk of perfect unity in all the fullest, deepest senses of the word. The question which the prophet asked was not, How can people walk together in an occasional or casual way, except they have agreed? Even in such cases there must be a measure of agreement; but if there is to be continual walking, perpetual walking, consistent walking together, there must be agreement which is profound and deep. This word "together" will help us to understand the word agreement presently. It is to walk as a unit, two persons to walk as though they were one.

What, then, is the conception? We all recognize that this is a figure of speech. What is the fact for which the figure stands? What is it that we intend to suggest, that Micah intended when he spoke about walking with God, that the Old Testament historian intended to suggest when he declared that Enoch walked with God, that the New Testament writers intended to suggest when they declared that we were to walk with God? What is the fact suggested by the figure? The conception is of God and a man moving together as a unit, in perfect time and perfect rhythm. Two lives, the life of God and the life of a man, united in volition, willing the same thing; united in effort, putting out strength toward the same end; united in direction, moving toward the same ultimate goal. A man walking together with God is a man willing one will with God, working one work with God, journeying toward one goal with God.

Therefore—for the moment leaving out of thought the Divine save as it influences the human—it is the picture of a man going toward the Divine destination, but it is infinitely more than that. It is a picture of a man moving toward the Divine destination along the Divine pathway, not choosing his own way to reach the ultimate goal, but marching along the pathway on which God Himself is marching. It is a picture of a man moving toward the Divine destination along the way of the Divine procedure in the power of the Divine fellowship. Therefore it is a picture of God and a man having identity of interest, having combination of resources, having fellowship of effort; God and a man having identity of interests, the master passion of the man that which is the master motive of all the Divine activity; God and a man having a combination of resources. Let me use the word that is haunting me, and which I want to use—and I halt only because it seems almost irreverent, and yet I trust it will not be so—God and a man *pooling* resources. We have become used to that phrase in recent days as we heard of three great nations pooling resources in order to reach one great issue. God and a man pooling resources! God bringing in all His infinite resources and placing them at the disposal of a man with whom He walks! That is the amazing thing. Never forget that if that is an amazing thing, there lies within it the claim that man shall place all his resources at the disposal of the God Who walks with him. Again, God and a man having fellowship in effort. This is a value full of wonder. A man making his effort with God; God making His effort, toward the ultimate goal, with a man.

One other thing is suggested, the last I am going to mention. The figure suggests finally mutual humility. The necessary humility of God, necessary, or He never could accommodate His goings to a man's slow footsteps; the necessary humility of man, necessary, or a man could never hope to keep pace with God. "Walk humbly with thy God" was the word of the text last Sunday evening. From the New Testament, in its most stupendous passage in some ways, comes this great word, "He humbled Himself, becoming obedient even unto death, yea, the death of the Cross." It may be that if I were discussing mutual friendship with a man I might not emphasize this so strongly, yet even in human friendship there must be mutual humility. If I am to walk far along life's pathway with you, my friend, my comrade, there must be humility in my heart and in yours. The very simplicity of the figure enables us to see that this must be so in the case of God and a man, God stooping, humbling Himself, accommodating His steps to the faltering, trembling walking of a man; a man humbling his spirit in order that he may walk with God along the pathway.

So we pass to the second matter, which, after all, is the supreme one in our present consideration. In order that there may be this walking together with God there must be agreement. Let us try to understand this condition.

The root idea of the Hebrew word is *to fix upon* by agreement or appointment. The marginal reading in the Revised Version runs: "Shall two walk together, except they have made an appointment?" I believe it was Dr. George Adam Smith who translated it, "Shall two walk together, except they have kept tryst?" That helps us, but it is altogether too narrow, it does not include enough. The idea of agreement is infinitely more than that of meeting at a certain point; it is that, but it is infinitely more. I take this word and trace it through the Old Testament, and see in what different ways it is used. It includes far more than our word "agreement." It is translated, to meet; that is what the margin suggests, to meet at a stated, fixed, time or place. We never use our word "agreement" in that sense. If I were going to make an appointment with you for tomorrow, using this word in this sense, I might say, We will agree at the British Museum at twelve o'clock. That would be in harmony with one Hebrew use of the word. It includes the place appointed, and the time fixed, and the fact of meeting there. The same word is used to indicate a summons in a legal sense to a fixed tribunal, and the thought is that of a judge who meets at an appointed place a person summoned to appear before him. It is translated also to direct, the idea being that of authoritative marking out of place and way by consultation, which consultation, when it has come to decision, is to be the binding law of the journey. Once again, I find the Hebrew word is translated to betroth, and within it lies the idea of that mutual surrender of life to life and love to love which creates the marriage relationship. All these things lie within the Hebrew word. As Amos used it, it was a far fuller word than our word "agreement" suggests.

What, then, is the general and inclusive conception of this word "agreement"? Ideally it refers to that perfect affinity and adjustment which makes one unit of two. That perfect affinity, not necessarily perfect likeness, it may be complementariness in nature, which brings two persons together into unity. That is the ideal conception. Initially the word suggests a method by which that is brought about; a place where those two persons come together; a time when they come together; and all that responsive habit of soul to soul and life to life that makes the coming together a perfect articulation, agreement, unity. So that when Amos asked his question it was no surface question. He did not mean merely, How could two persons walk together, except they met? He meant that, but something far fuller.

When we apply this idea to man and God, we see how deep this question is, and what profound things it suggests. Apparently it suggests a difficulty, for an insuperable barrier exists between man and God that never can be broken down or overcome by man himself. How can God and a man meet together, agree together, walk together except they have agreed? If I have said it seems to suggest a difficulty, let me now say something else concerning man. I am not now using the word *man* as it applies to myself, or to any man in this house; I am using the word in its ideal sense. I am using the word as I find it in the Bible: "Let Us make man." No man here is fulfilling the ideal that lay within that great word of Deity. I am now speaking of man ideally, as the idea emerges in the account of the creation, with all it there connoted. Then I make this declaration: man ideally, according to the first Divine intention and purpose, was in perfect agreement with God. The ideal of humanity that came out of the Divine mind, the thought that was in the mind of God when He said, "Let Us make man," was an ideal, a thought, of a being in perfect agreement with Himself, having closest affinity with Himself, being perfectly adjusted to Himself, being in absolute articulation with Himself. That is the meaning of the phrase that follows the words I have quoted, "In Our own image, after Our likeness." It may be that someone is challenging me and saying, You are basing a great deal on that word in Genesis. What right have you to say that was the meaning of that word in Genesis? I reply, Once in the process of the centuries and millenniums a Man walked across this human stage. Once one little part of this world was illuminated by the presence of a Man Who fulfilled the Divine ideal; it was the Man Jesus of Nazareth, Whose incarnation was not the incarnation of God only, but also of God's ideal in humanity. In Him alone we have seen what God meant when He said, "Let Us make man." It is because of that I say that man ideally is in perfect agreement with God, has affinity with God, is adjusted to God. The capacity for that affinity, that adjustment, lies within every human being. That is not the last thing to be said at that point; but it must be said and insisted upon. The trouble with our England has been that we have been thinking of ourselves, not as those who think too much of ourselves, but as those who think too little of ourselves; and the very selfishness which has been the root inspiration of so much of our living, leading us along pathways of childish triviality into things that have cursed and blighted and blasted us, that very selfishness is born of a low, ignoble, conception of life. O may it not be, may we not pray this prayer among our other urgent prayers today, that out of this darkness and this hour of calamity men may be brought back to a larger understanding of the tremendous dignity of their own manhood and womanhood! The Man of Nazareth is the revelation of that for which God makes man. So that if a man shall tell me that if he becomes a Christian he will have to run counter to all his natural propensities, I say, No, the propensities which lead him away from God are unnatural, things of evil, distortions, abominations, because they spoil him. A young man from Oxford once said to me, I am going to be a Christian because I believe it is right; but everything will go against the grain. I replied, No, sir; everything will go with the grain; you have been going against the grain all your life. The word of Augustine is sublime truth: God has fashioned us for Himself, and therefore the human heart cannot find rest until it finds rest in Him. When the prophet demands, and when we insist on the demand in a higher relationship than that in which the prophet made use of it, that there must be agreement, we are insisting that a man must come to himself, and in coming to himself he will discover that there are within him by Divine creation capacities for affinity, for adjustment, for articulation with God, for thinking with Him, living with Him, moving with Him; for being one with Him in a fellowship that is perfect.

To leave the matter there, however, would not be to be true to experience. Man actually is alienated from God, dislocated, in every way divorced. I said that a man walking with God is one who has identity of interest with Him, combination of resources, fellowship in effort. Take the life of any man today, apart from the regenerating work of the Spirit of God, and you find there is divorce of interest, divorce of resources, divorce of effort. Man naturally—and now I use the word in its doctrinal sense, in its Pauline sense—is not in affinity with God, is not walking with God. It may be that he sings about God, that he never takes the name of God in vain, that he worships externally in the house of God; but he is not seeking first the Kingdom of God; he is not placing the resources of mind, body, and estate at the disposal of God for the accomplishment of God's will; he is not moving in effort along the same line with God.

Therefore, what do we need, what does a man need? He needs some method by which he can be brought into the agreement for which he was made, but which he has missed. He needs some place where he and God can meet and meet anew. He needs a time of coming together. That is what every individual needs, and I pray you remember the message is an individual one. If I have used the word "man" generally, I have not intended to use it generically, but in the sense of the text of last Sunday evening, "He hath showed thee, O man"—always the individual man. My own soul is in review as I speak. Verily I am made for God. Yea, verily, I have not known God by my nature or by my choice, or by my will. Yea, verily, therefore, if I am to walk with Him I must find some trysting place where He and I can meet, and meet, not merely in a superficial, casual way, but in some profound action by which I can be again adjusted to Him in will, in thought, in purpose, in pattern, in life, in all the actualities of my being. "Shall two walk together, except they have agreed?"

I am going to say again as I close what I said last Sunday evening: This is not the Gospel. There is no Gospel in my text. It is investigation, it is inquisition. The whole time of our meditation on the text has been time—if there has been any true meaning and value in it—in which we have been finding out the need for the Gospel. The Gospel is not here. But we have a Gospel, and the Gospel begins with emphasizing the truth revealed in the investigation, for the Gospel begins with Jesus, of Whom I have spoken, Whose name we know so well, of Whom we thought in a passing moment as the one ideal and perfect Man. That is where the Gospel begins. But Jesus merely as Example brings me no Gospel. If you tell me that is the perfect Man among all the ages, and that if I will conform my life to His, then I shall walk with God, I shall say in answer, I cannot do it, I cannot conform my life to His, I cannot copy Him I love, I cannot reproduce in this life of mine all the fair and wondrous strength and beauty that shone and flashed and flamed in His life. I emphasize that further by declaring that if this Jesus of Whom men speak so often today, this perfect Example, has done no other than reveal that example, He has done no other for me than mock my impotence as He reveals my degradation. I cannot stand in His presence without knowing how entirely, utterly unworthy I am. Can you? Are you among the number of those strange men who write and talk of Him, and whom I sometimes meet, who admire Jesus and patronize Him? Whenever I meet Him I am compelled, as by comparison I look in on my own soul, to say I am unclean, I am a leper. I may have many things in which to boast if I compare myself with other men. I think I could compare myself with some of you quite advantageously; but, so help me God, I have given up the business, because I have seen the light that shone in Judæa and Galilee, and through all the centuries, and I am ashamed. There is a Man walking with God. There is a Man moving in the Divine direction, one with the Divine will, co-operative with the Divine purpose, in the Divine strength. God and a Man walking together! There is a Man in perfect agreement with God. All that He was in the deepest truth concerning Him I find that I am not. There is no Gospel in my text. There is no Gospel in Jesus as Example.

But we have a Gospel, for remember that the One on Whom we looked and grew ashamed, did not consummate His human life as He might have done if all He had sought was to give the world a perfect example. If Jesus had wished only to give the world an example He would never have descended from the Mount of Transfiguration. That was where His perfect human life was consummated. There in the light and glory He was prepared for entrance into the life that lies beyond, without death. The Sinless One had in Himself no reason to die. By transfiguration, metamorphosis, complete change, He might have passed out into the strange, wonderful, mystic life that lies beyond. But He came down from the Mount of Transfiguration. He trod the way of the valley where the lunatic boy was in possession of a demon, and He set His face steadfastly to go to Jerusalem, and gave Himself with all the strength of His purity to the buffeting and bruising of sin and malice and evil, and in a mystery unfathomable, and, therefore, blessed be God, sufficiently deep for all my sin to find in it cancellation and oblivion, He went by the way of the Cross and the way of Resurrection to the eternal and supernal heights. That is the Gospel!

Consequently, that Cross, my brother man, is the "trysting place where heaven's love and heaven's justice meet." That Cross is the place where I may come into agreement with Him, be reconciled to Him, discover anew the meaning of my own life, and receiving from Him absolution for all my sin, may receive also the energy and the life which will enable even me, tremblingly but yet surely, to walk with God.

Where shall I meet with Him? You may meet with Him right where you are. When may I meet with Him, in some special evangelistic meeting? This is an evangelistic meeting. In the after-meeting? There is no after-meeting; this is the after-meeting. Then by coming out? No, by sitting still. By signing a card and sending it in? No, by doing nothing that other men may see. There where you sit you may at this moment have direct dealing with God in Christ by saying to Him what I venture to declare you have sung hundreds, perhaps thousands, of times; but now by saying it and meaning it as you never have before, the central actuality of all your life:

> Nothing in my hand I bring,
> Simply to Thy Cross I cling;
> Naked, come to Thee for dress,
> Helpless, look to Thee for grace;
> Foul, I to the fountain fly,
> Wash me, Saviour, or I die.

If some in this congregation at this moment will make that the language of their inner life, then they will reach the trysting place, and presently, down these aisles and through yonder doors and along the darkened streets of London they may walk with God. And you also, young man, my brother, whom I honor as I see you wearing the King's Regimentals, presently in France, in the trenches, you may walk with God. But there is no walking with God unless there be agreement. There may be agreement through Him Who loved us and gave Himself for us.

CHAPTER V

HOW GOD HAS MADE POSSIBLE
WHAT HE REQUIRES

As therefore ye received Christ Jesus the Lord, so walk in Him.
COLOSSIANS 2:6.

IN READING THESE WORDS WE FIND OURSELVES IN THE SAME realm of ideas as that in which our thought has moved in the preceding meditation. The figure of walking is employed in dealing with the subject of living. The idea of a destination and progress toward that destination is at once the simplest and fullest suggestion. Life is considered as an effort toward a consummation. It is a walk along a highway that leads to a destiny.

In this text, however, we find ourselves in a new atmosphere. We have traveled far from the Old Testament, and are breathing the very spirit of the New. There we found the Divine requirement, and considered the agreement necessary to its fulfilment. Here we are in the presence of the Divine provision, and in its light are enabled to consider our responsibilities. There we had ever to end by saying that we had not found the Gospel, but only the need for it. Here we are beyond the Gospel, knowing its terms, realizing its benefits, and facing the obligations arising therefrom, "As therefore ye received Christ Jesus the Lord, so walk in Him."

The Gospel is implicated in the apostle's reference to receiving Christ Jesus the Lord; while the responsibilities and privileges of obedience are summed up in the command, "Walk in Him."

The line I propose to follow is to consider, first, the Person referred to, "Christ Jesus the Lord"; second, the relation referred to, "Ye received Christ Jesus the Lord"; third, the command, "So walk in Him."

In the first of these considerations we shall find the Gospel itself, inclusively and exhaustively implicated in the titles and name, "Christ Jesus the Lord." In the second we shall discover the way by which that Gospel becomes of real value to us, "As ye received Christ Jesus the Lord." In the third, we shall face the new responsibility of agreement with God it creates, and consequently of walking humbly with Him, loving mercy, and doing justly.

Let us endeavor, then, first to fasten our thought on the Person Who is here presented to us, and the way in which He is here presented, "Christ Jesus the Lord." Within these words as applied to the One Who bears the title and name the whole Gospel is implicated. In the first title and name, "Christ Jesus," Saviourhood in all its fulness is intended and affirmed. In the final title, "the Lord," sovereignty is declared. The Saviourhood leads to the Sovereignty, from which, indeed, it has proceeded. The whole description of the Person constitutes the fullest and most glorious designation of the Son of God. In the New Testament writings this name and these titles constantly recur; sometimes each of them alone, Christ Jesus, Jesus Christ, the Lord Jesus, Jesus the Lord, the Lord Jesus Christ, or, as in our text, Christ Jesus the Lord. I believe that the grouping is never haphazard. There was always some reason in the mind of the writer for the particular form in which the name or title occurred, and that particular reason invariably appears in the context if we take time to consider that context carefully. I believe that in this particular grouping of the familiar titles and name of our Master there is a revelation of supreme importance if we are to apprehend the Gospel.

The familiar title, "Christ," is supremely the title of His Saviourhood. This word "Christ" is but the Greek form of the old Hebrew word "Messiah," and its central thought is of anointing. The Hebrew thought of Messiah, as the Anointed One always had in it two elements, Kingship and Priesthood. The Messiah to the Hebrew was the King-Priest, both the One Who reigns and the One Who mediates. These two elements are perpetually united in suggestion when we use the word "Christ." The title "Christ" suggests government and grace, requirement and reconciliation, law and love, light and life. Consequently, in their very merging, in the fact that these two master ideas are both perpetually suggested by the word "Christ," that word becomes the supreme title of the Saviourhood of the Person referred to. He is surely King, governing, requiring, giving law, shedding light; but, with equal assurance, He is Priest, administering grace, bringing about reconciliation, expressing love, and communicating life to the souls on whom the light has fallen. The King is also the Priest. The King Who has supreme authority, and Whose law has been broken, is the Priest mediating between Himself and the sinner who has broken His law. The lawgiver—never for one moment lowering the standard of requirement, never consenting to condone sin or pass it over as though it did not matter—is yet the Lover of my soul Who comes to me in that state of bondage and pollution which results from my breaking of His law, and so deals with me that the chains are broken and the pollution is cleansed, and I can find my way back into the place of loyalty to His supreme Kingship. Consequently, the Cross is the trysting place where God and the soul meet, keep appointment, pass into agreement, for the Cross is the throne of the King and the altar of the Priest.

With equal separateness from every other part of the designation, let us fasten our attention on the next word, "Jesus." This word is supremely the name of human relationship. It is His name as Man. It is His name as friend of sinners. Jesus is the Greek form of the Hebrew name "Joshua." The name "Joshua" was a name especially created for a man. The man who was to succeed Moses in the leadership of the Hebrew people was named Hoshea, meaning salvation; but when he was to become the leader his name was mingled with the name Yahweh, or Jehovah, so that Joshua means the salvation of the Lord. In Old Testament history it was borne by two persons: the great leader who brought the people into the land, and the priest seen in the vision of Zechariah standing by the altar. When Jesus was born in Bethlehem long ago there were probably hundreds of Joshuas in Nazareth, Capernaum, Jerusalem. So when it was announced, "Thou shalt call His name Jesus; for it is He that shall save His people from their sins," the significance of the declaration was that in Him the intention of the name was to find fulfilment. Then bear in mind Paul's declaration concerning the name: "God highly exalted Him, and gave unto Him the name which is above every name; that in the name of Jesus every knee should bow, of things in heaven, and things on earth, and things under the earth." The name given to Him in babyhood, and carried by Him in boyhood and through manhood, was the sign of an intention. He received it anew when He ascended to the right hand of the Father as the sign of the fact that He had accomplished the intention. The name became the name above every name; but it is not a Divine name, it is a human name; it is the name that brings Him near to me in my humanity; it is the name borne by One Who looked out on life with eyes like mine, felt its emotions with a heart like mine, walked its way with feet like mine, did its work with hands like mine; it is so truly the name of a man of my humanity, that I feel that I may, without irreverence, lay my hand on His and call Him Brother-Man. That is the supreme significance of the name Jesus, and thus it expresses the truth the title Christ affirms, "for it is He that shall save His people from their sins." In its relation to the Person who bears it the name reminds us that He brings infinite things to our level in order that we may understand them. Jesus of Nazareth was the central, final, ultimate anthropomorphism. Because men could encompass a conception of God only by projecting their own personalities into immensity, God out of immensity contracted His personality to that of a human being, that men might see Him and know Him, grasp the infinite, fathom the unfathomable, and come through flesh into communion with the eternal spirit. In His manhood Jesus was the sacramental revelation of the things that are infinite in their splendor, their glory, and their magnificence. The name "Jesus" reminds me of the Man, and yet reminds me of the Man through Whom I am enabled to find my way into fellowship with infinite things.

It is the name, moreover, of One Who in that very nearness to me in His manhood inspires the love which inspires loyalty. How often young people have said to me, and with absolute reason, How can I love God? I can love father, mother, wife, child, brother, sister; but how can I love God? I can reverence Him, adore Him; but how can I love Him?

To such inquiries I reply, familiarize yourself with Jesus; walk with Him, talk with Him as He is seen in the Gospel stories, and you will love Him, and that is to love God. I am not now speaking of walking and talking with Him in those profounder exercises of the soul to which the saints come after long processes of discipline. I am speaking of the very first and simplest things. Take up your New Testament, read it, and think in the presence of the One of Whom you are reading; and I defy you to do that, without coming presently to love Jesus. The infinite tenderness of that great heart, the abounding strength of that great soul, the splendid courage of the Man Who dared confront all the vested interests and call them what they were, hypocrites, vipers; the exquisite tenderness of the voice which, tremulous with emotion, could say to weary souls, "Come unto Me, all ye that labour and are heavy laden, and I will give you rest"—these are the things that compel love. Idealize the reality revealed in the Gospel, get to know Him, and you will come to love Him, and love Him in spite of yourself, and in spite of your sin; even though you go on sinning, you must love Him if you see Him and know Him. But ever remember that loving Him will not bring you salvation. There are thousands of people who love Jesus but have no faith in Him, who never repose confidence in Him, never crown Him, never bend the neck to Him, never cast themselves in hopelessness and helplessness on His mercy.

We come, then, to the last title of the text, at which also we will endeavor to look in separateness from the rest. Yet not wholly can this be done, as we shall see. "The Lord." This is supremely the word of His Godhead, the word that reminds us that He is the Creator, the Sustainer, and the Accomplisher of human redemption. When we read this title it reacts on all that we have been thinking in the presence of the former title, and the simple name as it suggests the infinite value and nature of the things we have been referring to. "Christ" is the name of the Saviour, merging in the word the thoughts of Kingship and Priesthood. He is the Lord, which is to say, His Kingship is ultimate, final sovereignty. Mark what this apostle says about Him. The apostle calls Him the Son of God's love. He describes Him as the "Image of the invisible God." He declares that He is the fount and origin, the strength and goal, of all creation. The sovereignty of this King, then, is ultimate sovereignty, beyond which there can be no appeal. Consequently, His Priesthood is ultimate priesthood. He came to reconcile *all things* to Himself. This was done by the blood of *His* Cross. When we read that declaration the emphasis should be where I have placed it. Think not of the sacramental blood as being merely the blood of a man. It was the unveiling before finite, human eyes, of sacrifice in the heart of God Himself, ultimate in its values, universal in its reach.

This final title, moreover, illuminates the central name "Jesus," the symbol of manhood. This Jesus is the Lord, and so we learn the eternal glory of humanity: that humanity was in the purpose of God in His eternal thought, and that man was created to share the eternal life of God, that Man is to last while God Himself shall last, and so He has exalted Man to His own right hand, and given to Him the name that is above every name, the name of glorified humanity, "that in the name of Jesus every knee should bow . . . and that every tongue should confess that Jesus Christ is Lord, to the glory of God the Father."

So I say again in these hurried sentences that in the significance of the titles and the name the whole Gospel is implicated. What a Gospel it is! How mighty, how vast, how satisfying! If some soul, sin-burdened and undone, may be asking, How can it be that by the life and death of One two millenniums ago I should hope to escape the penalty and the power of sin? let that soul remember Who the One is, Who long ago appeared in this world of ours and wrought out into visibility the things of the eternities. He is Christ Jesus the Lord!

Now let me reverse the order, and employ that which we find in the earlier part of this epistle. He is *the Lord*, ultimate Sovereign, and ultimate Saviour; He is Christ, on Whom the holy chrism rests, the anointed King to reign, and Priest to redeem. And for me, that I may not be intellectually bewildered by the vastness of the provision, He is Jesus of Nazareth, man of my manhood, bone of my bone, flesh of my flesh, spirit of my spirit; man of trust, of temptation, and of toil. I come to Him as Jesus, and I find the Christ, and through Him I find God, and, behold, His Cross is the trysting place where He and I meet and agree in order that we may walk together.

So let us pass to the second part of our consideration, the relation between the human soul and this Person referred to in the text, as it is revealed in the words, "Ye received." In all evangelistic work the term "to receive Christ" is very familiar, and it is a perfectly accurate and strictly Biblical word. It is well, however, to consider what the New Testament writers meant when they spoke of receiving Christ. In a memorable passage John used the word and interpreted it, "As many as received Him, to them gave He the right to become children of God, even to them that believe on His name." By that added sentence of interpretation we have John's conception of what it is to receive Christ: it is to believe on His name. While that is fundamental, there are other things implicated. All are found in our context. Writing to these saints in Colossae, Paul said that he had heard of their *faith* in Christ Jesus, and of their *love* toward the saints, and of their *hope*. In that passage we have three very familiar words—faith, love, hope. Moreover, they occur in an order and sequence, suggestive and closely related to the grouping of the title and names in the text. Whether this was incidental or intentional on the part of Paul matters nothing; that there is spiritual value here I affirm, and of that we shall attempt to make use.

Faith is the word which supremely indicates relationship to Christ, that is, to the Saviour. Love is the word which supremely indicates relationship to Jesus, that is, to the Man Who is the friend of sinners. Hope is the word which supremely indicates the relationship to the Lord, that is, to the Creator and Sustainer. So that in the soul's relation to the Person presented, which is described inclusively as receiving that One, these great activities of the soul are found—faith, love, hope. To have faith in Him, to love Him, to hope in Him, is to receive Him. I should be very sorry to convey to the mind of any person the idea that this is a sequence in the sense that we mechanically start with faith, then, as a second blessing, have love, and, as a third blessing, hope. These things grow out of each other as the fruit grows out of the flower, and the flower from the root. There is one supreme and fundamental attitude of the soul toward this Christ which means reception of Him; it is the attitude of faith, and wherever that faith is exercised, it follows that love springs up in the heart; and wherever love growing out of faith in a human soul springs up in the heart, there begins the song which is the song of hope. Faith fastening on Christ as Saviour expresses itself in love to Jesus as Friend, and finds its hope and confidence in Him as Lord. So He is received.

Faith is supremely the word indicating relation to Christ as Saviour. Faith marks the soul's relation to the two elements that merge in the Saviour's work. He is King, He is Priest. Faith is submission to His Kingship, and confidence in His Priesthood. Faith is repentance, which is submission of the soul to Kingship. Faith is confidence in His Saviourhood, which is the determined risking of everything on His great words and abandoning forevermore the cares and anxieties about the past, with which we never can deal, but with which we may trust Him to deal. The answer of the soul in faith is response to the two elements that merge in His Saviourhood, submission to His Kingship, confidence in His Priesthood. This is to receive by faith.

Taking the other title I declare that Christ *may* be thus received by faith, because this anointed King and Priest is the everlasting Lord. I declare that He can be trusted, because this everlasting Lord, Who is also the anointed King and Priest, is Jesus stooping to my level, enabling me to put confidence in Him because He is Man of my manhood.' When, through the infinite simplicity of His true manhood, my soul enters into submission and confidence, lo, I find I have kissed the scepter of the eternal God, and I have trusted in the heart and passion of that self-same eternal One.

He is also received by love. Love is the word indicating the relation to Jesus the Man, the Friend of sinners. It marks the soul's response to Himself. Thus He is received by love. To know the man Jesus is to love Him, though you may not be able to accept the doctrine of His Deity. To know the Man Jesus is to love Him, even though you are puzzled by the mystery of His atoning work. As man, He is to be loved. The soul which thus goes out to Him in love does by that love receive Him. You will not become a Christian soul because you understand the doctrines of the Christian faith. It is possible to understand them in large measure, and yet never to be a Christian. Intellectual orthodoxy concerning the Person of

Jesus Christ will not make you a Christian. That which does so is relation to Him, submission of the soul to Him, the going out of the soul in love to Him, if that love become the inspiration of submission and surrender. Love becomes faith when it is submissive to the Person of the Lord Jesus Christ.

So, finally, we come to the reception of this Person in hope which is supremely the word indicating relationship to the Lord, the eternal One, the Creator, the Sustainer. It marks the soul's confidence in God. John said in one of his epistles, "Every one that hath this hope set on Him purifieth himself, even as He is pure." Am I not right when I say that there is no hope in this world worth having that is not set on God? It is the only hope that maketh not ashamed, because it is hope which is laid up in the heavens. Are we not learning this today through suffering and tears, through slaughter and through blood? * We centered our hopes on armament or disarmament, and both have failed us. There is no hope that maketh not ashamed but the hope set on God. But when this Christ is received, when the heart goes out to Him as Christ in faith and as Jesus in love, we find beneath and beyond the veil of His flesh Deity, Godhead. Then there begins—on the darkest day, and in spite of the most abject failure of the past, under the blight and mildew and blasting that have cursed the being—a song of hope, not hope trusting to my endeavor, but hope centered and founded on God.

I *can* hope in Him, the infinite One, because though I cannot encompass Him in my thinking, I find Him in Jesus. I must hope in this infinite One because, although I cannot understand how such a vastness of might and majesty can stoop to my level, yet in the Christ I have beheld the vision, and dare not despair.

This, then, is the relation and order of receiving Christ:

* During World War I—in the spring of 1915.

faith, submitting to Kingship, confiding in Saviourhood; love, fastening on that central Person represented by the name of ineffable sweetness, Jesus; and hope springing in the heart to sing its song and light the darkest day, because in Him the soul has reached God!

So we come to the last of our divisions, the walk enjoined. For the present we shall deal with this in broad outline only, "As ye therefore received Him"—in your faith, in your love, in your hope—"so walk in Him." The walk here enjoined is continuity of faith. Continuity of faith means persistent loyalty to Christ as King, and unswerving confidence in Him as Saviour. Mark the two elements: first, unswerving loyalty to His Kingship. I admit the necessity for that. I see it; I strive after it: but Oh, my God, I do not do it. I stumble and fall. Then let me never forget the second, unswerving confidence in His Saviourhood. The subtlest temptation that ever assaults the heart of man, of the struggling saint, is the temptation to doubt God's willingness to forgive. Unswerving confidence in His Saviourhood means that I make confession of my sin to God, and rest in the knowledge that He will forgive and put away and blot out. He does none of those things easily, for behind them lies forevermore the infinite, unfathomable passion and sorrow of His heart. To walk in Him is to walk in continuity of faith.

Walking in Him as we received Him is to walk forevermore guarding love. How are we to guard love? By yielding to the fear which results from the casting out of fear. When we know His perfect love it casteth out fear, but it inspires a new fear. No longer do we fear the consequences of our sin as it affects us, but we fear the consequences of sin as it affects Him. No longer do I fear that He will blast and damn me; but I fear lest I crucify my Lord anew, and put Him to an open shame. Strange, beauteous, paradox of the life of love; His love has banished all my fear for myself; but, oh, I am afraid lest I wound Him, grieve Him, cause sorrow to Him. To walk in Him is to abide in love by faith, in keeping the commandments. The experience must be cultivated in the secret place; and the expression will be manifested in public places, in my perpetual love of His name, and the kindling of my eye when He is referred to, and my readiness to speak of Him, and in my love to all the saints, and for all for whom Christ died, and who are near and dear to Him.

Finally, the walk is maintenance of hope. As in receiving Christ hope was born in the soul, so in walking with Him that hope is to be maintained. We shall maintain hope as we dwell in the light which keeps our vision of His ultimate purpose clear. Our hope will be maintained as we resolutely refuse to doubt Him on the darkest day. Paul talks about the things by which the saints would be surrounded and might be disturbed: vain deceits, rudiments of the world, traditions of men not after Christ. If we listen to the vain deceits of men, if we allow ourselves to be bound by the traditions of men, if we measure our outlook and inspire our thinking by the rudiments of the world, hope will surely die out. In proportion as we are walking in Him, though it be amid the furnace, we shall sing, we shall rejoice in hope of the glory of God. So that to walk in Him is to walk in faith, that is, humbly with God; in love, that is, loving mercy; in hope, that is, doing justly. All this is made possible to us by the Gospel.

This is the Gospel. This is good news. Here I find not merely that which God requires of me, not only that in order to fulfil His requirement I must be in agreement with Him; but that He has come to my level that we may agree together, and that in Christ He descends and walks with me in order that I may walk with Him.

This is based on God's faith in Himself and therefore in

man, on God's love, which needs no argument, love so amazing, so Divine; on God's hope in Himself and so for man.

The question of the moment, the last, the final question is, "Shall we receive this Christ?"

Let us begin where God intended man to begin, at the center, in Jesus. Let us remember that receiving Him does not mean, first of all, perfect understanding of all the mystery of His Person, or the doctrines of His grace. It means surrender of the soul to Jesus. That is the first thing. If we begin thus, where God intends us to begin, let us do so, including all that God intends us to include. This Jesus is the Christ, anointed King and Saviour. This Jesus is the Lord, the eternal, the immortal.

Is not that Gospel enough for you? Can you not trust yourself to the vastness of this strength? Sin not against the light by postponing thy reception of this Christ, but ere this day closes receive Him, and thus begin to walk in Him.

CHAPTER VI

OUR HOPE AND INHERITANCE

Blessed be the God and Father of our Lord Jesus Christ, Who according to His great mercy begat us again unto a living hope by the resurrection of Jesus Christ from the dead, unto an inheritance incorruptible, and undefiled, and that fadeth not away, reserved in heaven for you.

I PETER 1:3-5.

THIS IS A GREAT DOXOLOGY. IT IMMEDIATELY FOLLOWS SALUTAtion, and merges into consolation. This method of introduction is the more remarkable when we consider the condition of those to whom the letter was addressed. Peter, faithful to the compact he had made with Paul to devote himself to the circumcision, was writing to Jewish Christians in Asia Minor who were then passing through a time of "fiery trial." They were charged with being "evil-doers," enemies of the State. Their very name, "Christian," brought them persecution and oppression. Writing thus to these his brethren—his brethren after the flesh, and his brethren in the Lord Jesus Christ, writing to them to establish them, as his Master had commanded he should do when once he himself was turned back again— he began his letter with a vibrant note of praise and doxology. It is hardly the usual method. It is hardly the method that we should adopt ourselves. When we write to someone in fiery trial, misunderstood, oppressed, persecuted, we do not often begin with Hallelujah! But that is what this man did. His sentences are positively vibrant with joy.

The doxology consists of a celebration of life, the life from which it springs. What was the reason of the doxology? "Blessed be the God and Father of our Lord Jesus Christ, *Who . . . begat us.*" The life so begotten was the inspiration of the song, and the song celebrates that life out of which it springs.

Observe the movements of the doxology. God is praised, is worshiped—for that is the significance of the word, "Blessed be God." It is the language of a soul prostrate before Him, not in fear, but in courage; not in despair, but in hope; not in cowardice, but in high and holy confidence. It is praise for life, for life as the outcome of the mercy of God by the way of the resurrection, "Who according to His great mercy begat us again unto a living hope by the resurrection of Jesus Christ from the dead," and for life having a twofold value—"unto a living hope," "unto an inheritance incorruptible, and undefiled, and that fadeth not away." Thus we may say that the exultation of the singer centers in the abounding mercy of God, celebrates the resurrection of Jesus as the medium through which this mercy of God flows out toward men, and confesses the twofold benefit resulting from the outflow of that mercy by way of the resurrection.

Our theme tonight, selected from the many themes which the great passage suggests, is the relation of the resurrection to mercy and life. I propose two lines of thought only: first, what the resurrection of Jesus Christ meant to God; and second, what the resurrection means to us.

What the resurrection meant to God we will first state, and then attempt to consider. The suggestion is somewhat startling, that the resurrection in itself could mean anything to God. Yet, if one thing is most clearly revealed in this passage, and, indeed, in all the New Testament writing, it is that God had great gain by way of the resurrection, that the resurrection made possible in the activity of God that which apart from it had not been possible. We here view the outworking in time and into visibility of the profound fact by which God was enabled to do, what apart from this fact He could not have done. Take Peter's words once again, leaving out the subsidiary clauses: "The God and Father of our Lord Jesus Christ . . . according to His great mercy begat us again . . . by the resurrection of Jesus Christ from the dead." The declaration of the apostle is that by the resurrection God created the possibility for the outflow of His great mercy in the gift of life to needy souls.

This assumes, first, the fact of the mercy of God. That mercy was not created by the resurrection. The resurrection made a channel through which it could flow. It also assumes the restraint of the mercy of God. It could not move; it could not act according to its own desire. By that of which the resurrection was the symbol in time all the barriers were broken down; and the eternal fact of the mercy of God found restraint ended, and the consequent possibility of outflow toward the sons of men.

What is mercy? Our word is a rich and beautiful one; but in order that we may make no mistake, in order that our interpretation may be neither too narrow nor broader than is warranted, let us see what the word really means which here is so translated. It is a primitive word whose history is unknown. It always had one particular significance, being always used in reference to compassion in activity. There may be compassion which never becomes active, which is always passive, the nursed sorrow of the heart; but that is not mercy. Mercy is compassion struggling and determined to reach out, and become active. The root significance of the word translated mercy in the Old Testament is apparently at the first a very simple, insignificant one; it means to bend, to stoop, to bow. Mercy is compassion bending, stooping, bowing.

Mercy, then, presupposes a state of need in those toward whom it moves, or over whom it stoops. Herein we distinguish between love and mercy, between grace and mercy, between compassion and mercy. I grant that apart from love, grace, or compassion there can be no mercy; but there may be love and grace, and even compassion, without mercy. Love does not necessarily connote sorrow or suffering in the case of the one on whom it is set; but mercy does. Love becomes mercy in the presence of the suffering and sorrow of the soul on whom it is set. Without love, there is no mercy; but whenever we employ this great word "mercy" we are conscious of a shadow over the brightness, there is a sigh and a sob, the sigh and sob of need; and mercy is that effort of love to go out to the needy one and lift and heal and bless. The mercy of God, then, is God's desire to heal and help, to deliver and save those who are wounded and in need, who are bound and in the place of destruction.

The apostle writes of the "much mercy of God." Here is a case in which all grammar is defeated. When I went to school I learned, positive, much; comparative, more; superlative, most. Which is really the greatest of these three? The superlative? By no means. The superlative is only the ultimate in comparison. The positive is the greatest, for when left alone it admits of no comparison. We may speak of the *most* merciful God when we are thinking of someone else; we think of God as being *most* merciful when we think of ourselves. When we think of any quality of God comparison is impossible. There is nothing with which to compare it. In that phrase "the much mercy of God," so easily passed over, the apostle has brought us face to face with the fact that God suffered; and suppose—a supposition which is entirely unwarranted, but in which I will indulge for the sake of argument —suppose God had found no way of saving men, He still would have mercy, compassion reaching out toward need. "The much mercy of God." None is unreached by that mercy, so far as it is desire on the part of God to save. If you rather question that statement I will enforce it by another Biblical quotation, God is "not willing that any should perish, but that all should come to repentance."

But there is a sense in which that "much mercy of God" must be, and is, held in restraint; there is some reason why it cannot flow out to men, some reason why it cannot act on behalf of those who are in need. This reason consists in the impossibility of conferring benefits on those who are in sin, that is, who are in rebellion against holiness, and under the mastery of evil. God cannot give the gifts of His love to souls who are under the mastery of sin. This restraint is not the operation of justice as opposed to mercy; it is the operation of mercy itself, and of mercy in the interest of its own object. To bestow benefits on such people would be to defeat the intention of mercy. An angel is seen with a flaming sword at the gate of Eden guarding the way. Why? "To keep the way of the tree of life," lest man should eat of the tree of life and live forever. You say, That is judgment! No, it is mercy! To confer the gift of life on a man who has sinned would be to perpetuate his sin, and his pollution, and his paralysis, and his agony. Guard the way to the tree of life, and guard it by a flaming sword; and that flaming sword is mercy delivering men from the unutterable penalty of continuity in the condition into which they have brought themselves as the result of their own sin. Mercy is not weakness, not sentiment, not mawkish sympathy. Mercy will never try to deal with sin by the application of rose water! The old Hebrew singer understood this:

> He smote Egypt in their first-born;
> For His mercy endureth forever.
> He smote great kings;
> For His mercy endureth forever.
> And slew famous kings;
> For His mercy endureth forever.
> Sihon, king of the Amorites;
> For His mercy endureth forever.
> And Og, king of Bashan;
> For His mercy endureth forever.

The mercy, the going out of God in desire to heal, cannot confer blessings on men in sin. The gates of the city of God which the Seer of Patmos beheld were of pearl, every several gate was of one pearl; and the infinite significance of the pearl is its purity. The flashing splendor of the gates of the city of God forever says, Nought that defileth can ever enter here! Why? Because if that which defileth be permitted to enter into the city of God, then the very city of God is insecure, and the very conditions which mercy seeks to establish are denied and made impossible. By reason of the profundity of the Divine mercy, by reason of its intensity, of its marvelous greatness, it can make no truce with sin. The much mercy of God is, therefore, held in restraint.

Listen, then, to the doxology: "Blessed be the God and Father of our Lord Jesus Christ, Who according to His great mercy begat us again unto a living hope *by the resurrection of Jesus.*" What, then, was the resurrection of Jesus? First, the resurrection of Jesus was the necessary, inevitable sequence and culmination of the Cross of Jesus. The resurrection of Jesus was the perfecting of that which took place in the mystery of His passion, of that passion wherein sin was dealt with in a way so profound that we have never been able to understand it perfectly, but in a way so Divine that two millenniums have rejoiced in the experience of it. The resurrection was not something separated from the Cross, or in opposition to the Cross; it was part of the Cross, the completion of it, the last movement in it. To that conception of it all the references of the Lord Himself give witness. Whenever He spoke of His Cross, the last thing He said was about resurrection. We cannot find a single occasion on which Jesus spoke of His Cross but that He ended by speaking of His resurrection. The evangelist tells us that when Jesus and Elijah and Moses met on the mount they "spake of the *exodus* which He was about to accomplish at Jerusalem." That is more than the Cross; it is the Cross and the resurrection. When Luke tells the story of Jesus going to the Cross, His determination to journey to Jerusalem to die, he does not say Jesus is going to die, he says, "When the days were wellnigh come that He should be *received up,* He steadfastly set His face to go to Jerusalem." Jerusalem was an incident by the way, the Cross was part of the journey, the resurrection was its completion. In that hour of resurrection, therefore, we come to the culmination of the Cross, and so to the ending of sin, the breaking of its power, the canceling of its obligation, the quenching of its fires, the disannulling of its bonds, the devitalizing of its poison. When that is done, the abounding mercy of God can move out toward suffering and needy humanity.

The second thing has been involved in the first. The resurrection was the initiation of a new and living way. The resurrection was that which, resulting from the Cross, meant that the life taken from the dead, having been voluntarily laid down therein, was now at the disposal of others. Christian life is Christ's life, communicated, shared, and mastering our own lives. That is the new and living way open for men, made possible for men. Mercy can operate, indeed operates in this very activity, and brings men into the new and living way. The sinner is cleansed from that with which God can make no terms, and energized for that which God demands in His holiness because He is a God of love. The sinner is lifted from the depths, loved out of the pit of corruption, and saved, in the full and gracious sense of the word. The resurrection stands in human history for our eyes to look back at its light and glory, and know that through it, that is through all those infinite and spiritual mysteries and wonders of which it was the outward symbol, God has gained a way by which His great mercy may flow out for the help of such as are in need.

What the resurrection, therefore, means to us is revealed in the doxology by two co-ordinate clauses, each one beginning with the word "unto," one before the declaration as to begetting, and the other after it: "Unto a living hope . . . unto an inheritance incorruptible, and undefiled, and that fadeth not away, reserved in heaven for you."

"A living hope" is a hope that is alive, that is not mortal, perishable. Hope always deals with things unseen, with things which are not demonstrable to the senses. What a man seeth, why doth he yet hope for? We are saved by that hope. What, then, is hope? What I have said about hope I might surely say about faith. Indeed, it is difficult to keep the two things apart. Yet there is a difference. Hope is a greater word than faith. Faith does not always involve hope. In the first place, God has conditioned our salvation on faith. Hope is not always involved in faith. When faith operates simply it grows into hope. Faith is always involved in hope. Hope is therefore to me the greater word. Hope is the element of joyful expectation in faith. A man can have faith by a strenuous effort of the will. When faith has a song at the center of it, a song of assurance, then it becomes hope. Our word is a beautiful one, coming from the Anglo-Saxon *hopa*, which meant not merely anticipation of something ahead, but the effort of the life to reach it.

In what sense has the resurrection given us a living hope? Hope, as we have said, deals with unseen things which cannot be proved by the senses, not being demonstrable to the senses. Let me name two such. The resurrection of Jesus is a new interpretation of personality, such as the world had never had before, such as the world has never had, apart from the resurrection, and the works which our Lord Himself did work. Do not be foolish enough to try to get rid of the last two chapters in John's gospel. They are absolutely necessary to the interpretation of the gospel. Do not try to get rid of the post-resurrection stories. You need them. Think of them as a whole. What do you see? Jesus the same, and yet different. Human personality is revealed as superior to physical death. He died, but is alive. By that sign and token our heart is sure that the last word has not been said about personality when over the sacred dust we repeat the words, dust to dust, earth to earth, ashes to ashes. We are referring then to the transient abode of personality, but not to personality. We know, moreover, that personality means continuity of essential individuality. It was the same Jesus they had known before Whom they knew after. Shall we know our loved ones in heaven? Surely, absolutely yes. There is no question about it. That is what these post-resurrection stories show. He was the same, the same Jesus. Yes, but there is more in this new interpretation of personality. I see in the risen Jesus change, and enlargement of capacity and potentiality, even within the realm of that of which, for lack of a better term, I speak as the material. In the resurrection the body of Jesus was raised; it was such a body that He was able to light a fire on the shore and prepare breakfast for tired fishermen who had been out all night, such a body that He was able to sit down with them in the upper room and eat of broiled fish, yet so different a body that He was there in their midst without the shooting of a bolt or the opening of a door, so different that for a long way along the road to Emmaus He could walk with two of them who knew Him well without allowing them to discover Him. So much the same that when He so chose, they saw and knew that it was the Lord. Are these stories speculations? No, they are revelations; your philosophy cannot explain them, no human philosophy can; but God has given us this one picture of personality beyond the grave for the cheer and courage of our souls. The grave does not end everything. Beyond it we continue the same, yet with a personality so changed, enlarged, and beautified, that as they read the story men are inclined to doubt. I do not wonder. Do not treat these stories as though they were in any sense small. Some man says: Do you really think that someone came into that room without anyone opening the door? Do you really believe that? I reply: Would not you like to be able to do it? I think you would. I think you often sigh within the confines of this material body. I know there have been moments when I would have given anything, not to be out of the body, but to be suddenly present where I could not come by traveling. That is only a rough and almost brutal suggestion. We have no definite, detailed revelation; but here are great whispers, wonderful whispers, giving us gleams of personality beyond the tomb. I think Jesus tarried those forty days with bereaved souls in order that straining, tear-bedewed eyes might know that the life on the other side is the same, only ennobled, glorified, beautified.

The resurrection is also for us the pledge of our redemption. The death of Jesus was vicarious. He died for others. The resurrection of Jesus was vicarious. He rose for others. Men die in Him and live in Him. This is the great value for time with its vicissitudes, for earth with its limitations. We are born again unto this living hope.

The text, then, takes us across the line, and suggests to us the things that lie beyond. "An inheritance." That means a place and possession in the heavens, interpreted, as I have said, by the risen One, and guaranteed by the ascension of that risen One. Let us pause ere we call in question the accuracy of the declaration that this Man ascended as Man, and that this Man, as Man, sat down at the right hand of God. If you deny me that, then I am not sure about myself and the future. While that remains to me as a truth in the power of which I live day by day I have hope indeed. At the right hand of God—the mystic phrase suggests a definite location—is Jesus of Nazareth even now, not limited in His Deity by His location, but located in His humanity, while by the Spirit His Deity is with us everywhere. In that ascension of the Son of Man I have man's guarantee of place and possession in the life that lies beyond this: where He is we shall be also.

That inheritance is reserved by the power of God. Reserved, what does the word mean? Withheld! That does not sound quite so pleasing. It means something else. Secured! The infant in the eye of the law to the age of twenty-one does not enter into his inheritance and patrimony, but it is reserved for him. Withheld from him in the days of infancy, it is secured to him at the period of his manhood. So the ultimate in our life in Jesus Christ is withheld from us for the present; but it is secured to us; it is reserved for us. "Beloved, now are we children of God, and it is not yet made manifest what we shall be. We know that if He shall be manifested, we shall be like Him; for we shall see Him as He is."

The experience is reserved for those who are kept. The picture here is that of the power of God on sentry duty, the power of God watching over us and guarding us, keeping us for the inheritance which is withheld from us, but secured to us in Jesus Christ. Kept by the power of God through faith, that is through faith operating in that power, trusting it, and obeying it.

The apostle employs language full of poetry as he gives us the characteristics of the inheritance, "incorruptible, and undefiled, and that fadeth not away." There is something of the poetry lost in the translation. As he wrote it, there is a beauty and dignity which we miss in the translation. Our inheritance is unwithering, unsullied, unfading! Unwithering —that speaks of its deathlessness, nothing is in it of the element of destruction; it cannot die; that is eternal life. Unsullied—that speaks of its sinlessness, nothing is in it that prevents the perpetual development of the Divine life; it is perfect in purity. Unfading—nothing is in it that dims the glory or tarnishes the beauty; it is fadeless.

Lift your eyes, ye sons of night; for ye are also sons of light! On beyond the gloom is the gleam of the glory! Beyond the fiery trial is the day of emancipation! A larger and more stupendous life lies beyond!

For today amid the strife we have a living hope. An inheritance is reserved for us in the undying ages and limitless spaces of eternity. To these things He begat us when His abundant mercy was enabled to flow forth through the resurrection of His Son.

The theme is a very pertinent one for today. I have found it so in meditating on it. This is a time of fiery trial to

Christian souls. So far we are preserved from physical suffering; but these our sons are enduring, and we also with them. Our spiritual and mental stress is great. We need some great comfort of God today. Moreover, I think there is another line of similarity. It seems to me that it is even so that prophets of Christianity are in danger of being called enemies of the State today. There is a subtle peril abroad of supposing that Christianity should be postponed to some more convenient season. I hold no brief for Dr. Lyttelton. I have not read his sermon; but from what I gather from the criticisms of it I agree with him almost entirely. I think that very probably he was unwise in some of his illustrations; but if Christianity is not to be proclaimed in the Spirit of Christ today God have mercy on the Church and the nation. We are in dire peril lest we be afraid to say the great things of our faith because we shall be supposed to be enemies of the State. It is also certainly so that in some quarters the very term "Christian" is suspect. We need comfort, we need help. Where shall we find it?

This Easter day has come to us in the midst of fiery trial, misunderstanding, difficulty, perplexity, and agony. If Easter day does nothing else, it should bring to us the capacity for singing a great doxology. Mercy is the inspiration of judgment. While God's judgments are abroad in the earth men are learning righteousness, and that is the purpose of mercy. God will, and does, remember mercy in the midst of wrath. It is the reason why His judgments are operative. Our hope today is still living. No slaying can destroy it. No grave can hold it. Our inheritance is still reserved, and through death, defilement, and decay, we move ever onward toward the unwithering, the unsullied, the unfading. We look, as Peter said in another of his letters, not alone for the things that lie beyond, we look for new heavens and *a new earth* wherein dwelleth righteousness.

We march listening to the music of the reserved inheritance; we march in the energy of the living hope, to both of which we have been born anew in the much mercy of God by the resurrection of Jesus Christ from among the dead.

CHAPTER VII

INDIVIDUALITY IN RELIGION

Behold, all souls are Mine.

EZEKIEL 18:4.

THE BIBLE IS UNIFIED BY THE ETERNAL PRINCIPLES WHICH IT reveals. Every great principle of religion finds explicit statement somewhere in the Sacred Writings. Elsewhere that particular principle is always implicit, and has occasional manifestation in some special application. In the words of this text I find the central Biblical statement of the fact which demonstrates the supreme importance of individuality in religion, and that, of course, means the supreme importance of individuality everywhere. The words were uttered by the prophet in correction of the mischievous suggestion of an entirely false and untrue proverb, which, by the way, is still current in common speech notwithstanding its absolute falseness. "The fathers have eaten sour grapes, and the children's teeth are set on edge." These people were blaming their fathers for their sufferings in exile; the inclusive answer to the false proverb is in the text, "All souls are Mine"; the particular application of it to the heresy embodied in the proverb is found in the chapter.

My present purpose is to examine the truth contained in the text, not in this particular application, but in the very broadest way. We shall consider, first, the explicit statement of the text, "All souls are Mine," and then one or two relative truths which must be borne in mind lest we misapply the teaching of the statement itself.

Still by way of introduction, let us note the two principal terms of the text: the word "souls" and the personal pronoun "Mine." The Hebrew word here translated "souls" is a very common one in the Old Testament. There are occasions on which it is used concerning the beasts, but the occasions are few. There are occasions on which it is used in reference to the spiritual nature of men; these occasions are more, but by no means in the majority. There are occasions on which the word is used concerning personality in its entirety, and these far outweigh all other uses in the Old Testament. All souls, that is, all persons, all individuals, are Mine. The possessive pronoun "Mine" is related to the title immediately preceding it, "As I live, saith the Lord God," that is, the sovereign Lord, Who is in Himself the essential One, of unlimited might. The double title suggests the might of God, and the fact that He is sovereign in His Lordship.

From that explicit statement we make three deductions which seem to me to be supreme, and inclusive. If this indeed be true, then every individual soul has personal relation with God; every individual soul has personal rights in God; and it follows by a sequence from which there can be no escape that every individual soul has personal responsibilities to God. These are the facts which the text suggests, and the recognition of which—if that recognition produce a corresponding attitude of mind, will, and heart—will issue, first, in revolutionizing the life of the individual who yields to the truth, and ultimately in reconstructing society as a whole and realizing the great Divine purpose in humanity.

First, every individual has personal relation to God. I do not say *may have*, but that every individual *has* a personal relation with God. That personal relation consists, first, in the fact of being; second, in the potentialities resident in the being; and, third, in the peculiarities that mark off the individual from all other individuals.

I am what I am, not by my own choice, not by the choice of my parents after the flesh, but by the choice and election of God. That is fundamentally true of human nature. I am speaking of human nature essentially, not as we know it experientially, but of what it is in itself. In the deep, essential fact of human nature there is intimate first-hand relationship to God. The underlying fact of every human life, the spirit, has an immediate relationship with God, which is independent of everything that has gone before. The writer of the letter to the Hebrews says, "We had the fathers of our flesh to chasten us, and we gave them reverence; shall we not much rather be in subjection unto the Father of spirits, and live?" I have nothing to do now with his question, or this argument; I have something to do with the essential conception of humanity which there finds incidental expression. It is that the individual has had a parentage on this earth which is of the flesh; but that the individual in the deepest, essential fact of his or her personality has but one Father, who is God. In an infinite mystery, God has united Himself with the human race in the process of its procreation, so that wherever a child is begotten, God acts, and creates its spirit-life. It is equally true that each human being has relationship with God in capacity. The capacity of the individual is partial, but it also is definite. Every man has something that he is qualified to do naturally; every woman has something she is qualified to do naturally. Happy is the man or woman who has discovered the one thing he or she can do, and is doing that one thing well. It does not matter whether it is working in a carpenter's shop, or preaching the everlasting Gospel, or sewing with deft fingers—the great thing is to know the capacity, and remember that it is a Divinely bestowed gift.

All human beings have relationship with God in being and capacity, which implies relationship with God in potentiality. Potentiality is more than capacity. It is the force in capacity that makes it, not dynamic merely, but kinetic, that makes it do the thing it is able to do. That living force in his nature which enables the individual to do the thing for which he is fitted is also a Divine bestowal. The supreme, final heinousness of sin, therefore, is not that men do what they like with their own, but that they prostitute Divine gifts to base and terrible uses.

Peculiarity also marks Divine relationship. By that I mean that the very partial nature of the individual which speaks of incompleteness, nevertheless speaks of relativity, and, therefore, is Divinely arranged. I am incomplete; there are things I cannot do; but there are things I can do. My friend who stands by my side cannot do what I can do; but he can do things that I cannot do. Both what he can do and what I can do are necessary in doing some greater thing. Peculiarity is a Divine gift, and lest I forget it when I come to the application, let me now say, no man should allow himself to be laughed out of his peculiarity; it is his glory; it creates the possibility of his contributing something to the general good.

The individual soul, then, has personal relationship with God in being, in potentiality, and in peculiarity.

Every individual has also personal rights in God. This is of His grace. So far as human thought can go—and it goes a very little way unilluminated by revelation—it is conceivable that such a God as is revealed in the Bible, a God of might and wisdom, might have created individuals in His own likeness, having capacity, potentiality, and peculiarity, and then have left them to themselves. The Biblical revelation, however, declares that what God has created He has not abandoned, that He retains His relationship, and gives to all human souls rights in Himself. These rights may be described in three ways. The individual has the right of access to God, the right to all the resources in God, and—in view of the condition in which men are living today—the right to redemption in God.

Every individual has the right of access to God, and that by the grace of creation. God's grace did not begin with sin, it antedated sin. In the presence of sin it took on a new form, that marvelous form that wrought redemption. But grace existed before sin, and in the grace of creation God put Himself at the disposal of all souls, so that every soul has the right of direct, immediate access to Him, that is, access without mediation. He is to be found of them that seek after Him. He has placed Himself at the disposal of the individual. While it is an almost vulgarly awkward way to put it, it is still true that I have God all to myself when I need to have Him so. Indeed, I never really find Him until I find Him so. He is so infinitely and beautifully jealous in His love of the lonely one that He will brook no interference of any other if He is to reveal Himself in His glory to the one who is seeking Him.

Every soul has this right of access, and this includes the fact that every soul has a right to the resources in God. Here grace is seen in government. All the wisdom and all the strength of God are at the disposal of each individual life, that it may find itself, realize itself, and contribute its part and portion to the great whole which is included in the mind of God. All the wisdom of God is at our disposal; then we need not blunder. All the strength of God is at our disposal; then we need not stumble. All the resources of God are at our disposal; then it becomes base iniquity, arrant blasphemy to blame our earthly fathers because our teeth are set on edge. Nearer and closer than any earthly relationship is that of the God Who places His unfathomable wisdom at our disposal, and also the resources of His inexhaustible strength.

So far, I can conceive that in the heart of some Christian people who are thinking theologically, and also in the heart of some who are not Christian people, but who are thinking out of the agony of their own souls, there is protest against what I am saying. The protest is that men do not find their way to God, do not avail themselves of the wisdom and might of God, nor can they. They are right in the protest insofar as we have gone, but do not forget that there is another fact. God has provided and placed at the disposal of all sinning, failing souls what I cannot more adequately or better describe than by a phrase of the Biblical revelation, "plenteous redemption." Every individual has the right to the redemption provided for Him in God and by God. Through the appropriation of that redemption he passes into the place where he may avail himself of the resources in God, and, finding that the veil is rent, may have access immediately to the presence of God.

These two things involve a third—every individual has personal responsibilities to God. We have intellectual responsibilities to God; we have emotional responsibilities to God; and, finally, we have volitional responsibilities to God.

Our intellectual responsibilities toward God are perfect honesty and yielded obedience to whatever of the essential light of truth shall break in on our lives. Perfect honesty intellectually is the first responsibility. The one type of mind against which God Almighty has set Himself, as the revelation proves, whether in the old or in the new covenant, and supremely in the Person of Jesus, is the hypocritical. We have but to remember the burning, scorching, blasting words of Jesus to recognize that they were all spoken against hypocrites, people who act, who play a part, who dissemble, who try to keep up an appearance which is false to the inward fact of their personality; people who profess to believe something that they do not believe. With the hot and angry protest of honest agnosticism God is never angry; but against the calm, canting profession of belief by a man whose heart is away from his lips, God makes His protest. The first responsibility of the soul toward God may be expressed in other words: God requireth truth in the inward parts, which means intellectual honesty in dealing with Him. Then He also requires ready obedience to whatever light or truth may break out in the individual soul. God does not ask you to walk in the light He has given me. God does not require of me that I shall walk in the light you have received. God does require of me and of you that each of us shall follow the gleam the moment it breaks on our souls as the result of our honesty in seeking to know His mind and His will.

Our responsibility is not intellectual alone, it is also emotional. We are responsible for surrendering ourselves to this God in the proportion in which we discover Him, and for having our surrender take the true form, adoring worship. Someone may say, Surely that is a condition which is not essential. That is the mistake we have made too long. We have treated worship, adoration, and prayer, as though they were nonessential things. Perhaps we have been willing to admit that in certain circumstances, and in certain places, they do add something of beauty to the life. Yet, really, these are the essential things of life. No man has found the real meaning of his own life until he has yielded to God in adoring worship. The soul prostrate before God is never prostrate anywhere else. The man who knows what emotional surrender to God is—prostration, true worship, and absolute adoration—comes out from the presence chamber erect, strong against all the forces that insult God and blast humanity. Our responsibility, therefore, is emotional.

Centrally, and finally, it is immediately admitted, and therefore not argued, that our responsibility is volitional; and this expresses itself in appropriating our rights in Him, choosing His redemption in order that we may take hold of His resources, and that in order that we may practice the presence of God and find constant access to Him.

The whole point of the discourse and declaration is that every individual is to say for himself or for herself, The Lord Almighty has said, "All souls are Mine"; then I have relation with Him, I have rights in Him, I have responsibilities toward Him.

In conclusion, and as briefly as we may, let us attempt to group the related truths. Let us endeavor to encompass the Divine thought, not only as it is here in the text, but as it is interpreted by the Biblical surrounding. "All souls are Mine." Every unit is related to the unity. All souls are God's; but He has not made a mass of individuals who live alone, or are intended to live alone. Trench says that the phrase, "the solidarity of humanity," came into current coinage after the French Revolution. That may be so, as it was so; but the idea behind the phrase was not born then. If the idea behind the phrase had been realized by humanity, there would have been no French Revolution. If the idea behind the phrase had been realized by humanity, there would have been no war at the present moment. The solidarity of humanity means that in the Divine economy every individual soul is related to the whole race. That great, wonderful word, too often almost sneeringly employed today, *the commonwealth*, has within it this thought of the interrelationship of souls. Every soul, having individual relation to God, rights in God, responsibilities to God, is, nevertheless, incomplete; and for the completion of the individual life the lives of all others are necessary. The capacities within me are not for me, they are for you, for others. The capacities resident within others are not for those who possess them, but for me. God's outlook on humanity is not on an aggregate of individuals, but on a great corporate whole, a race, a family, in which, if one member suffers a tremor, the pain reaches to the extremity of the commonwealth; in which if one member rejoices, the ripple of the merriment spreads over all the faces. Every unit is related to the unity in the Divine creation.

Consequently, the law that God imposes on me is not merely for the perfecting of my personality, it is in order that I may fit into the body corporate and fulfil the meaning of my life in right relationship with my fellow men. There at once we touch the whole question of the limitation of individual liberty. There is no such thing as individual liberty if by that we mean enslaving other people, and wronging other people. I am free, always provided that my freedom does not mean the harming of my brother man. I repeat, therefore, the law of the unit is in the interests of the unity. Of course, it is for the realization of individual fulness that God imposes His law on me. By law here, I mean not merely the Decalogue, but that law which is immediate, the light that shines on me that you cannot see, that you are not intended to see, and have no right to see; that inner word of God to my own individual spirit that meets me, halts me, checks me, encourages me. God deals with me in law, that I may realize all my own life, and that in order that I may fit in with all the other lives, until from the whole realization of humanity there shall come the possibility of the expression of the whole fact of Deity.

Again, the claim God makes on all is for the sake of each. There we have the other side of the great ideal. The limitation of corporate freedom is found here. There is no such thing as corporate freedom which excludes the rights of the individual. No association of employers or union of employees is to be free to interfere with the individual conscience of individual employer or employee. I know this is a difficult thing to say; it is a problem in economics, but it is a Divine law. No nation in its corporate State-life has any right to say to an individual man, You must sacrifice your individuality, and give yourself up entirely to the will of the dominant power. There are limitations to corporate freedom in order that there may be realization of corporate fulness and beauty. God has set the bounds of the habitations of the nations of the world spiritually and mentally, as well as geographically; and in every national idea there is a contribution to international realization. We cannot, in the last analysis, do without anything that is other-national than our own. It may be an amusement for half an hour that you and I should sometimes laugh at the liveliness of a Frenchman, or that he should make merry over our dulness. When God has done His business with the race, He will need the glory of the mercurial temperament of the Frenchman as well as our own stolidity. Or, to take the narrower outlook, that peculiarity of a man's conscience that you are trying to destroy by your machine is needed in order that your machine may have in it the last touch of excellence and beauty. The claim on all is for the sake of each, as the claim on each is for the sake of all.

From that glance at the Divine thought I make one or two human deductions. In view of this belief no man can judge his brother. I do not believe there is a person who objects to that view as a view; but I wonder how many of us live by it. We are always judging each other, passing our condemnation on others, on the views they hold, the clothes they wear, their peculiarities. If we once grasp this Divine teaching, we shall forever be silent, we shall never again pass judgment on our brother. Every man will rather judge himself in the interest of his brother. Every man will sit in severe judgment on his choices, his actions, his deeds, in the interest of other men. All judgment is finally before the throne of God. I must not judge my brother, because we must all appear before the judgment seat of God; but I must judge myself, and it must be done before that judgment throne, for it is the only judgment throne.

This conception of life—so vast as to include the whole race, so intensive and particular as to grip the soul of every honest individual—is an everlasting condemnation of unjust attitudes towards others. In the fourteenth chapter of Romans there are very suggestive applications of this great principle. Paul there says that we are not to judge our brother because he eats meat and we are vegetarians. He says we are not to judge our brother because he is a vegetarian and we eat meat. He says we are not to judge our brother because he observes holy days—let me be modern—saints' days. Free Churchmen are not to object to the man who observes his saints' days, and those who observe saints' days are not to hold in contempt those who observe no particular days, because they observe all days. There is to be no contempt, no judging. Paul says of every man, "To his own Lord he standeth or falleth"; and then Paul utters the great word of his Christian confidence, "He shall be made to stand." We thought that man would surely fall because he is not a vegetarian. No, he will not fall; his Master will make him stand. We thought that man would surely fall because he was so particular to observe saints' days. It is not so. God fulfills Himself in many ways, and He fulfils human lives in a thousand different ways. Let us be done with unjust attitudes toward others.

There is one other thing we learn. From this vast conception of life so particular and intensive in its application, I learn the necessity for cultivating individuality, always remembering the larger relationship, and always leaving God to deal with others. The individual is to define and yield to the facts of relationship with God, to realize and use the resources that are in God, which may be done by appropriating the redemption that is provided for him in Christ Jesus. So may we enter into the spacious life to which men pass only by the narrow gate and the straitened way.

I address my last sentences to the peculiar person (whom nobody quite understands) whose spiritual apprehension is certainly strange to my thinking, whose mental attitude seems all at an angle. Dear heart—man, woman, youth, maiden—deal with God! Give Him His chance to fulfil Himself in you and you in Himself! Remember that all souls are His, and in your separate individuality respond to His government, claim His resources. As individuals do so; then, lo, without any acts of Parliament, and without any more strife, the strange chaos of aggregated individualities will merge into the cosmos of the Kingdom of our God.

CHAPTER VIII

HOW THE WALL IS BUILT

So the wall was finished.

NEHEMIAH 6:15.

THESE WORDS CONSTITUTE A DECLARATION OF SUCCESS. THEY are vibrant with triumph and joy. So far as the actual event to which they refer is concerned, they record what I may term an incidental victory. Nevertheless the story is microscopic. It is suggestive of vaster truths than the actual narrative in this wonderfully fascinating book of Nehemiah contains.

Our purpose is to find out the secrets of that remarkable success. I shall take it for granted that the story is well known. How came it that such desolation was turned into so excellent a construction within seven weeks? What were the secrets of success?

The wall was intended to enclose a Divine idea, and to preserve it until the hour for its development should arrive. Zerubbabel had come back first, and had erected an altar, and immediately following thereupon had commenced building the temple. For long years the temple, rising but a few feet from the ground, had remained until it had become overgrown with weeds, a picture of desolation. Under the ministry of Haggai and Zechariah men had turned again to its building, and it had been completed. Thus life was gathered round the altar and the temple in the city of God. As Paul said long after, in writing to the Galatians, referring to this very fact: "Before faith came, we were kept in ward under the law, shut up unto the faith which should afterwards be revealed." Within those walls was to be gathered, and preserved, the Divine idea, until after four centuries had run their course the coming of Christ should be the first movement forward to the accomplishment of the Divine purpose.

There arose a prophet in those times, named Zechariah, who saw a young man going up to measure Jerusalem, and heard an angel declare to him that Jerusalem cannot be measured. Eventually, Jerusalem will not be contained within walls; it will enclose villages, and its only walls will be the glory and fire of the Divine presence. Long, long centuries after, another seer beheld the city of God coming down out of heaven to earth, and described the walls as great and high, and made of jasper, the symbol of conflict, including a new order. So the figure of the city of God runs through the Book, and the figure of the walls recurs again and again. In the narrative of Nehemiah we have the account of how in seven weeks walls were rapidly flung round the city, and the deed was celebrated by the writer in the words of the text: "So the wall was finished."

Looking at the work of those seven weeks, observing the man who came up to do it, observing his method with those who surrounded him, observing their response to his enthusiasm, watching them carry out their work, seeing them as difficulties presented themselves and were overcome, I want to find out what were the elements that made for the success.

The first element I observe is that, in the case of Nehemiah and under his influence, in the case of the whole of the people for those seven weeks, there was the element of forgetfulness of self in the presence of the passion for the accomplishment of the great end. When the need for building of a wall was manifested and these people came to an understanding of the need, each sank himself and worked for the common weal. The vastness of the work to be done filled the souls of the people, and created a natural, unstrained spirit of self-abnegation. That is always the first secret of success. It must be by natural, unstrained selflessness. When a great passion fills the soul, when some high, holy purpose is to be accomplished, then a man forgets himself. In working as a community this is very necessary. It is an element that moves to success whether it be for good or evil. Along the line of individual self-denial that became a corporate self-abnegation the men moved to the building of the wall, and so it was finished.

That involves another element. It is unity. Unity was not sought, not mechanically arranged, it was not the outcome of consultation. I read of only one consultation in this book. I will quote it: "I consulted with myself, and contended with the nobles." That is the consultation that arrives somewhere. There is no other consultation here at all. Here each man built over against his own house; every man did the piece of work that was nearest to his own dwelling. As self-denial was unconscious, born of the vision of the importance of the work, so the unity was unconscious as to any effort to produce it; it was born of the passion for the accomplishment of the great object. It is an old saying—but we need to be reminded of some of the trite sayings today—that unity is strength. All the fibrous strands of hemp are of no use, but weave them together, and by their very entanglement, skilfully arranged, you create the cable against which the mighty ship will strain in vain. For the best illustration of unity outside the Bible that I know I recommend that all, young people especially, read Rudyard Kipling's *The Ship that Found Herself.* When that ship started on her voyage across the sea, how the parts talked to each other! The rivets grumbled at the bolts; the planks objected to the upheaval of the beams; but through stress and strain and storm and tempest, at last the ship arrived, and the grumbling voices of the bolts were silenced, the complaints of the rivets were heard no more; all the parts had forgotten themselves in the realization of the unity of the ship that found herself.

Apart from such unity there can be no success in toil. Too often, we have been busy building, and we have tried to build the piece of wall near at hand, but we have been so busy building it high that we have not broadened it to touch the building of our neighbor; and the devil passes through the gaps, and laughs at us and destroys our building.

I look at those builders again during those busy weeks and I am impressed by their consecration. What is consecration? The expression of real consecration is the perfect discipline of life as it submits to the law created by the necessity of the case. These men were doing their work by hard discipline. At the heart of all real consecration there must be discipline, submission to authority.

I remember as a boy how I read with almost breathless interest the story of the taking of Quebec by Wolfe. It comes back to me almost with the scent of the flowers under a Gloucestershire hedgerow, where I sat to read. I remember, too, how vividly it all came back to me when I stood on the Heights of Abraham and saw the place where it was done. How was it done? By discipline. How was discipline expressed at the taking of Quebec? The boats dropped down the St. Lawrence, and the one order issued to every man in every boat was to be absolutely silent, not a word was to be spoken. That army, comparatively small, must climb the Heights of Abraham by way of a narrow defile which could easily be held at the top by twenty men. They dropped down the river without speech, with scarcely the sound of oars; they climbed silently to the heights, and waited in silence until the order to charge was given. That is consecration. "So the wall was finished."

I watch them again, and I am further impressed by their consistency, their cohesion, their holding together. I do not now mean the holding together of all in unity, but the consistency of every man, the all-roundness of them. The whole thing is graphically suggested by the use of a phrase that we always think of when we think of this building of the wall—*the sword and trowel.* These men were girt with a sword ready for conflict, while the trowel was busy. Every man was building, but every man was ready for battle. That merging of caution and courage, that splendid bringing together of the sense of danger and the readiness to meet it—that is consistency. Under Nehemiah's inspiration these men were ready to bring every part of the forces of their personalities into this one work. The whole thing is condensed into a statement of the book: "We made our prayer unto God and set a watch." These men neglected no side that was necessary to completeness, left nothing undone that must be done. What wonderful cohesion is manifest in the activity of every man, and this consistency within each personality, multiplied by all the workers, made for the finishing of the wall, until Nehemiah was able to write, "So the wall was finished."

But there was something more than all this: there was that indefinable, wonderful force which we describe as earnestness or enthusiasm. That is expressed in one sentence from the pen of Nehemiah: "The people had a mind to work." The work lay near their heart and captivated all their powers, so that it was commenced, continued, and completed. They were men who believed in the possibility of that to which they set themselves. They knew the importance of that completed wall and all that it meant to their city. That earnestness was the central secret of all their success. Men who lack enthusiasm will never do anything for God. Men who lack earnestness will never build any wall for God. Not by the dilletante discussions of committees will work eventually be done. I am not undervaluing committees, provided they are small enough! Certainly not by disparaging the work in hand, nor by declaring that the wall never can be built, will the wall be built. It is only when the fire that inspires construction and perfection fills the heart that a man can do God's work. When the fire in the individual heart is multiplied by the fires of united, consecrated souls, then the work of God goes forward.

Out of the fire of their enthusiasm emerges another quality making for success—stability. When Paul was writing of Christian work he said, "Be ye steadfast, unmoveable, always abounding in the work of the Lord." The two words do not mean the same thing. Steadfastness is that square-backed quality of fidelity that stays at work however long it take, however hard it be, however much drudgery there be in it. Unmoveableness is the same thing in the presence of opposition. If ever a man was hindered in his work Nehemiah was. Sanballat, Tobiah, and Geshem, sent four times to lure him from his work, but his answer was quick and sharp, "I am doing a great work, so that I cannot come down: why should the work cease, whilst I leave it, and come down to you?" Opposition arose within the city when Shemaiah advised Nehemiah to hide in the temple. He indignantly refused, "Should such a man as I flee? and who is there, that, being such as I, would go into the temple to save his life? I will not go in." The spirit of the leader permeated them all. Nothing moved them, nothing hindered them, because their enterprise was deeply rooted. The secret of stability is to have the life so completely rooted in the Divine enterprise, the Divine will, the Divine power, that life becomes unmoveable in the presence of opposition. By stability of this kind that wall was built.

Yet again, the wall was built, finally, by the sobriety of the rank and file, by the quiet, steady, plodding work of all the men whose names certainly are not mentioned in the record, and probably were hardly known at the time. Great enterprises are always won by that element of sobriety and self-control, with its quiet, steady, plodding work. That is the work that tells in the building of the city of God and the building of the wall around the city of God. It is so everywhere. There is a place in nature for the volcanic; but it is occasional, not regular. Some of you, perchance, have sailed across the great Pacific, and have seen the thousand islands that gem its waters, all things of beauty and joy. How came those islands there? Ever and anon a volcanic island is seen; it was flung up in a night by some convulsion; and it is sure, stable, beautiful; but the majority of the islands were not so flung up, but were formed by the tedious, persistent work of coral insects through long millenniums. When at last God's city is built and the wall is finished, there will be recognition of the volcanic men who did things explosively, and suddenly and magnificently; but if there had been none but they the wall had never been built. It is the quiet, steady workers, going on through what would seem to some of us the hopeless monotony and dulness of days and years who build the wall. How I could illustrate where I stand tonight, as I think of the work of this particular church through all its history. There are those here today who were here fifty years ago, who through stress, and toil, and storm, hoped, prayed, believed, and wrought with God for the building of the wall! These are the men and women that the Church needs if she is to do her work. That is the element that builds. "So they finished the wall."

If we have really seen these things we have discovered that the note on which I began is the note on which I must end. These people had perfect confidence in the work they were called to do. They saw the whole of it. There was one man who went down to the dung-gate and built there, where nobody wanted to go; but he built there until he had finished the work; there was another man who, perchance, had to cover a larger piece of work, and his daughters helped him, they went and built with him; one chapter gives us many such details. The secret of every individual effort was that of the vision of the wall itself, the absolute confidence of the people in its importance, and the integrity of the one appointed to lead them in building the wall. In answer to that vision they wrought, and the wall was finished.

In God's great economy two processes are going forward still, as they have been through all the centuries and all the millenniums: the processes of building and of battle, of destruction and of construction, of the sword and of the trowel. As I said before, this is a story, an incident by the way; but it is microcosmic. The whole Divine process is revealed in the picture of these men and the seven weeks of building the wall.

Are we engaged in this business of God? If we are, how can we prosecute it so as to be perfectly sure of ultimate success? The day will come when the city of God shall come down out of heaven, when its jasper walls shall flash with beauty, and its streets shine with gold—all figurative and symbolic language, figurative because the fact is so fine that it can be expressed only in figurative language. God's victory is yet to be won. That we believe with all our hearts. Are we doing anything to hasten it? Are we engaged in the building? Are we doing anything in the battle?

There are times when the question reacts on the soul and almost scorches us as with flame. There are days when looking ahead to the ultimate victory one feels as though one would be ashamed to share it if one had no scars of battle and had never known weariness in the process of building.

All this is most pertinent today. Surely we have felt as though the walls were broken down and the gates burned with fire; all the fair things that we had hoped and longed for lie about us in catastrophic ruin; but to sit and lament is to be disloyal. Our business is to hear the cry of the leader, Come and let us build again the walls of Jerusalem. If we hear the cry of the Leader, then with our eyes on Him, and our eyes fixed also on the consummation toward which His lovelit eyes are ever looking, let us bear in mind that we shall do our building only as we learn the secrets of this lesson and yield ourselves thereto.

Self-denial is the first necessity if we are to succeed, and that must be after the pattern of Christ's Cross, which was the supreme revelation of self-emptying in the interest of God's high enterprise. That Cross leads the sacramental hosts!

We must also know unity in Christian service. Could anything be more ghastly today than that this nation should divide itself as within itself, and begin internecine quarrels in the presence of a common foe? Yet we are in a little danger in that very direction, and I say to you here and now publicly that I would suppress half the newspapers that are keeping up this unholy strife in the national life. At the heart of the struggle today is this supreme spiritual necessity for unity in the Church. I think there can be nothing more disastrous than that the Church of God should emphasize its divisions today. Oh for such a vision of God's purpose and of the necessity for building the wall and the restoration of Jerusalem that would bring every section of the one Catholic Church side by side to stand for the Christian ideal of the compassion and grace, the righteousness and justice, of God. Under the stress of the present conflict we are seeing many things as we have never seen them. We are seeing drink as we have never seen it before, but it has been here all the while. There has been no more drinking in the aggregate, but rather less because of the war; yet if a newspaper refers to the fact that a deputation waits on the Chancellor of the Exchequer with regard to this question it points out that they were no *teetotal fanatics!* Is *fanatic* ever the proper word with which to describe men who see the dire disaster that drink has wrought in the commonwealth? At least there must be no internecine strife. The Church must come into unity for the process of righteousness if the wall is to be built, or perhaps I should say, if the wall is to be rebuilt, for it seems to lie in ruins, burned and blackened with devilish fire.

There must be new consecration under the authority of Christ's Lordship expressing itself in discipline and obedience to every command that falls from His lips or is whispered by His Spirit to the soul of a man.

There must be a new consistency in the communion of Christ's Spirit holding together in balance and proportion. There must be the sanctifying of all life and the secularizing of all religion. Religion must proceed from the high altars of the Church, the cloistered quietness of the sanctuary, into the market place, the legislative halls. Wherever men go they must carry the force of religion in order that the walls of the city may be rebuilt.

We must also know that holy enthusiasm in the enterprise of Christ's Kingdom which may be analyzed by the use of three words: faith, fervor, fidelity.

We must know stability. We must have our lives rooted in the things unseen and eternal, or we shall be entirely unable to touch the things seen and temporal. This we may find in the fulness of Christ's eternity, and only as we live in that relationship with Him can we ever hope to be stable in the midst of the stern and terrible conflict.

We want as we never wanted before all the quiet, persistent sobriety of the unnamed workers. In this hour of national crisis and religious catastrophe we depend most on the multitudes who are unknown and inconspicuous, and on their remaining quietly in the home, the office, or the shop, doing in the strength of Christ's patience the commonplace drudgery of the darkened days.

Mistake me not. As God is my witness, there is no panic in my heart and no fear in my soul. The walls are yet to be built. The city of God is yet to come down out of heaven. The triumph of our God is assured. Whatever Armageddon there may be ahead of us in some dispensational, prophetical sense, the central Armageddon of the ages is accomplished, and the victory was with God. In that hour of loneliness when the universal Man, gathering into His own personality all types and temperaments and nationalities, trod the winepress of the wrath of God alone, in that hour when He bent to death and by dying slew death, in that hour He won the victory. Every subsequent catastrophe is by comparison with that but the administration of victory already won. The ideal of the Christ is the master ideal, the all-conquering ideal, only I want to have some share in the travail that makes the Kingdom come, I want to have some part in building the wall so that when at last He who came first to visit the ruin and inspect it—taking counsel with no man but Himself—when He shall write as the summary of the battle and building of ages, "The wall is finished," I want to have some share in the thrill of His triumph, some partnership in the joy of His victory. These things I can have only as I stand by Him building, and stand by Him fighting until the work is done.

CHAPTER IX

REGENERATION

Born not of blood, nor of the will of the flesh, nor of the will of man, but of God.

JOHN 1:13.

THE PRINCIPAL AND INCLUSIVE THOUGHT OF THE TEXT IS CONtained in the phrase "begotten . . . of God." By this phrase we are ushered into the presence of the central miracle of Christianity, the first, fundamental work of the Holy Spirit. All the powers and the wonders of Christianity proceed from this center. The new social order which ought to be established within the limits of the Christian Church, the influence on the world which the Church exerts, its message to men—of all these the power ultimately results from this initial, central, and fundamental miracle of the new birth of the individual soul. The dynamic in each case is that of the new life in the individual. That new life, mutually related in the Church, becomes the heavenly nation, and enables that nation to show forth "the excellencies of Him who called them out of the darkness into His marvellous light." That new life in the sacramental host creates the force of the Church's aggression in the world.

Therefore, although it is indeed the old, old story, and a theme most familiar in many of its aspects, it is perennially new; and the application of it can never be exhausted nor its consideration ever be out of place.

In order that we may think intelligently on all that is suggested by the phrase, I shall ask you to notice with me with some amount of care the interpolated negatives of this text, "not of blood, nor of the will of the flesh, nor of the will of man." I shall ask you, in the second place, to consider the immediate statement in all its sublime brevity, recognizing the mystery but insisting on the fact, "begotten . . . of God." I shall ask you, finally, to consider the instructive context, for in some senses my text is wrested from its context, not in order to forget it, but to return to it.

In the first place, then, we turn to what I have described as the interpolated negatives. A threefold negative statement breaks in on the general phrase and demands attention by the centrality of its position. These words sweep away all false ideas concerning the nature of personal Christianity, and leave the mind clear for contemplating the sublime fact itself. The theme is that of the origin of life. Christianity here is looked on properly and necessarily as life, something infinitely more than creed, something infinitely more than a cult; life, ultimately perfected in the whole Body of Christ, which is the Church; life, fundamentally realized in the individual soul. The subject is the origin of that life. In the whole text I find the answer to a question of Nicodemus. He said to Jesus, "How can a man be born when he is old?" People who criticize Nicodemus for that question, and think that it was flippant, have surely never understood the deep agony of soul out of which it proceeded. This question men must always ask when they come to any sense of God, of themselves, of sin. It is a question that suggests impossibility: "How can a man be born when he is old? Can he enter a second time into his mother's womb, and be born?" How can a man start anew untrammeled by the past? How can a man escape from the insistent, haunting pressure of the things that lie behind him in his own life? How can a man be born anew? The answer is in my text; he can be "begotten . . . of God." Now all the difficulties are really suggested by these negatives: "Not of bloods, nor of the will of the flesh, nor of the will of man." In these three phrases we have a revelation of the only methods of which any man could think when he began to consider the possibility of a new beginning in his life. All man's theories concerning the origin of life are suggested by these phrases. Not of bloods, which is to say that the new, peculiar life of the Christian cannot be accounted for by the combination of anything that is material. If I may borrow a very modern phrase, this life cannot be accounted for by the fortuitous concurrence of atoms—"not of bloods." "Nor of the will of the flesh"; this life is not generated naturally, in any sense of the word. "Nor of the will of man"; its origin is not even in the rationality of humanity. That threefold line covers the whole ground of philosophic discussions on the origin of life. Within the three phrases of the inspired Word lie all the suggestions that have ever been made on the origin of any form of life. The apostolic word sweeps them all away and says, This life is not so to be accounted for.

In my text, in these negatives, I find, however, recognition of spiritual conceptions. I believe here is the answer of inspiration to sincere souls who are earnestly desiring, as was Nicodemus, something higher, nobler, earnestly desiring to escape from the bondage of the past and the paralysis of the present. How can a man be born again? Here are three ways in which it is impossible.

"Not of bloods," that is, by no mere process of nature. In that statement lie at least two suggestions: not by descent from our forebears after the flesh, and not by the evolution of anything that is homed within the material. A man begins his life again in the power of an entirely new life. In the first place, these gospels were written by Hebrews and undoubtedly were largely studied by Hebrews, and it was necessary that they should understand that this new, mystic, Christian life could not be begotten in the soul of a man by the fact of his relationship to what lay behind him, by descent, for instance, from Abraham. The truth abides. I am not a Christian because my father was a Christian. I cannot transmit my Christianity to my children. "Not of bloods." We may make our boast in our blood, and may even name it by certain colors, which seem to suggest some kind of aristocracy, but there is nothing in any blood inherently of the spirit-life, and there is nothing in any blood which secures to the man in whose veins it runs the possibility of the new birth and the new beginning.

Again, "nor of the will of the flesh." This suggests the sincere and passionate desire after the better, which expresses itself in personal effort, so that here we are taught that the new birth does not result from the determined throwing off of the evil that is within or from the persistent imitation of the good that lies without. Not by any natural force can a man enter into the new life. I am not undervaluing the attempt a man may make in his loneliness, apart from the revelation of the gospel, to master evil forces; I am not undervaluing the attempt a man may make to imitate that which is high and noble. In the final dealing of God with men I have no doubt whatever that the heathen who has never heard our gospel and has never walked in our light, but has answered the light within him, fighting against the beast within himself and climbing after the higher ideal, will have a far better chance than the man who names the name of Christ and sings the songs of the sanctuary and is content with some orthodoxy of the intellect, but has no response within his own soul and no obedience in his own character. Not thus, however, can a man be born anew.

Once again, "nor of the will of man." No decision of man generates life. Even though Christ is presented to me, and I will to believe in Him and honestly do so, it is not of my willing that I am born again. The act of my will is not that which generates new life in me. Neither can any man bestow by life on man. These negatives completely sweep everything false from beneath us, and leave us face to face with the one and only method by which the soul can be born anew and enter into the Christian life. The gateway into the Church is the gateway of a life which never comes through blood, through effort, or as the result of rational and intellectual activity; which never comes by the soul's own effort.

So we come necessarily to the central fact itself: "Begotten . . . of God"! We have no explanation of the process of the mystery. We must not be deterred from the consideration because that admission is properly made. That is true of all life. The methods of the generation of life are absolutely hidden. The secret of life in every realm is unfathomed today, and in spite of all scientific investigation. Life eludes analysis and definition. The mystery of the budding and blossoming flower is as profound as the mystery of the new birth of an immortal soul. Involved within your personality as you know it, apart from spiritual things, there is a mystery which is as profound as the mystery which you have to face when you hear the central Christian doctrine of the necessity for the new birth. The phrase of my text speaks of the Agent, God; and of the begetting and the beginning of new life. It is for us to consider what the phrase suggests, remembering here also that "the secret things belong unto God: but the things that are revealed belong unto us and to our children forever, that we may do all the words of this law."

The communication of life is from God; it is new life, different in quality from the life which we have lived until we receive it; but it is life as definite and positive as any life, finding its demonstration in the results that follow its possession. The mystery of its coming none can explain. When Nicodemus asked his question, the Lord employed the simple symbol of the wind to help him to understand that he could not understand: "The wind bloweth where it listeth, and thou hearest the voice thereof, but knowest not whence it cometh, and whither it goeth; so is every one that is born of the Spirit." The thought of the text taken in its simplicity is that the life bestowed is of a new quality, different from any other life, the very life that is needed if a man is to begin again and is to realize all that in which he has previously failed. In the discourse contained in the tenth chapter of this gospel our Lord made this declaration: "I came that they may have life, and may have it abundantly." In the course of the same address He said: "I lay down my life, that I may take it again." His argument and teaching is that His life was laid down in order that that very life might be communicated to others. Again, the mystery of the process abides; but here is the declaration of the fact, and the demonstration of its accuracy to be found in the results produced. Peter, James, and John were never born again until the day of Pentecost. Until then they were disciples, the Hebrew disciples of a Hebrew Messiah, following His teaching, obeying His commands so far as they had light, naturally shrinking from His cross as the natural man forever shrinks from the cross—but pressing after Him with fine loyalty though with much trembling. In the strict sense of the word they were disciples only. They never shared

His life while He was among them. They never saw with His eyes, though they saw His eyes and the love light shining from them. They never heard with His ears, though they heard His speech and were astonished. They never felt with His heart, though they loved Him and knew the warmth of His affection. There was no identification with Him in those early days. They were never born anew, until on the day of Pentecost there came the Holy Spirit, by which they were baptized into union with Christ. This union was not of a common sentiment, not a union born of a common admiration; it was a definite, positive, real, though mystical, union in life. From that baptism of the Spirit they began to live one life with Jesus Christ; He, now ascended, glorified, Man of their humanity, at the right hand of the Father; and they, on the earth, in the world, in the midst of its temptaions and its sins and sorrows, burdens and responsibilities; but their life was His life, His life was their life. They were living one life with Him.

You say that is theory. No, it is a fact, demonstrated by the change in the men. Look at these disciples in the gospels, and then look at them in the Acts of the Apostles: the change is radical, and marvelous. They were changed from men, struggling, climbing, endeavoring, failing, to men new-born, living one life with Christ, mastered by love, illumined by light, doing exploits in the power of the dynamic actually communicated to them, of which they were devoid until that time. I look at them before Pentecost, and I hear them saying in the presence of the Cross and passion, the shame and suffering, Not that, Lord; that be far from Thee! I find them almost immediately after, their backs waled with rods, bruised and bleeding, and I read that they were "rejoicing that they were counted worthy to suffer dishonor for the Name." They were new-born men, men mastered no longer by their own lives according to their first birth, but by this mystic life which did not destroy the capacities of the first birth, but fulfilled them, glorified them, ennobled them. This being born of God is the communication to the soul of the very life of Christ which is at once human and divine. The new-born soul is one who has received into his humanity the humanity of Christ in its perfection and the Deity of Christ in its fellowship, and so that soul has become, to use Peter's illuminative word, a partaker of the Divine nature. That new life never comes of bloods, or of effort of the flesh, or of rational, intellectual struggle. It comes directly from God.

This new life means renewal of the dead. Here is its supreme wonder. The Christ-life, given to the individual, shared by the Church aggressive in the world, is always life bestowed on those who were dead. This Christ-life God bestows not on sinless beings but on sinners, so that the great and marvelous fact is that the new birth, the new creation, is life out of death.

The new creation is after the pattern of the story we find in the book of Genesis. In the first verse I read, "In the beginning God created the heaven and the earth." That is a complete story in itself, there is nothing else to be said. Then what? "And the earth was waste and void; and darkness was upon the face of the deep." That is not how God made it. Isaiah declares, "He made it not waste and void." Between verses one and two in Genesis, something happened, some cataclysm, some catastrophe, some upheaval. God has not revealed to us what happened. It may be that this very earth of ours was the place which angels first inhabited, where their probation was spent. I do not know. Between the original creation of God and the picture of the second verse it is certain that there was a cataclysm. Perhaps some day, in the fuller light, we shall discover that back there is the solution of the problem of evil and the genesis of it. What next? "The Spirit of God moved upon the face of the waters. And God said, Let there be light: and there was light." In all that remains of that chapter we find, not creation, but restoration; a new creation out of a dead creation, the bringing forth of cosmos out of chaos. Things did not begin with chaos. God is not the God of confusion. Chaos never originates with God. It is held in His grasp and never allowed to escape that grasp; but the first thing is cosmos, order, beauty. Then, somehow, chaos; and then what? A new creation, restoration; the brooding Spirit of God, the uttered word of God and the first fiat, "Let there be light."

That is a perfect picture of the new birth of a soul. This Christ-life, with all its glories of grace and truth, its final, absolute, wondrous perfections, is not bestowed on perfect souls. God is not gathering into His heaven essentially new creations, having formed them in the likeness of Christ, without relation to past failure; He is bestowing this mystic, wondrous life on souls that may be described as waste and void, in darkness; on which souls He comes by the Holy Spirit, brooding on them, touching them with new life; communicating it to them, so that they rise to the realization of all that which in themselves was waste and void, to the fulfilment of all that which lay in chaotic disaster. The new birth is for finding and fulfilling every distinct capacity created by God in the first birth. To the individual soul born of God is communicated the very life of Christ, which, being possessed, takes hold of that life to which it comes, cleansing it, purging it, renewing it, energizing it, enabling it to rise to the fulfilment of that which lay within it, but in destruction; and, higher yet, to a range of being which is far beyond anything possible to humanity apart from sin, and apart from the redeeming work of Christ. The great possibility of that birth was that for which God became flesh and tabernacled among men. To make that birth possible He granted the Holy Spirit on the day of Pentecost. The first thing in the Christian fact is the new life of a soul; it is also the fundamental thing in the Christian witness in power by the Church in the world.

In the third place, and finally, let us notice the instructive context. The previous statement is linked to the text by the word "which," "which were born." Who are they that are thus born? Let us read. "He came unto His own, and they that were His own received Him not." In that declaration we have the whole account of the rejection of the Lord Jesus Christ by those who were His own, and there is a sense in which all men were His own, all races were His own. As presently all things are to be summed up in Him because all things proceed from Him, then all were His own. The verdict against Him was the verdict of humanity. It was the angry refusal of chaos to crown the King of order. It was the hot, rebellious refusal of the human soul, generically in revolt, to give Him His right of way. "But as many as received Him, to them gave He the right to become children of God." Preliminary to the birth, then, is the reception of the Christ. The people who received Him were born of God. There is a parenthetical word which interprets this: "Even to them that believe on His name." We may take for the illumination of our own souls whichever of these words does most profoundly appeal to us, for they are mutually interpretative. Believe on Him—what is that? Receive Him. Receive Him—what is that? Believe on Him. Only we must understand that belief here is not mere intellectual assent, it is reception of Him. All this is theory, not therefore untrue, but perhaps not powerfully appealing. Let us go back to the picture suggested by these words of John: "He came unto His own, and they that were His own received Him not." Of that rejection the Cross was the ultimate expression. The rulers have said: "We will not have this Man to reign over us." Will no one receive Him? Yes, there is one soul who will receive Him. A dying malefactor, nailed to the cross, in extremis, there and then came to faith, than which there is no more wonderful faith in the whole of the New Testament or the Bible itself. Illuminated in his dying, he saw the Crucified coming into a Kingdom. Can anything be more impossible than that? Can a crucified peasant ascend a throne? Can a murdered reformer ever come to the imperial purple? The only crown He wears is one of thorns, the only throne He has is a Roman gibbet, the only purple is that of His own blood as it flows from His wounds. He is the despised and rejected of men. But one soul crowned Him: "Jesus, remember me when Thou comest into Thy Kingdom." That is believing on Him; that is receiving Him. With infinite, majestic dignity, and all supreme authority, the answer came from the dying One to the man who received Him: "Today shalt thou be with Me in Paradise." He opens the Kingdom of heaven to all believers! In answer to that act of faith, by which that soul did receive this Christ, that soul received the gift of life. Presently the King was dead to all human appearance, and then in all probability they broke the legs of the malefactor that he might die swiftly; and now He was dead. So the world looks on, and goes its blind and ignorant way, measuring reality by the transient and trivial things that appear on the surface. Just out of sight the King meets the malefactor, and they are together in Paradise. And not to that dying malefactor only, but to others, and yet others; and on down through the ages the mystic wonder runs, and the sacramental host of God has been multiplied:

> Part of His host hath crossed the flood,
> And part is crossing now;

and the great, holy Catholic Church of the first-born grows into the holy temple of the Lord, always by the gift of life to individual souls who were dead, and always by the communication of the dynamic of infinite order and beauty to souls that were ruined and in chaos. It seems to me that heaven must be silent with wonder, and the angels forget to sing in silent adoration, as they watch the wonder of the process by which the Church grows to its finality, as individual souls are born again.

All this is worth while only when it becomes personal. If our Christianity falls short of that experience, then remember we are not Christian in the New Testament sense of the word. We may be admirers of the teaching of Jesus, we may most sincerely hold that His example was perfect, we may even be trying in our own strength to obey His teaching and imitate His example; but nothing short of new life creates the Christian soul.

To any who are asking the question sincerely, not with the flippancy born of intellectual arrogance, but with the earnestness begotten of spiritual agony, How can I be born again? my message is this: There is new life for you which God alone can bestow. That life He does bestow without favor on all souls who crown His Son Lord and Master of their lives, and trust to Him their destiny, and yield to Him their weakness, resting wholly on His merit, confiding only in His mercy, going forward alone in His might. So may it be ours, all of us, to know this life which is begotten of God.

CHAPTER X

THE ETHIC AND EVANGEL OF JESUS

Ye, therefore, shall be perfect, as your heavenly Father is perfect.
MATTHEW 5:48.

The Son of man came to seek and to save that which was lost.
LUKE 19:10.

HERE WE HAVE TWO SUPERLATIVE UTTERANCES OF JESUS, which, at first glance to the thoughtful man, seem contradictory, yet, as a matter of fact are most closely related. They condense into the briefest declaration the sum total of Christ's teaching. On the one hand, we have a word of superlative truth; on the other, a word of ineffable grace. One is a word of light, searching, revealing, shaming, filling the heart with fear; the other is a word of love, caressing, healing, lifting, filling the heart with hope. The apostle John declared of Jesus, "We beheld His glory, glory as of the only begotten from the Father, full of grace and truth." Here the two things find expression from His lips. If we take a larger outlook than that of the text in each case, we shall immediately see that there is no contradiction. While the first word is a word that demands perfection, it is set in relationship to declarations of love. The definition of the Divine perfection in the context is this: "He maketh His sun to rise on the evil and the good, and sendeth rain on the just and the unjust." In the atmosphere of the demand for love flashes the great word of light. On the other hand, the story from which the second text is taken is purely an ethical story. Jesus entered the house of Zacchæus, a notorious wrong-doer, and within a short period of His entry the most marvelous moral reformation had taken place. In the presence of that mighty ethical change Jesus said, "The Son of man came to seek and to save that which was lost." So that when I set each text in its context I find the value of the other constituting that context. The first text is a text of light set in an amosphere of love; the second text is a text of love set in the shining of light.

For these two things Jesus stood in all the days of His public ministry. For these two things the Lord Jesus Christ stands at this hour. His demand is for perfection, and if He says no more than that to me He leaves me on the highway of life having discovered my failure and unable to realize the high ideal; but His gospel is that He finds the man whom His ethic condemns, and enables him to fulfil that ethic—"The Son of man came to seek and to save that which was lost." These two things must never be separated from each other. The proclamation of the evangel which even suggests that the mission of Jesus in the world was to persuade God to excuse sin is a blasphemy. The proclamation of the ethic which declares that God has set a high standard to which He demands that a man shall climb ere He receive him is equally a blasphemy. When, on the one hand, we realize that Jesus Christ, in the days of His flesh, through every successive century, and at this hour, calls for absolute perfection, and then see Him holding out to the condemned soul hands in which are the arguments which declare His power to realize in the life of the failing man the very thing He demands, then we have begun to understand the real message and mission of Christ.

A generation ago there was a phrase which was largely the phrase of the schoolman, the phrase of the scientist. It has become the phrase of that ubiquitous and remarkable individual we describe as "the man in the street," whom no one has ever seen but everybody knows: *the survival of the fittest*. With strange, intuitive accuracy, humanity has fastened on that phrase, and now applies it everywhere. Whatever it meant when it was first used a generation ago by the physical scientists, today it stands for the conception that only fit things ought to survive. Men have been applying it physically and mentally, and the Church has, or ought to have, been applying it spiritually. It embodies an essential truth. It reveals a profound necessity. It reveals a principle apart from which our life is not worth living. Only fit things must survive; the unfit must go to the wall. I go further and declare that it is a law of God, and that the chief exponent in human history of that particular law and that particular principle is Jesus Christ. There never passed the lips of Jesus a single plea for the excuse of incapacity. Through the centuries He is not leading into some heaven that lies beyond an army of mental, moral, and spiritual cripples. He demands perfection. In the presence of such a word as this we must not indulge in any of that kind of criticism which is far more destructive than the higher or the lower criticism—the profane criticism which says that Jesus did not mean exactly what He said when he uttered the words, "Ye shall be perfect." If we want to know the severity of the demand we must remember the location of the text. There never was a day when the context will search us more than today. "Ye shall love your enemies." "Ye, therefore, shall be perfect, as your heavenly

Father is perfect." This is Christ's demand for the ultimate fitness, the fitness of the soul, love baptized, love inspired; the fitness of the soul that cannot stoop to untruth or to meanness, cruelty or devilry, because it is mastered by love. The last spiritual, mental, physical, fitness of humanity is created by the mastery of love. Christ stands with that great word forever sounding in the listening ears of astonished, ashamed, confounded humanity, "Ye shall therefore be perfect"; and, lest there should be some lowering of the ideal, He interpreted His meaning, "as your heavenly Father is perfect."

What does all that mean? It means that I stand in the presence of Christ and say: "If that be the standard, then, verily, I am guilty and a failure! Oh, it may be, my masters, that by the ordinary standards of respectable society you will pass; it may be that even by the standards of the Christian Church you will pass; but if you come to that solemn loneliness of spirit which is the self-consciousness of a man in the presence of Jesus Christ, you also will say: If that be the standard, God help me, I am not that. Yet that is Christ's demand. I declare that if that is all Jesus Christ has to say to me, it is a word of condemnation, and there is no help in it for me.

Now I listen to Him again, the same Christ; and with no lowering of the standard, I hear Him say, "The Son of man came to seek and to save that which was lost." He bends over me, the man whom He has condemned; He bows over me, the soul whose unutterable failure is revealed; and as I lose all heart and hope, and feel that if that be the standard, not only have I not attained it, but I cannot attain it, He whispers to my heart this word of hope. Forgive me if I change His wording that I may express His meaning—I have come to make you the very thing that I demand you shall be

—"to seek and to save the lost." Here, then, we have the ethic of Jesus. Here, then, we have the evangel of Jesus.

Let us consider a little more carefully this ethical ideal of Jesus. I think we must try to understand it by trying to understand Him, for if John declared that the glory which shone from Jesus' Person was "glory as of the only begotten from the Father, full of grace and truth," it is also recorded by John that upon occasion Jesus said, "I am the truth." Not, I teach it, not I declare it, not I explain it; but "I am the truth." That is to say, He claimed to be the incarnation of that perfection which He demanded. I am not going to defend His claim. Believing it to be true, I want to see the perfection, first, by listening to His teaching; second, by observing His example; and, third, by noting one stupendous fact of Divine relationship to Him.

First, then, by listening to His teaching. The first of my texts is taken from His ethical manifesto. It breathes the spirit of that manifesto. It catches up the ultimate claim, appeal, demand, thereof. Yet, because it is so inclusive and so vast, let us think of the manifesto itself, not in detail, but in general outline. First, we find in this manifesto of Jesus that He insists on supremacy of character, and of character of a particular type. As I read I am impressed with the fact that no blessing is pronounced on any human being for having anything, or for doing anything; every blessing is pronounced on men for what they are in themselves. Then I discover that Jesus reveals the nature of the character on which He pronounces His blessing. He declares that character is a matter of the soul, a matter of the hidden life, a matter that is entirely inward. There may be external attitudes and actions which convey the idea of rectitude; but if the heart be wrong there is no beatitude. He declares that the character must be purity in the inward parts, "Blessed are the pure in heart;

for they shall see God." Not the overt act of sin is that which is supremely to be condemned, but the inner lust after it. God does not shudder and tremble where man does, in the presence of the murderer with blood on his hands; God shudders at those movements of the soul which are of contempt, of hatred, and which presently may express themselves in murder. While the man who does not inflict bodily harm on his neighbor will escape the law of humanity, the man who speaks in terms of contempt of his fellow man is judged in the courts of heaven as being iniquitous and unholy. This is the ethic of love. These are the demands that love sets up on the human soul, and which can be realized or answered only when love masters and inspires the life. Life must be true and gracious, it must be according to light and according to love. It must be stern and hard with irrevocable justice. It must be tender and sweet with unfailing compassion. A man must steadfastly refuse to bend the neck in the presence of any oppression and wrong; and yet he must be ready immediately to embrace the wrong-doer with the love of a great forgiveness. That is the ethic of Jesus, all contained in the ultimate conception of likeness to the God Who is love, and expressed in the terrific word of my text, "Ye shall therefore be perfect, as your heavenly Father is perfect." In the manifesto, moreover, something is added which is entirely peculiar to Christ and Christianity. Jesus says that the true value of character is not that it secures safety to the men who possess it, but that it scatters blessings on other men. Those who have this character are the light of the world, are the salt of the earth. Men are to be men of holy character, true and gracious, not that they may secure their own safety, either for time or for eternity, but in order that from them light may fall on the pathways where men stumble and are lost; in order that they may exert the aseptic influence of salt,

salt that hinders the spread of corruption and gives goodness in other people its chance.

When I have done listening to this Teacher I look at Him. When I look at Him I am more than ever impressed with the awful glory of the standard, for the purity of Jesus is something that fills the soul with ever-growing awe. There came a day when Paul was writing a letter in which he declared, "The grace of God hath appeared, bringing salvation to all men." That is the value of the second text. Then he continued: "instructing us, to the intent that, denying ungodliness and worldly lusts, we should live soberly, righteously, and godly in this present world." That is the value of the first text. The words Paul used I reverently use of Jesus Himself. "Soberly"; that means with perfect inward self-government. It is a word that refers to the individuality, and describes life as held in check, in poise, in restraint, none of its passions destroyed, but all held in check by principle. Look at Jesus. We cannot find in the records a single instance in which he lost control of Himself. I can find instance after instance in which He surged with passion as He denounced hypocrisy in language which even at the distance of two millenniums is white-hot and scorching. But He was always Master of His language; no word passed His lips that He had to recall. I have seen Him, His bosom heaving with emotion, and His wondrous eyes of matchless beauty suffused with tears; but I never find Him sickly in sentiment. Thrilling through the threnody of His complaint is the thunder of His righteousness. "O Jerusalem, Jerusalem . . . how often would I have gathered thy children together, even as a hen gathereth her chickens under her wings, and ye would not! Behold, your house is left unto you desolate." He lived soberly, that is, with personality powerful, but controlled. That is perfection.

The word "righteously" here defines human interrelationship. It refers to the world around. To live righteously is to maintain the relationships of justice and mercy with our fellow men. Righteousness is supremely merciful. When our Lord commenced His ministry He said to John the Baptist, "Thus it becometh us to fulfil all righteousness." He said that when He was bending, stooping, to a baptism that was symbolic of the death whereby He would extend mercy to men. Even His enemies never attempted to bring against Him any charge of ever having wronged man, woman, or child. They did charge Him with profaning the temple, with violating the Sabbath, with being overfriendly with sinning men and women; but never with wronging man or woman, or being unjust to a child. When at last they would murder Him, they must lie in order to do it, and procure false witnesses to trap Him. They charged Him with the violation of the trivialities of their ceremonial in order to nail Him to the Cross; but they could not charge Him with being unjust to His kind.

The last word, "godly," reveals relationship with the great over-world, the ultimate world of the human spirit, the world with which man essentially has to do, whether he admits it or not, for in the hand of God is man's breath, in the government of God are all man's ways. No life is perfect that has no traffic with heaven, no commerce with eternity, no dealings with God. The godliness of the life of Jesus was revealed, not conventionally, not according to the religious standards of His day. The supreme trouble was that He was not a religious man in the thinking of the religious men of the day. He broke the Sabbath, He violated tradition, He failed to give His hands ceremonial cleansing before eating food. But He was godly. Hear His own beatitude, and discover in it a chaplet of glory and beauty that found its first resting place on the head of the Man Who uttered it: "Blessed are the pure in heart: for they shall see God." See God! Where? Everywhere. See God! When? Now. Jesus saw God everywhere, in the beauty of the lily, in the safety of the bird, in the glory of the harvest field, in the faces of men and women, in the vast movements of history. The vision of God was the inspiration of His humanity. His life was adjusted to God with a familiarity that often fills the soul with wonder. He spoke of God as Father, and declared His unity with Him, and His submission to Him; made the declaration that He never said anything of Himself, but uttered only the things He heard whispered in His soul by His Father, God; that He never did anything on His own initiative, but only as the Divine will constrained and controlled Him. That is godly life, perfect life. The ethic of Jesus was incarnate in Himself.

Once again, and finally, the perfection of Jesus was demonstrated by that supreme and final act of God wherein He raised Him from the dead. On the day of Pentecost Peter for the first time became a truly seeing man, all the blindness gone, understanding as he never had understood, by the sudden, glorious coming of the Holy Spirit apprehending the meaning of the Man in Whose presence he had been for three years. Referring to Jesus' resurrection, Peter declared, "It was not possible that He should be holden of it." Why not? Because of the perfection of His righteousness, the righteousness of His godly life, the righteousness which He perfected in the mystery of His dying. When God raised Jesus of Nazareth from the dead He said to humanity by that act, This is the type of human life acceptable to heaven. By the resurrection of Jesus Christ from the dead He rejected every other ideal of human life and every other conception of human greatness. By that raising from among the dead of One Who had bowed to buffeting and sacrificial death God declared in human history that the man who desires to rise to power by the oppression of others is rejected of heaven and doomed in the ultimate economy of eternity. By that raising from the dead of this Man God declared that merely intellectual attainment can never be the final ground of humanity's acceptance. By that raising from the dead of Jesus He declared that every ideal and every conception of man that does not harmonize with the perfection of that wondrous life is rejected. The raising of Jesus from the dead is God's signature to the perfect glory of the human ideal that had been incarnate in the Man of Nazareth.

Now I listen again to His second word, so familiar is its ineffable music, and so has it comforted the hearts of multitudes that perhaps there is need to do little more than repeat it: "The Son of man came to seek and to save that which was lost." The seeking involves the whole of His mission, not merely the earthly mission, but His mission through the Spirit, the methods by which He approaches man's soul and makes His great appeal, seeking, ever seeking. The saving involves not merely the initial act whereby a soul is received, but all the disciplinary processes which follow, until that soul is perfected and presented faultless before the throne of God.

He came to seek, and why to seek? Because of the distance between those whom He came to seek and the God from Whom He came. But God is not far from any one of us. In Him "we live, and move, and have our being." He is "the God in Whose hand our breath is, and Whose are all our ways." Our distance is that of inability to know and apprehend the near. It is the distance of the blind man from the glory of the picture that is in front of him. It is the distance of the deaf man from the beauty of the symphony sounding round about him. It is the distance of the insensate man from all the movements of life in the midst of which he lives. Men live and move and have their being in God, and do not see Him. His voice, broken up into a thousand inflections, is ever speaking in their ears, but they do not hear them. He is close at hand, and they do not feel or touch Him. This Man saw God everywhere, heard Him always, and always touched Him. Man's distance from God is the distance of death from life in the midst of life. How appalling is the fact that men everywhere are near to God but never see Him. There are men who never see God in a flower, never see Him in a bird; who never see God on the mighty ocean or amid the vastness of the eternal hills. There are men who cannot see God in the war today. They are blind souls. God's judgments are abroad in the earth. His grasp is on all humanity, making humanity work out its own choice to inevitable expression, that He may correct the wrong and bring the light of life to light. Yet men do not see Him. Therefore, He came to seek, to open blind eyes, to unstop deaf ears, to touch the hard heart until it thrills and throbs with emotion. Those who are thus at a distance from God have become unlike God. He seeks them that He may restore to them the Divine image, and them to God Himself. Souls who are remote from God by reason of death are at enmity against God, hating, not God, but what they think is God. He came to seek them, to shine through the gloom, and destroy all false conceptions of God by being Himself incarnate Deity, revealing to men through the glance of the eye, the strength and tenderness of human speech, the glory of human life, all the perfection of grace and beauty, the wonders of what God is in Himself.

He came not only to seek, but to save. He begins with that central, essential fact of human personality, the spirit, linking it again to God, opening blind eyes, unstopping deaf ears, making it keen of scent in the fear of the Lord. He renews the mind also, transforming it until it becomes spiritual. The body He preserves as a temple of the Holy Ghost, and promises that at last there shall come to all trusting souls the infinite wonder that came to Him, resurrection from among the dead.

The announcement at the beginning thus becomes not a command, but a promise. Because He bends and stoops to me in my low estate, and lifts me notwithstanding all, and takes me into His fellowship while as yet I am a polluted man, sitting down to eat with me, a sinner; because He does this, I dare look into His face with reverent awe, and glad emotion of soul, and I dare say to Him in spite of my growing consciousness of failure and weakness, "Thou wilt perfect that which concerneth me."

God help us to submit ourselves to the measurement of His standard. Let us be done with comparing ourselves with ourselves, or finding some crumb of paltry satisfaction in the fact that we are not worse than other men, or a little better than a few. Let us press into His presence that He may measure us and condemn us, for by that process we shall be led to press nearer and yet nearer to His wounded side of ineffable love, that we may know His restoring and healing power, and at last be presented faultless before the throne of God.

CHAPTER XI

THE CONDITIONS OF COMING TO GOD

He that cometh to God must believe that He is, and that He is a rewarder of them that seek after Him.
HEBREWS 11:6.

THE TEXT IS PART OF A VERSE WHICH BREAKS IN ON THE CONtinuity of the chapter from which it is taken. That chapter constitutes the roll of honor of the heroes and heroines of faith. The second name on the list is Enoch, of whom it is said, "By faith Enoch was translated that he should not see death; and he was not found, because God translated him: for before his translation he hath had witness borne to him that he had been well-pleasing unto God." Then it is declared, "Without faith it is impossible to be well-pleasing unto Him: for he that cometh to God must believe that He is, and that He is a rewarder of them that seek after Him." In this interpolation on the continuity of the chapter we have the one clear Biblical statement for the necessity of perpetual and fundamental Biblical assumptions. Everywhere the Bible assumes the two things that here it is declared must be believed if man is to come to God. The Biblical literature from its first majestic sentence, "In the beginning God created," to its very last sentence, "The grace of the Lord Jesus be with the saints," assumes that God is, and that He is a rewarder of them that seek after Him. For these things it never argues. Of the men whom it presents to us, whether they be the great historical figures of the old covenant or the new, whether they be lawgivers, or prophets, or psalmists, none argues for the existence of God, none ever attempts to prove that He is a rewarder of such as seek after Him. This is supremely, finally true in the case of the one supernal figure, Jesus. He never argued for the existence of God. He never argued for the truth that God is available to souls that seek after Him. These Biblical writers argued for the love of God, for the justice of God, for the care of God; and some of them, in the midst of agony, questioned the love of God, questioned the justice of God, questioned the care of God; but none of them argued for Him, or for His availability to certain souls in certain conditions. The man who denies the existence of God is almost contemptuously dismissed, "The fool saith in his heart, There is no God." In my text, then, we are face to face with fundamental things.

Let us consider, first, the central idea suggested, that of coming to God; second, the declared condition in its twofold application; and, finally, the involved teaching which may be of profit to our own hearts today and always.

First, then, the central idea of coming to God. Simply and inclusively the thought is of approach to God, drawing near to God, or of putting oneself into communication with God. In expression and in experience the thought is of speaking to God in praise and prayer and of hearing God speak. Of these two exercises of the soul in addressing God, prayer is the first in experience, but praise is the higher. I believe that praise may become so profound and so continuous that there is hardly any room left for prayer. But the experience of the soul in speaking to God is, first, of prayer, then of praise. In experience and expression, drawing near to God is not only speaking to Him, whether in prayer or praise, it is hearing God speak. That is the more difficult exercise, conditioned in silence and experienced in the reception of what God has to say. Of these, the second, the reception of what God has to say to the soul, is assured to all those who keep silence before Him. But again I say it is far harder to be silent before God than to speak to God. This is one of the lost arts of the Christian Church and of the Christian soul. We have almost forgotten how to listen for God. That is the reason why we so seldom hear Him speak. I would urge all young Christian people, at whatever cost—however busy the days with pressing duties, however important it be that you do something for God—not to fail to make time in which to cease praising and praying in order to cultivate the silence of the soul. That is the condition to which God addresses Himself directly and immediately. These are the highest aspects of the expression and experience of coming to God. Light on the conception comes to us from the context. "By faith Enoch was translated that he should not see death; and he was not found, because God translated him: for before his translation he hath had witness borne to him that he had been well-pleasing unto God: and without faith it is impossible to be well-pleasing unto Him: for he that cometh unto God must believe that He is." Immediately in connection with the great declaration we have this illustration: "Enoch walked with God: and he was not; for God took him." That is coming to God. "Enoch walked with God" in a godless age. Enoch was the seventh from Adam through Seth. The seventh from Adam through Cain was Lamech. Lamech and his sons were the originators of the arts and sciences, and of the enfranchisement of women. It was a wonderfully successful age, but godless. One simple soul walked with God in the godless age. That was coming to God. It involves leaving a good deal, cutting oneself off from many things; it means being out of date, peculiar, behind the times! Enoch walked with God in a godless age. With what result? God took him, took him out of the godless age while he was still in it, became his boon companion, making up for the loss of all such friendships, satisfying the inner cry of his soul, though all other things were denied him. At last God took him away from the age by translation, so that men sought for the strange, peculiar character who had been separated from all the progress of the age, and they found him not, for God had translated him. What was the deep secret of it all? Enoch believed "that God is, and that He is a rewarder of them that seek after Him." Answering his belief, he found God, he gained the reward; he marched with God through the weary years, and at last walked out into light and life forevermore. That is coming to God.

What, then, is the condition of coming to God? I pray you note the simplicity of the statement, and its sublimity. We "must believe that God is, and that He is a rewarder." Nothing can be simpler in statement, nothing more sublime in conception; for to believe that God is, and to believe that God is a rewarder, is to have all life conditioned by that belief, to see everything personal, relative, social, national, racial, set in the light thereof. To believe that God is, and that God is a rewarder, is to have solved the riddle of the universe, and then to march along the line of the solution, knowing that presently every tangled web will be made straight, all the mists will melt, and the discords of the straining and the tension will merge into the last and final harmonies of perfect order and perfect music. It is so simple that a little child will understand it, and agree that no one will come to a person he does not believe exists, no one will come to a person he does not believe will receive him and reward him. It is quite simple; and yet fundamentally, finally sublime.

The inclusive condition is to have faith. Faith is infinitely more than intellectual conviction. Faith is intellectual conviction expressing itself in volitional obedience. To me, trust is a greater word than faith. Faith is belief, conviction; trust puts conviction into practice. There is a chair, I have faith in it; when I sit on it I trust it! I have an intellectual conviction that the chair will bear me, I could argue it, demonstrate it, lecture on it: that is faith; but when I sit on it I am trusting it. That is the faith that is demanded of men who come to God: not merely intellectual conviction, but abandonment of the whole life to the truth of which the soul is convinced—that is faith.

First, we must believe that God is. I have said in my introduction that it is never argued for in the Bible. I will stand by that declaration. Therefore, is it necessary, or wise, or will I do any good if I argue for it, seeing that the Bible never argues for it? Yes, I think it may be well to discover the reasons of our faith, for the faith demanded of us is not blind, foolish credulity. Therefore we will inquire if there be any grounds for this great assumption of the Bible.

I first declare that belief in the existence of God is the most natural activity of the human soul. Effort is required to disbelieve rather than to believe. Wherever you find a person who does not believe that God is you have a person who has come to that condition of mind as the result of effort. I am not speaking disrespectfully of such; they may be honest; the disbelief may be the outcome of agony, but it is the outcome of effort. The human soul naturally believes in God, in the fact that He is. Is there anything more beautiful or wonderful than the story of Helen Keller? She was blind, dumb, deaf from birth, a soul imprisoned; yet with infinite, beautiful patience another soul took time to communicate with that imprisoned soul. Without the aid of eyes, or ear, or tongue, but with the touch of tenderness and delicacy of sensation, Miss Sullivan at last found Helen Keller's beautiful soul. In the process of that training, Bishop Phillips Brooks was asked to see her, and communicate to her the idea of God. With patience the great Bishop gave himself to the business. After a long while Helen Keller responded. She said to the Bishop, "Oh, I know perfectly well what you mean; I have always known Him; but I did not know what you called Him." That is a rare illustration, but by reason of its rarity the more powerful; a soul shut up in prison always knew God. It is perfectly natural to believe in God. Every child believes in God, unless you in your unutterable folly have told the child there is no God; and even then it does not believe you at first. Every child believes in God. All simple souls believe in Him. I say it is the natural attitude of the human soul.

If you are not for the moment prepared to accept that, or it may be that in your struggle after truth you have got away from that, then there are lines of proof that it would be well for you to consider. I should be inclined to ask a man who told me he did not believe in God first to appeal to his imagination. I wonder how many of you young people have read Paley's *Natural Theology*. You young men, lay preachers, have you read it? I find no exercise more helpful when I am preparing a sermon than to get down some old book and read it again. I have been all through Paley's *Natural Theology* getting ready for this sermon. It was written in 1802, and contains the argument from design, which I am asked to believe is out of date. It may be out of date, but it has never been answered or refuted. The first argument, on which he bases all the rest, is the argument of the watch. Paley says that if walking across the moorland his foot struck against a stone, and he should inquire whence it came, it is possible that he might say, That has been there forever and forever, and not be able to demonstrate the absurdity of the reply. If, instead of a stone, he found a watch there, it would be impossible to say that it had been there forever and ever. The watch argues a watchmaker. That has never been answered; it has been laughed at, counted out of date: today I do not know that there is a theological college or seminary in the world where it is studied; but it has not been refuted. I appeal, then, to my imagination. The fact that watches are improved and that the skilful watchmaker would laugh at the old-fashioned mechanism does not disprove the argument; the more complex the mechanism, the more secure is the argument for the man behind the mechanism. Since that book was written what strides we have made in our understanding of the universe! It has been discovered to us to be far more complicated, mystical, marvelous than our fathers ever suspected; but that does not invalidate the argument from design; rather this additional knowledge accentuates the argument and makes it powerful. If there can be no watch without a maker and a mind, will your imagination allow you to be satisfied to believe that the universe so rhythmic, so wonderful, so beauteous in its processes, so regular in its irregularities, so irregular in its regularities, is a mere accident, a creation without intelligence, an order without arrangement? Take a twig from an apple tree and look at it; the leaves are set in spirals, and number five is always exactly above number one. Why is number five above number one? I do not know, I have no idea; but it proves regularity, order, design. My apple trees, with their spiral blossoming, make it impossible for me to believe that there is no God. An odd number of rows will not be found in any single ear of corn, among all the multiplied millions. I do not think these things are accidents. If I try to think of creation without intelligence, of order without arrangement, of man, the most marvelous thing in all the universe, without the God Who thought him, created him, my imagination is in revolt. Consequently, my appeal to imagination becomes an appeal to reason. I declare that for myself it is far easier to believe that God is than to believe that He is not.

I make my appeal finally to the manifestation of God which He has made of Himself in human history in a Man named Jesus, Who claimed to be one with the hidden God, Whose influence through two millenniums has been to make men believe in the one hidden God, Whose most glorious victories in the two millenniums have been the victories of the growing beauty of man's conception of the God Whom He claimed to reveal. We cannot decide whether God is until we have dealt with Jesus of Nazareth, have listened to His claims, and have begun to consider the influence He has exerted. Countless millions of souls have walked with God because they have trusted in Jesus, have found infinite comfort in the Divine compassion because they have dared to follow the lonely Galilean peasant; have felt the force, the energy of God sustaining them in conflict and in suffering because they have loved Jesus. We must remember also that the great conception men have of God, even though they may be denying Jesus His Deity, has nevertheless come to the world as the result of His presence therein and His teaching of the sons of men.

But there must be more than believing that God is. There must be belief "that He is a rewarder of them that seek after Him." The general idea is that this means that man must believe in the moral government of God. Of course, that is involved. It is impossible to believe that God has abandoned the highest results of His creative power, man, and the moral element in man. It is impossible to believe that God rolls the seasons round, decks the sod with beauty, clothes the trees with verdure, maintains the equilibrium of all things in the great process of His order, and has nothing to do with man. It is impossible to believe that God cares for man on the physical side of his being and nothing for his moral nature. All that is involved, but that is not the declaration of the text. The declaration is of the availability of God to certain souls on certain conditions. Those souls and conditions are revealed in the words rendered in the Revised Version, "them that seek after Him," and in the Authorized Version, "such as diligently seek Him." I think the Revised Version has lost something by omitting the word "diligently." As a matter of fact, there is but one word in the Greek, but it is a strong word, and we need something more than the ordinary word "seek" to convey its meaning. The word means to investigate, to crave, to demand. God is a rewarder of such as investigate, crave, demand Him; or, in the simpler words of Jesus, such as ask, seek, knock. The attitude of soul described is persistent determination to approach God. God is not found of men who indulge in dilletante fooling. When the soul feels its need, when the soul gropes in the night, and, knocking, inquires, then God becomes a rewarder, a Payer of wages—that is the word, a Remunerator, one who gives what is demanded, pays over what is asked. God comes to the soul that comes to Him.

What proofs have we that God is a rewarder of them that seek after Him? There are hours in which the soul seems unable to find God. Said Eliphaz to Job, "Acquaint now thyself with Him, and be at peace." Said the man in his agony in reply, "O that I knew where I might find Him. . . . Behold, I go forward, but He is not there; and backward, but I cannot perceive Him: on the left hand, when He doth work, but I cannot behold Him: He hideth Himself on the right hand, that I cannot see Him." The human soul knows that experience; but let us never forget that Job did find Him. Through the very process in which he thought he could not find God Job was preparing himself to find Him. By the strenuousness of his endeavor, by the stress of his agony, by the strong crying of his soul after God, he was preparing for the coming of God. The very pain and suffering and tribulation and unrest which seem to prove that God cannot be found may be the exercise of soul through which He will be found.

I find in the nature of man the first proof that God may be found. Man is made to ask, to seek, to knock. In her beautiful book, *Laddie*, Mrs. Gene Stratton Porter makes one of her characters say of man that he is a praying animal. Though he never prays, if he be in sudden peril of shipwreck, fire, or death, he will pray. Man has a natural capacity for prayer, and there is no half measure in this universe. Has that bird a wing? Then there is air in which to poise it. Has that fish a fin? Then there is water in which to use it. Does your soul go out in prayer? Then there is a God to pray to Who will answer prayer.

Another proof that God gives Himself to such as seek Him is to be found in the experience of men. If testimony is to be accepted as evidence on any subject, why not on this? Why do men rule out the testimony of souls who declare that they have prayed and have been answered. It is unscientific to rule out such testimony. There are tens of thousands who know what it is to pray and to be answered, to ask and to have, to seek and to find, to knock and to see the door swing open. Their testimony is not merely the testimony of their avowal. It is also the testimony of their lives, transfigured by their belief, and made beautiful, pure, compassionate, glorious.

The final proof is the testimony of the Man of Nazareth, Who, whatever doubts we may have concerning the meaning of some of the things He said, has left no room for doubt that He believed, and intended men to believe, that God is available to souls, will answer them, will reward them, will come to them in grace, in succor, in strength, in love, in help —when they seek after Him.

To believe that God is, is to believe in One Who knows all, is infinitely wise, is always close at hand, is all powerful, and is love. If that be true, then how easy it is to come to God. There is nothing to explain when you come, He knows it all. There is no journey to take to reach Him:

> Closer is He than breathing,
> Nearer than hands and feet.

Effort is unnecessary; in silence, and in the quietness of the soul that has ceased its struggling God makes Himself known. "Perfect love casteth out fear."

To believe that God is a rewarder is to believe, first, that He is interested in me. I can think of Him as interested in the universe, but to learn the corollary of that, that nothing is too small for His attention is the wonderful thing. God is great not only in the infinitude of immensity, but in the exactitude of littleness. Consequently, He is interested in me, in what I wear, in what I eat, in where I live, in my amusements. Think how easy it is to come to Him; no persuasion is necessary. That whole conception of prayer that declares we must persuade God is erroneous. Jesus gave us the figure of the importunate widow to prove that we need not be importunate. Importunity was necessary in the case of the unjust judge; it is not necessary in the case of God. Refusal is not possible in the heart of love, except that love will refuse what would harm us.

Nevertheless, the text reveals the need of urgency. The belief necessary involves conviction of the necessity for demand, craving, seeking. Such is the only condition to which God can give Himself.

Finally, do not let us forget the opening declaration of the letter from which the text is taken: "God hath spoken . . . unto us by His Son . . . the effulgence of His glory, and the very image of His substance." Christ stands to me in the place of God, and He is God. So that when I would come to God I come to Christ, the Man of my humanity, so that this frail imagination of mine may go out to Him apprehendingly. As I do so, I find I have included in the grasp of my comprehension the vastness of God and eternity. I come to God because I believe that He is, having seen Him in Christ; because I believe that He is a rewarder of them that seek after Him, having seen Christ receive publicans and sinners, and heard Him say to them as they thronged to Him, "Him that cometh to me I will in no wise cast out." Believing these things I come to Him, and He comes to me, and we walk and talk together.

CHAPTER XII

THE OPPORTUNITY OF CALAMITY

Redeeming the time, because the days are evil.
                              EPHESIANS 5:16.

IN THESE WORDS WE HAVE A REMARKABLE REVELATION OF Christian privilege and responsibility in days of calamity. In the text are outstanding words which arrest our attention: first, the opening word, "Redeeming"; then the word almost immediately succeeding, "time"; and, finally, the word used to describe the days, "evil." The word here rendered "redeeming" literally means to buy out or to buy. The base of the word is the market place. The word itself suggests keen business acumen, the ability to know exactly what to buy, and when to buy. It is a strictly commercial term.

The second word, "time," has a particular significance. It indicates a special occasion, and therefore a special opportunity.

The third word, "evil," refers to evil in the effect it produces: evil is that which is hurtful, harmful, calamitous.

From this examination of words we immediately discover that in the thought of the apostle evil days constitute special occasions or opportunities for the prosecution of the commerce of the Kingdom of God, that such evil days can be bought out, bought up, turned to account; and, finally, that if they are to be rescued from their evil nature or from that which is calamitous, if they are to be turned to account in the interest of beneficence and goodness, they must be bought up, they must be purchased. The element of sacrifice is involved, the giving up of something, in order that the opportunity may be seized. Of course, involved in that is the larger thought that all such giving results in getting. As in the market place in the olden days, as in the market place today, the man, keen and shrewd and honest and upright and true, is ever prepared to give, but he expects also to gain.

The whole conception of the apostle, then, is that to certain people days of calamity offer special opportunities for the prosecution of great enterprises of the Kingdom of God.

Let us first notice the thought of the apostle concerning the days, "evil days." It was a revolutionary idea. If we had found our way into Ephesus, one of the cities certainly to which this letter was sent, and had talked to the men of Ephesus, the men in authority, if we had told them that someone had said that these were evil days, they would have laughed at us. They were very prosperous days in Ephesus, the days of her wealth, the days when the Temple of Artemis was also the banking house of the merchants, the days of that strange relationship between commerce and religion that made Ephesus materially great. We shall understand the apostle only as we remember the people to whom he was writing. When I glance at the opening of the letter I find this description of them:

> "Paul, an apostle of Christ Jesus through the will of God, to *the saints* which are in Ephesus, and *the faithful in Christ Jesus*."

He was writing, then, to those whom he described as saints, those set apart to God in Christ, separated to God for the specific purpose, not of saving their own souls, but of carrying out God's enterprises. When Paul described them as "the faithful in Christ Jesus," the word does not suggest they were always faithful in the sense of fidelity, but that they lived on the principle of faith. These people to whom the apostle wrote then judged things not by the seen but by the unseen; these were people who saw not merely the things that were seen, but all those vast things of the spiritual world and of eternal measurements in which all near things were conditioned; they were people who lived on the principle of faith. Writing to such Paul said, the days are calamitous.

In the chapter from which this text is taken we have a yet further description of these people: "Be ye therefore imitators of God, as beloved children; and walk in love." In that injunction we have a revelation, not merely of what these people were in themselves, but of their supreme responsibility. They were to imitate God; they were to behave as God would behave in Ephesus; they were to live according to the standard of Divine love in Ephesus. Love was to be the master passion of all their thinking, all their speaking, and all their doing. It must be the love of God, not a mere weak, sentimental anemic emotion, evanescent and passing, but love, that high outgoing of the soul that acts as surely in judgment as in mercy, that is based forevermore on truth and is always suffused with light.

To such people these days in Ephesus were evil days, and wherever that ideal of life Paul gives the Ephesians is accepted and followed the days are evil days. This world is not a friend of Jesus Christ. It may speak respectfully of Him, it may even patronize some of His teaching, but it is not a friend of Jesus Christ. In proportion as men are truly trying to live and love like God, on the principle of faith, the days are always evil days. Take any ordinary day. I do not mean the days of the moment in which we are living, but those days before we were plunged into the catastrophe of the hour. The ideal of life among the mass of men in the city or in the country is godless. Men are living without relationship to the claims of God—rather, I should say, without recognition of that relationship. The bulk of human activity is material, even our own activity. It is so of necessity. I am not saying this is wrong. The majority of our hours are necessarily given to things that are material, transient, perishing, the things that presently we shall drop and leave. The rush and speed of life today are against man's development and the character of love. The hurry and the jostle and the crush of life do not help the development of Christian character. There is a sense, I say, in which all the days in which we are called on to live are evil days if the ideal of life be that described by the apostle, and if its master passion be that of living as God would live, and walking forevermore in love. To the majority of saints the general atmosphere of the ordinary days is against Christian character, and not helpful. When that is declared on a Sabbath morning in the sanctuary by a preacher of the truth men are almost surprised to hear it. Yet it is the thing they are constantly saying in the subconsciousness of their inner life.

I think that we shall all agree that these are evil days, days of calamity. The things that hurt and harm and spoil and destroy seem rampant everywhere. The Christian man must be conscious that this whole war* is in itself evil, that it is calamitous. Christian men cannot rejoice in war for war's sake. We may be divided in our opinion on this particular war, on the relationship of our own nation to it; but as Christians we must agree that war itself is calamitous. It can

* World War I.

be none other than a calamity. This ghastly destruction of human life is dire calamity. And Dr. Saleeby is perfectly right, even though some people label him today as fanatical, when he persistently reminds us that we must think of the long cost of the war. That is not the cost of money but of men, and not of men alone, but of the impoverishment of the generations ahead. Surely there is no man in this country who can rejoice in war for the sake of war. They are evil days for the world.

I go further now, and here is the great burden on my heart, inspiring the message I would deliver. At the present moment the days seem to be almost more evil to us as a nation and people than any that have preceded in the war. Let me hasten to explain that, so as to leave no misunderstanding of what I am thinking. We are all conscious that there is abroad just now a spirit, shall I say, of pessimism. I confess I have been burdened and oppressed during the last week with reading papers, religious and secular. I also confess that there is some ground for the present attitude, that this particular hour is a very serious one, from the beginning of August last until now. I do not propose for a single moment to speak as one having any knowledge which is not available to the everyday reader, but as one who has been attempting to follow the whole movement, reading the writings of such men as Mr. Hilaire Belloc, Mr. Garvin, Mr. Spender, and Sir William Robertson Nicol, and I declare that I do not consider the hour at which we have now arrived is any darker than any hour through which we have passed since August 4 last. That is a personal opinion, which you may dismiss. What I do think is happening—and I think it is a great gain—is that we are beginning to understand how serious and terrific is the task before us. What I am trying to do now is to face the fact that the days are evil days. What then? What, then, is to be the attitude of the man of faith? How are we to look on these days? And what is our duty in this particular hour?

Now, for the moment leaving all this reference to the present situation, I go back to the text. Having then in mind the apostolic description of those days and those saints at Ephesus, I ask you to notice that the whole meaning of this text is that evil days constitute peculiar opportunities for the prosecution of the enterprises of the Kingdom of God. Let me touch on the things I used a moment ago as illustrations. Every godless man is an opportunity for godly men. Godless men come into contact with godly men in the economy of grace in order that they may pass under the influence of their godliness. Immediately there breaks on us the conviction of the wrong we have done if in the company of godless men we have consented to lower the standard of our own godliness in thought and speech.

I am not suggesting that a man of business is to ask every man who comes into his office if he is a Christian. That is not my suggestion. I am not suggesting that a man on his professional duties shall offer tracts to men. That is not my suggestion. If I were a business man and you talked to me about my soul when I am doing business with you, I should show you the door immediately. A tract enclosed with an invoice is an insult to religion. When a godly man does business with a godless man he must see to it that his business is done in a godly fashion. The godly fashion is not merely the fashion of the man who is strictly just; it is also the fashion of the man who is walking in love. The godly fashion of doing business is not merely the fashion of the man who will refuse to misrepresent his goods. The godly fashion is the fashion of the man who will not allow the other man to sell him something for less than its value in order that he may get the advantage.

Oh! you say, I had a great bargain this week. Did you? What was it? I bought a picture and the man did not know its value, but I did. That is not godliness; it is godlessness. Godliness in business means more than integrity and uprightness of purpose. The actually godly man will see that the other man is not wronged or harmed. Every godless man is an opportunity for our godliness to shine forth. All material things—I have said that the majority of days are filled with material activities—all material things are a basis for our spirituality to shine on, the carbon on which the electric current of our relationship with God must flash out. The very things that make it hard to be a Christian are the things which enable us to shine, are opportunities to display the meaning of Christianity and the value of our relationship to God. It is a day of rush and jostle and hurry, when it is hard to be quiet, and calm, and tender, and merciful. The rush today is our chance to reveal the quietness of God.

I go back again to the thing that is on all our hearts. These are dark days, serious days. May I remind you, then, children of God, sons of the Most High, faithful in Christ Jesus, those who are called to be imitators of God and to walk in love, that panic today is the result of the overwhelming sense of the might of brute force. Courage demonstrates confidence in God. Courage is never foolhardiness. Courage will take every precaution. But courage will never sit down and utter its dirge in the hour of darkness. I find men today looking out over the present situation, and suggesting that the ultimate issue of the struggle, however long and however ghastly, may be the defeat of righteousness and truth and justice and honor and compassion. The men who make such a suggestion must, for the moment, be overwhelmed with the force of brutality, and have lost their vision of God. I declare here publicly this morning, with great solemnity, that if the forces that trample order under foot, and violate the common things of humanity should triumph, then in the day of their triumph my preaching would cease in despairing silence, for my faith in God would be utterly broken. The thing is impossible. The thing can never be. We must take the large outlook. We must remember that even in this hour we also are suffering by reason of our sins. These things of suffering are disciplinary. I look toward the issue, and I cannot bate one jot of heart or hope. I must move right forward and believe that God Who acts in truth and love and mercy must prevail. The true attitude for the man of faith today is that attitude of courage which demonstrates confidence in God.

It may be said that perhaps these things need saying to those who are writing in the papers, but not to Christian men and women. I do not agree. The thing of importance is how Christian men and women talk after they have read. By ordinary conversation, in homes, and stores, and clubs throughout the length and breadth of this land today, more is done to influence opinion than is done by all the writers in the press. Therefore it may be well to remind ourselves of so simple a matter as this, that when we read articles in the press, in magazines, daily papers, weekly papers, we should attempt to find out the temperament of the men who write them. When we do that we discover the reason for a good deal of foolish optimism and pernicious pessimism.

There is, however, a common bond uniting these men who are interpreting the hour, and that is the passion for the success of truth and justice and right. When we have listened to them and taken their outlook, let us remit everything to the Biblical revelation that good shall be established. If we waver it is because our confidence in God is not the confidence that it ought to be. "Strengthen ye the weak hands, and confirm the feeble knees"—that seems to me to be a message we supremely need to hear at this particular time.

I go back to one of the least known books of the Old Testament, the Song of Solomon, that wonderful, mystical love song, purely Eastern in its gorgeous coloring and in all its speech. In the course of it I find these words, and I resolutely adopt the old Puritan method of making use of them as an illustration of the highest relationship between Christ and His people: "As the lily among the thorns, so is my love among the daughters." That is the bridegroom's description of His Bride, Christ's description of His Church: "As the lily among the thorns." The lily is of gorgeous beauty, of light and splendor, of loveliness; the thorns are rank and dank and poisonous. Yet the lily grows among the thorns in the soil in which the thorns are reared. The lily is fanned by the breezes that blow on the thorns; on the lily falls the rain that falls on the thorns. The difference is the difference between the nature of the lily and the nature of the thorns.

All about us are the things that are against us, evil days, days of darkness; and men's hearts are failing them because of fear. Evil might is attempting to master a world of love by putting it under the heel of cruelty. The lily is to grow in that soil, and in that atmosphere, full of beauty, full of grace, full of courage, full of confidence, full of assurance. Christian people are not to be aloof from the age in which they live. They are not to separate themselves from the endeavors of others. In order to win victory in this struggle we must unite. We must not be guilty of abating hope, of sitting down in ashes, of suggesting that at last that which began best is going to end worst. We are to demonstrate our belief by our courage, by our certainty, by our hope.

Through the fulfilment of this obligation in the midst of such opportunities the enterprises of God will be carried forward, men will be won for Him, and the victory will be on His side. Men are rallying to the flag from the north and the south, and the east and the west, from all the lands within this great Empire. But something more than material force is needed. There must be intercession, the activity in the secret place, if there is to be spiritual courage. These are the things needed today as never before, and these are the contributions which we can supremely make in this hour of our calamity and our need.

Never must the men of faith allow themselves to be confined in their looking to the horizon that appears. There was a man of old time who endured as seeing Him Who is invisible. And this is the question I think we need to ask ourselves today. Do we see God? You remember the story from the classics, how, when news was sent to Antigonus that an army as of ten to one was mustered against him, he looked at the messenger and said: "And for how many do you count me?" I lift the lesson into this higher realm. We are told of the enemy that they have more men, more munitions, more strength, more preparation. I affirm, then, that the question God is asking of the men of faith is this: *For how many do you count Me?*

Ah, yes, but we must see to it that we are on His side. We must see to it, in all our praying and our thinking and our enduring and our sacrificing, that we seek, first, right, truth, justice, mercy, compassion, and that these be the main motives of our endeavor. Then may we calmly wait amidst the furnace blast, knowing what the issue must be. The measure of our investment is the measure of the return that will reward us presently. The measure in which today we are putting into the awful business of the hour all the forces of our life, temporal, mental, spiritual, is the measure of the victory that will come to us presently.

One glance at the context in conclusion. The true attitude for heavenly commerce is a threefold one, and the apostle has carefully marked it for us. "Look therefore carefully how ye walk, not as unwise, but as wise"; "understanding what the will of the Lord is." "Be filled with the Spirit." If the saints of God, the faithful in Christ Jesus, who are to imitate God and walk in love, are indeed to buy up the opportunity of the dark and evil day these things must not be neglected. Their walk must be with care, with caution. Let us be very careful now to put a guard on our lips, and in the matter and the method of our everyday conversation let us walk circumspectly. Let there be a great silence when silence is better, quiet speech when speech is called for. The Christian man who runs round his place of business and among his friends wailing over the apparent neglect of the Government, or of this general, or of that admiral, ought to be imprisoned till the war is over. Lift up the hands that hang down, confirm the feeble knees; your God will come with a recompense!

The true attitude must also be that of the shrewdness that understands the will of the Lord. In the midst of our waiting there must be the patience that recognizes the necessity for discipline. There must be no forgetfulness of that past which was characterized by forgetfulness of God. I am driven to declare to you that as I climb the heights and look out on this England of ours, this land so honored and dear to our hearts, I feel it is better this than that we should have drifted still further away into our luxury, and our ease, and our trivialities, and our indulgences. Better this, for out of it all is coming a great sense of the vastness of life, and of the reality of God. Men are discovering that the only resting-place for the heart is the belief that over the battle and the slaughter, over the waiting and the weariness God presides, and that out of it all at last shall come the new era, cleaner, purer, better.

Here also are words which, of course, have a much wider application: Be filled with the Spirit. It is true, however, that in proportion as Christian men and women today are filled with the Spirit of God, they will co-operate with Him in this hour of calamity, and the evil day will be bought up in the interest of God's Kingdom.

This is what we need to do today in order to serve our nation: to walk circumspectly as those that know the will of the Lord, and that in that fulness of the Spirit that enables us each in his place or her place, in public work, in Parliament, in the home, about our professional duty, not to be pessimistic, nor optimistic with the optimism that is foolhardy, but strong and courageous with the courage that is built on our confidence in God. So today may we redeem the time, because the days are evil.

CHAPTER XIII

PREPARING THE HIGHWAY

The voice of one that crieth, Prepare ye in the wilderness the way of the Lord, make straight in the desert a high way for our God.

ISAIAH 40:3.

THESE WORDS ARE TAKEN FROM THE PROLOGUE TO THE SECOND part of the prophecy of Isaiah. That prologue consists of the first eleven verses of chapter 40, and this chapter contains the keynote of the twenty-seven chapters here beginning and closing with the end of the book. The burden of this second part of the prophecy is comfort, and the comfort which was to be brought to the people of God in those olden days was to know that Jehovah was acting on behalf of His people. Nevertheless, there was a responsibility which they were called on to fulfil. That responsibility is revealed in the words of my text.

By bringing together the first verse of chapter 35, with which the earlier prophecy closes, and the charge of the text, light will be thrown on its meaning.

> The wilderness and the solitary place shall be glad; and the desert shall rejoice, and blossom as the rose.
> Prepare ye in the wilderness the way of the Lord, make straight in the desert a high way for our God.

The abiding principles revealed in the text and in all its context are these: first, that God never abandons man to the result of his own folly; second, that He interferes, arresting, changing, restoring; and, finally, that in His interference He always calls on man for co-operation.

In order that we may gain the present value of this Old Testament call let us examine carefully the scriptural applications of it, and apply this scriptural examination to our own circumstances and conditions.

The prophet heard a call, the voice of one that crieth, and this was the cry: "Prepare ye in the wilderness the way of the Lord, make straight in the desert a high way for our God." When we turn to the New Testament we find that each of the evangelists, Matthew, Mark, Luke, and John connected this prophetic utterance of Isaiah with the ministry of John the Baptist as the herald and forerunner of Our Lord Himself. Consequently, we have a double illustration of the real meaning of the text, and so are helped to apply it to ourselves.

In the twenty-seven chapters which constitute the second part of the prophecy there are three great movements. In chapters 40 to 48 the prophet was contrasting Jehovah with idols. We may summarize the contrast thus: that the difference between Jehovah and all other gods is just this: other gods men make and carry; Jehovah makes men and carries them. Having thus contrasted Jehovah and idols, beginning with chapter 49 and ending with chapter 57, there comes into view, first indistinctly, then gradually with a wonderful distinctness, a Person Who is the Servant of Jehovah. We see Him suffering and triumphing, the Person through Whom Jehovah is to reveal Himself in His superiority to all idols. In chapters 58 to 66 the prophet again leads us along the line of contrast, contrasting faithful souls and hypocrites. The whole movement has to do with peace, the purpose of peace, God's Prince of peace, and the program of peace. Peace is seen ultimately established, not by the abandonment of any principle of truth or honor, but through battle and smoke and turmoil under the leadership of the great Prince of peace. The twofold preparation which the prophet pointed out as necessary for this activity of God through His Servant was, first, that people should turn from idols to Himself, and, second, that they should turn from hypocrisy to perfect confidence in Himself.

Then, as we come to the New Testament to consider the message of that wonderful man, the last of the long line of Hebrew prophets, again we discover three movements in his ministry which may thus be summarized. First, he came denouncing sin; second, he came announcing the near advent of the Messiah; finally, he came to present the Messiah to men in that statement: "Behold the Lamb of God, Which taketh away the sin of the world." When they asked him who he was himself, he answered that he was a voice, and uttered the words of the text.

The twofold preparation on which John the Baptist insisted may thus be described: repentance, a change of mind expressing itself in reformation, a change of conduct; and faith in the coming of One, expressing itself in following Him. He fulfilled his ministry when he indicated Jesus to his own disciples and sent them after Him, and when, at last, he said, "He must increase, I must decrease."

Now, the value of this glance at the old-time illustration and the illustration in the New Testament is that each reveals the fact that those who hear it can obey the call, and prepare a way in the wilderness for God, a high way in the desert along which God can travel. The accomplishment of the divine purpose is wrought out by God Himself, but He always asks for co-operation from men. In the ancient time the little remnant gathered round the prophet of the Theocracy is seen helping God's progress, making a high way, casting up a way in the wilderness and in the desert along which it was possible for God to move in order to accomplish His final purpose. In the case of the herald, the little group of disciples that gathered about him, loyal to his preaching in the midst of the corruption of the age in which he preached, constituted God's vantage ground. Out of their number the Messiah Himself at last selected His own disciples at the first, and so moved forward.

And if we follow through we find the principle obtaining in all subsequent history. The apostles of Jesus, hearing the call, obeyed and prepared a high way for God, and through their loyalty God moved forward to all the victories of the centuries.

In the dark ages in the history of the Church the cry went up again, and the Reformers heard it, and made a high way for God. Later on in the history of our own country, amid lasciviousness and frivolity and corruption, the Puritans in the Established Church, and the Independents outside it, constituted that little group of souls who felt the agony of the wilderness, and made therein a high way for God. A little more than a hundred years ago, when once again darkness had settled on the Church in this country of ours, the Holy Club at Oxford, so-called in uttermost contempt, in which were found the Wesleys, Whitefield, and other kindred spirits, constituted a remnant who in the dark wilderness made God's opportunity, who in the desolate desert cast up a high way for the triumphant march of Jehovah.

Now I come to that which of course is principally on my heart, the immediate application of the call of the text. We lift our eyes in the midst of worship and look out on the world. As we do so we see the world today in the throes of the most terrific and appalling upheaval that it has ever known. The measure in which our eyes have seen the vision of the glory of the divine ideals for humanity is the measure in which we are conscious of the tragedy of the hour in which we live. I go back again to this passage in Isaiah, and see in the 35th chapter a most glorious picture of restoration: "The wilderness and the solitary place shall be glad; and the desert shall rejoice, and blossom as the rose." If we reverse the picture contained in that whole chapter we find a picture of desolation, an exact picture of the circumstances in the midst of which we are living today.

But that is not all the outlook, that is not all the truth. That is not the highest truth or the deepest. So let us look again. What does the man of faith really see today when for a moment he resolutely climbs the mountain, and looks from the standpoint of his living fellowship with God?

First of all, he sees God. Ah! but that is the difficulty today. That is where we halt. Well, if you and I, living in the comparative quiet of this England today do not see God, the men in the trenches see Him, and the men who keep their long and lonely vigil on the high seas see Him. There is nothing more wonderful than the fact that letters are coming pouring in everywhere today from these men, who, in different ways, in different language, are telling the same great truth, that they are seeing big things and know it, that they are finding God as they never found Him before, and are being tremendously impressed with the reality of God.

But all the faithful see Him, and they see Him still in Himself as Love. God is Love. That fact has been forever made sure in human history by the Cross of Christ. That God is love never can be denied by all such souls as have really seen that Cross and have really come into fellowship with it in their own lives, and know its matchless power in the lives of other men. Therefore we know today that we must interpret circumstances by God, and not God by circumstances. The peril of the hour is that men and women of faith may be trying to account for God by the circumstances of affliction. It cannot be done. That is not the true outlook. The true method is that of interpreting the circumstances by the fact of God. Under the shadow of the Cross of the world's Redeemer, in the presence of all that Cross has wrought in personal life and in history, we are compelled to look again at this dark hour from the standpoint of the abiding, unchanging certainty concerning God, that He is the God of love. When we begin to do that we find that we see God not only in Himself, but in His activity.

In Isaiah 63 the prophecy is of conflict. "Who is this that cometh from Edom with dyed garments from Bozrah?" The answer was given, and another question was asked. Why are thy garments red in their apparel; why is there blood on thy garments as thou swayest forward in the majesty of thy strength? Then came the great answer, "I have trodden the winepress alone." The figure is daring, illuminating, inclusive, final. Look at the treader of the winepress in those Eastern countries and see what he does. He presses the grapes so that their own lifeblood may be poured out, so that their own very nature shall be manifested. That is what God is doing today, pressing out the inwardness of things to manifestation in the sight of angels, in the sight of men, in the midst of human history. Nothing has happened yet in all this strife but that potentially, its inspirations lay within the human heart and the human mind ere the strife began. All the brutishness and godlessness lay like a smoldering fire under the veneered rottenness of a false culture, and all the strength and heroism of the faith that is prepared gladly to die in defense of honor and truth lay unrecognized as the inspiration of life before the war broke out. In this hour God is compelling humanity to express itself, and in all the terrific scenes in the midst of which we live God is treading out the winepress, compelling the inward things of human life to express themselves. He has not inspired the slaughter, He is not responsible for the iniquity of war. All the potentialities that have grown into experience have been generated within the heart of man. God always compels man to be outwardly what he is inwardly. He gave Judas the bag, knowing that he was a thief, which is a graphic, terrific illustration of an abiding principle, that God compels a man, a nation, a race, into circumstances in which they will manifest outwardly the true inwardness of their character. He is treading the winepress.

But the true man of vision climbs higher yet, and sees the issues resulting. Every valley shall be exalted, and every mountain and hill shall be made low; that is the ending of all inequality—valleys exalted, mountains made low. All the unevenness shall be made level and the rough places plain; that is the restoration of the highway that has been lost, over which ravenous beasts have been passing. Finally, is seen the divine Hegemony, the revelation of the divine glory, which all flesh shall see! God Himself is winning His victory, which ultimately is the victory of humanity as it marches out into the larger, grander, nobler life, a life to which it cannot come until the poison is pressed out in the winepress, until the forces of life have been poured out in the winepress. So God is seen, even today, not exiled, not indifferent, but active with the master impulse of infinite love to humanity; the hour of His vengeance is come, and that is the year of His redeemed.

Now we come back to the call of the text: "Prepare

ye in the wilderness the way of the Lord, make straight in the desert a high way for our God." Observe that way is to be prepared in the wilderness, in the desert. It is in an hour of desolation that this work is to be done; it is through darkness that this toil must be endured. The results will be seen when presently the desert is blossoming with beauty, and the wilderness has become a cultivated way; but we are to do our work while it is still a wilderness, while it is yet a desert.

That brings us to the very practical question: How are we to prepare a way for God? What can we do? I say the question is practical. It is a large question. Yet sometimes the most practical and the largest questions may best be answered by the simplest forms of statement. Therefore, in two declarations, I want to give the way of preparation as I see it today. First, we have to prepare His way by standing for God with men; and, second, by acting with God for men. This is an hour in which the men of faith must stand for God with men, must stand for the sovereignty of God, for the absolute rights of God. Does that really need saying? Is it not so patent that there should be no need of saying it, certainly no need of argument? Yet, on the other hand, have we not been in grave danger of wandering from it? That old fundamental bedrock of Calvinist theology is the bedrock to which the Church must come back, the sovereignty of God. In this flippant and decadent age of ours, someone has positively written something about "If I were God"! The almost blasphemy of the suggestion! We have to take our stand anew today, for the final sovereignty of God, for the fact that there is no appeal from His decision, for the fact that whether it be a man or a society or a nation or a race, if either or all of these seek in any way to act apart from His law there is nothing for man or society or nation or race but irrevocable and irremediable ruin. That is a bedrock assumption to which we must get back from all those anemic interpretations of Deity which seem to think Him as merely some sentimental Being with Whom men can trifle and then escape. We must get back to the rock conception of God, and know that, whereas on that granite Rock a man or humanity may build eternal dwelling places, if man or humanity trifles with it, it will grind man and humanity to pieces.

I go further. The Church of God today will prepare a high way for God as she insists not merely on this fundamental fact of His Sovereignty, but on the revealed character of God. The Church is to insist on it that God is, as He has revealed Himself to be in the Word. The Church must lift her perpetual protest against any false conception of God. God is not Moloch, God is not Baal, God is not Mammon. God is God as He unveiled His grace and glory in the Person of Christ, terrific in His wrath, overwhelming in His compassion. The God of truth, the God of justice, the God of righteousness, the God of long-suffering and patience, the God Who will make compromise with evil under no circumstances, but the God Who will divest Himself of His dignities to die for a lost and ruined humanity.

Included in this is the fact that today the Church must stand everywhere for the law of God as that law is laid down, for individual rectitude of life, a rectitude of life the Pattern of which has been given to the world in the humanity of Jesus, in all the interrelationships of humanity for the value of truth, the necessity for justice, the maintenance of honor, and loyalty to obligations.

Forevermore the Church must stand for the infinite mystery of the love of God, so that as she helps men to make their policies, as she sustains men in the hour of their strife, as she prepares men to live or die for righteousness, she must forever more instruct and inspire them with love as the central, final meaning of all life.

The Church is also called on to act for men with God. That means, first of all, that she is to lift holy hands in perpetual prayer. I wonder if we are ceasing to pray as the days go on, or are we praying more? When this war broke out meetings for public intercession were held here and there much more so than today. I have had correspondence recently on whether we are right, or whether something should not be done to bring the Christian people together for public intercession. I am not anxious for this, but I am anxious that the individual soul in holy fellowship with God shall never cease to pray. I am not anxious to assemble a crowd. I am anxious for the mystic fellowship of all the saints in all congregations in unwearied intercession on behalf of humanity. We are to act for men with God. Men will understand our activity presently when we go out and act for them in actual deeds. I am coming to that. But the Church's first business is prayer. So far as I have influence, so far as my message may reach, I would urge, not that men will waste time trying to get up a meeting, but that they get to business in private, that whenever their minds go to the fields of slaugher, to the suffering homes, to the rulers of the nations and their counselors, they give their thoughts wings and lift them Godward. So shall we prepare in the wilderness a high way for God.

Then, of course, there must be much more than that. We must act for men in the actuality of the strife, in all ministry on behalf of those who are sorrowing, in guiding all diplomacy in the compass of the divine wisdom and the divine thought. This is an hour when prayer must have its expression in actual service. In proportion as all men and women of faith are realizing these things, and doing them, we shall prepare a high way for God.

In conclusion, let me say some things that are on my heart. Recently an interview with Benedict XV, the Pope of the Roman Church, appeared in our newspapers. He is reported to have declared that he stood for spiritual neutrality at this particular hour. I hasten to say that we have no right to judge any utterance of the Pope by newspaper reports. At the same time, when a man occupies that august and terrible position, any opinion to which he gives utterance demands attention. I notice that the Organ of the Vatican has said that in that report there are "various inexactitudes." I observe that Cardinal Bourne has said that in the report he discovered "much embroidery." I note also that Father Bernard Vaughan said, in his own more vigorous method, that the whole thing is "a wicked fake." Let us hope that it is so. I do not suppose that anything I say will influence the Pope any more than anything he says will influence me. Yet, because people are reading this report, and the mind of men has been moved by it, as the correspondence in the newspapers has revealed, I should like to say that the Pope has the means of definitely correcting the inexactitudes, removing the embroidery, exposing the fake. However, that is beyond the consideration of the present moment. The idea which shocks my soul is the idea of spiritual neutrality. I declare to you today that this is impossible. Because the Church of God is supernatural, she cannot be spiritually neutral. She must distinguish between right and wrong, she must distinguish between truth and a lie; and she must speak. The necessity for her distinguishing, and for her public speech today, is the greater because the rationalization of theology has issued in the destruction of the elementary moral sense in certain theological quarters. Perhaps it is so—I suppose it is so

—that organized Christian testimony is impossible. Then let all individual Christians and those prophets who are responsible to God alone utter no uncertain sound today. Let it be declared, and insisted upon, that we stand, not first for our own nation, but first for the Kingship of God and for the Kingdom of God, and for all those things which are involved in the divine government of right and truth. Only as by our praying and by our toiling, and, if necessary, by our sacrifices, our tears, our suffering, we stand for the spiritual ideal are we helping. But as we stand for that ideal, in the wilderness the way of God will be prepared, and in the desert the high way will be flung up.

CHAPTER XIV

MANIFESTATIONS OF THE RISEN LORD

After these things Jesus manifested Himself again to the disciples at the sea of Tiberias; and He manifested Himself on this wise.

JOHN 21:1.

OUR SUBJECT IS THE WHOLE OF THE TWENTY-FIRST CHAPTER of John in the light of this first verse. Whatever there is in the story is qualified by this opening statement, and especially by the word which is twice repeated in the course thereof, a word which is well rendered in the Revised Version, "manifested." The literal meaning of the word is "to shine forth." In this particular verse, moreover, the verb is in the active voice, thus showing that John considered that it was the intention of the Lord to reveal Himself in some special way. Taking this, then, as the keynote, we find the viewpoint for our meditation.

The story is another of the Post Resurrection stories. It would seem to have been added after the conclusion of the narrative in its more systematic form. The verse with which chapter 20 ends formed a natural ending to the scheme of the Gospel. The probability is that the Gospel did end there, and that at some later period, perchance for some very special reason, John added this chapter. I am not going to argue about the writer. I take it for granted that John wrote it. I think the internal evidences are absolutely conclusive that whosoever wrote the first part of the Gospel wrote this also.

In very many ways this chapter is peculiarly beautiful, and its different parts often have been considered in detail. I now propose a quiet meditation while we attempt to see the Lord as in the fresh light of early morning, He is manifested in the whole movement by the sea of Tiberias. In order to do this, we will first consider the succeeding incidents that make up the whole movement, and then notice some facts which here have special manifestation and outshining.

First, then, let us look at the incidents. There are three. First, the Lord is seen directing fishermen in their fishing, then providing breakfast for the toilers, and, finally, dealing with Peter—here, as always, the representative disciple—on the future.

As I thus merely name the three incidents, there is almost a shock of surprise in the mind. Directing fishermen about their fishing, preparing breakfast, and uttering high and wonderful words concerning a spiritual campaign! It seems as though, after mentioning the first two incidents, we have to readjust ourselves to speak of the third. That sense of incongruity is our fault, our failure, and an immediate revelation of one of the marvels and glories of the story. Here our Lord is seen relating these things to each other: a common calling—fishing, a very persistent necessity—breakfast, and some of the most wonderful things He ever said about the whole campaign of His Church. The three follow naturally and regularly and beautifully. There is no real break in the story. The break comes in our mind, because we think we must put some gap between breakfast and spiritual work, that we must put some great gulf between fishing on

Saturday and worshiping on Sunday. So we are face to face with one of the values of the story at the very beginning, to which we shall have to come back presently.

Let us, however, look at the Lord. First, we see Him standing on the beach directing fishermen in their fishing. Now, whether these men ought to have been fishing does not matter. I know there are different opinions as to whether Peter, on this occasion, when he said, "I go a fishing," was warranted in doing so. I am very willing to give my personal opinion for what it is worth, and then it can be dismissed. I think he was wrong. Our Lord distinctly told the disciples to wait until they were endued with power from on high. But this must be added: whatever the Lord felt about their going, He did not rebuke them.

These men knew the business of fishing, at least it is certain that three of them did. Peter and the sons of Zebedee, James and John, were fishermen. They knew the Sea of Tiberias well, just when it was likely that the fish would be best taken, where the currents ran, what effect the driving wind would have on the waters, how to cast the net, how to be silent, and how to act. They were fishermen, and yet that night they had failed. I do not say that they were to blame. It was fisherman's luck. They had taken no fish; there was no harvest of the sea that night. There, on the beach, in the gleam of the morning, stood a stranger. They did not know Him. They were only about a hundred yards from the shore at the time. Then Jesus' Voice came across the waters: "Children, have ye aught to eat?" The answer came back clear and sharp, and, perhaps, with a slight tone of disappointment, "No." "Cast your net on the right side of the boat, and ye shall find."

Now, whether this was miraculous or not does not matter. Whether our Lord here may have been exercising His sovereignty over all nature; or whether He was merely observing the sea and saw the shoal of fish there does not signify anything. The great value of the story is that He was interested in the men fishing, He directed their operations, and He gave them success. The most obvious thing here is the most important. He Who did this was the Risen Lord of Life and Glory. He was interested in the fisher folk while they were fishing, and directed them in the hour of their failure, so that they became successful.

In the next incident Jesus is seen providing breakfast for the toilers. When these men found their way to land, they saw a fire of coals there. I would like to use a more literal translation, They saw a fire of coals *laid*. In that word *laid* there is the simple significance that the fire had been carefully prepared; it was built, it was laid. Moreover, fish was laid thereon, and bread was provided.

Now, again, whether in all this there was anything supernatural or miraculous, to use our very imperfect words, I care nothing. Here is the fact. Jesus is seen on the seashore building a fire and preparing food for hungry fishermen. The Risen Lord of Life and Glory, Whose persistent mission had been to ransom a race and establish the Kingdom of God is seen on the seashore, while men are absent fishing. What is He doing? Getting breakfast ready for them! One man on that boat knew Him, and said to his companion, "It is the Lord." Immediately that splendid man, that impulsive man, the friend, girt his outer garment about him and flung himself into the sea and reached the shore. At last they all arrived. None of them durst ask this stranger who He was. They were afraid. Then Jesus came nearer and invited them to sit down and eat, and waited on them. That is the second picture. Jesus was manifesting Himself; He was shining forth on these men. A mystic glory had enveloped His Person in consequence of His Resurrection which seemed apt to remove them from Him and Him from them. Here He was seen understanding their hunger, sympathizing with their necessity, serving; and in the Hands that built the fire and placed the fish thereon were wound prints! It is a picture of the world's Redeemer getting breakfast ready for cold, tired fishermen.

There is yet another scene, equally familiar and equally wonderful. Finally, Jesus is seen here dealing with Peter on the future—dealing with him, as I have already hinted and will now again remark, as a representative man. All the way through Peter is the representative disciple; he is more intensely human than is any other man; he is a man in whom all the elemental qualities of humanity are discovered—intellectual, emotional, and volitional. When the breakfast was ended, Jesus began to deal with this man, and to challenge him three times in order to utter to him a threefold commission, which covers the whole of the Church's campaign to the end of the Age. It is not sufficient only to declare what has been declared, that at this point our Lord handed to Peter the Crozier—that is, the Staff of Office of the Pastor of the flock when the flock is folded. In other words, He was not thinking only of the Church when He spoke of "My sheep" and "My lambs." He was thinking of the race.

Now, whereas I am perfectly sure there is a close connection between the threefold denial uttered in the presence of a fire the enemies of Jesus had built and this threefold confession made in the presence of a fire that Jesus had built —I do not think that our Lord was especially concerned with that matter. He had had a private interview with Peter before this, since His Resurrection, in which the whole business of Peter's deflection had been once and forever settled. Our Lord does not go back on such settlements. That is the mistake we too often make. When He forgives He blots out. It was in view of a larger commission that a threefold confession was necessary, because of the threefold character of the work it included.

What is the first thing our Lord wants to say to the Church through Peter? "Feed My lambs." In the view of Christ all the lambs are already included in the flock, and the business of the Church is to feed them. The second phase of the great commission is, "Shepherd My sheep," that is, gather them, guard them, guide them. When speaking of His own work, Jesus said, "I am the Good Shepherd." The Good Shepherd layeth down His life for the sheep. The Good Shepherd layeth down His life that He may take it again. The Good Shepherd entereth into conflict with the wolf, and when the wolf can be destroyed only by the Shepherd's dying, then the Shepherd dies to destroy the wolf. All that was surely in His mind when he said, "Shepherd My sheep." Finally, He said: "Feed My sheep." In these commands we have the whole commission. In order that Peter may be able to do it, in order that the Church may be able to do it, there is one supreme necessity, which is revealed in the challenge: "Lovest thou Me?"

In the next place, the Lord proceeded to deal with Peter about his personal pathway of service. He told Peter what lay ahead of him in the consummation of his earthly service:

> When thou wast young, thou girdest thyself, and walkedst whither thou wouldst; but when thou shalt be old, thou shalt stretch forth thy hands, and another shall gird thee, and carry thee whither thou wouldst not.

With all reverence, if I may change the wording, this is what Jesus said to him: In the days of thy young manhood thou hast made thine own choices, and thine own decisions; even in the days of thy fellowship with Me thou hast asserted thy will, protesting against My Cross, that yoke under which I serve. But now thou must walk My way, and the culmination of that walk shall be that thou wilt, at last, suffer apparent defeat. The Cross waits for thee actually. But Follow Me.

As Peter heard Him say this he remembered that the Lord had gone to the Cross, but that the Cross had not been the end. Jesus was alive from among the dead. Peter understood there and then that if he himself must go by that restricted, pressing, agonizing way of the Cross, it was a way that led out into life and fulness of victory.

Then all the glory and the beauty of the story once again seems to switch back, almost with vulgarity, to the commonplace. When Jesus said: Follow Me, evidently He began to walk away, and Peter, literally following Him, turned round and saw John. Then he asked Jesus: What shall this man do? Will he die, too? Will he suffer? With swift suddenness Christ definitely and sharply rebuked Peter. What is that to thee? Follow thou Me. If, again without irreverence, I may translate into the language of today, this is what Jesus said: "Mind your own business! Follow *thou* Me!"

In this simple looking at the story, as it seems to me, there is almost all we need of help and encouragement. Yet let us pass to the second and the last line of consideration, and notice some of the facts that are revealed as we look at the manifesting of the Lord in this page of incidents.

What first impresses me as I watch Jesus is the sanctification of all life, and the cancellation of many false human terms. Let us remember Who this One is, and where He stands; that He is the Son of God and the Son of Man; that He stands on the other side of the forces of sin and sorrow and death against humanity. As I watch Him I know that all life is sanctified. I know that fishing is sanctified, and not merely as a figure of speech concerning spiritual work, but as an actual occupation for every day in the week. That would appeal to us more strongly if we were fisher folk. And yet why? We shall destroy the beauty of it if we think only of fishing boats. I will try to make the lesson superlative by saying that Jesus Christ would never have said to me, I will make you a fisher of men. He knows perfectly well that I am no fisherman. He did come to me one day, when I sat at a desk with boys around me teaching, and He said: Follow Me, and I will make you a teacher of men. I went after Him on the line of my capacity. Suppose He had not called me to this work as I sat at the desk. Then that work would have been as sacred as is this. Or suppose He has not called you to give up your office in the city, but to stay there. Then your office is a holy place, if you are a holy man. Suppose you are called on every day of the week to work at the carpenter's bench, to superintend the building of houses, to place brick on brick therein! It is all sacred. The Lord is watching you when you are fishing, watching you as you write your letters, watching as you build your house, as you do your work. Then all life becomes sacred. If we could but realize this, then we would go back to a week radiant with light and glory. Ah, yes, that particular work that is so very commonplace, hidden away in some quarter in London, up some back stairs—that work and that office would be radiant with glory if you remembered that the Lord is watching, that all life has become beautiful since you stood on the seashore and watched Jesus taking an interest in fishermen.

Yes, all life is sacred, and here I want to speak with reverence. I say this, not in pleasantry, but with real reverence. The greatest work that is done in London on any given day is that done, not in the office, but in the home. The place of drudgery, the place of the commonplace, of monotony, is the home. You men, think of the commonplace of having to get breakfast ready in the morning. My sisters, I speak to you with reverence. You who preside over our homes and our households—and not only those of you who preside, but also those who serve therein—when tomorrow morning you are up betimes, laying a fire, preparing a breakfast, remember that the Lord of Glory built a fire and cooked a breakfast. This is a wonderful sanctification of life; this is an illuminating glory that transfigures the commonplace and makes it the special. Let us cancel the word, "secular," or at least some of our uses of it. There is nothing secular. Our Lord transmuted the commonplace, base metal, and made it the fine gold of the sanctuary of God, when He prepared that breakfast and waited upon those hungry men.

He has sanctified human life in its larger outlooks also by the fact that when He looked out with those wonderful Eyes of His, He saw humanity, and He said, "My sheep." Oh, but you say, surely He meant His people! Yes, but who are His people? We must interpret our Lord's word here by our Lord's thought and teaching elsewhere. In a superlatively revealing passage, at the dividing of the ways, when Jesus was about to send these men out for the first time, Matthew has told us how our Lord went through all the villages and cities teaching, beholding the multitudes, and was moved with compassion for them. Why? They were *as sheep* without a shepherd. Here, then, in the simple words, "My sheep," "My lambs," He includes all humanity—the bruised, the degraded, and the vicious.

> Then on each He setteth,
> His own secret sign.

That secret sign is not merely on the brow of the saints worshiping; that secret sign of a love ineffable and a passion unfathomable is on the brow of every man and woman and child. Our Lord sanctified humanity when He spoke of the multitudes as "My sheep" and "My lambs." He sanctified all human life. Let us never again think contemptuously of any human being.

Again I look, and I see Jesus manifested here, not only as the Sanctifier of all life. He is also manifested in His Sovereignty. It is seen in that first incident in the direction of the fishermen, in the fact that He told them where to fling the net. Whether His sovereign will impressed the strange harvest of the sea, or whether it did not, He knew how to direct the fishermen, and in the act I observe the easy grace and equal beauty of a Sovereign Lord and Master. I hear the strong authoritative note of His Sovereignty also in the tender terms by which He described humanity: "My sheep, My lambs!" when I put the emphasis on the possessive, "*My* sheep, *My* lambs!" Our Lord had entered into conflict with the wolf, and had destroyed the wolf; and now He claimed authority over the sheep among whom the wolf had ravened. It was the tone of His sovereignty.

I find that evidence of supreme sovereignty, moreover, in the test He imposed on those who will serve Him, revealing as it does the one and only fitness necessary for spiritual ministry: "Lovest thou Me?" Observe the superlativeness of this, for, said Jesus in effect to this man, If you love Me, then you are fit for this high and holy office to which I appoint you. He made Himself the spiritual Master of the affection, claiming that in love to Him there was transforming and transmuting power, enabling a man to do the most glorious work of the centuries.

Yet once again His sovereignty is revealed in this narrative in the fact that He taught Peter that the one and only business of His followers is to follow. Peter, there is the *Via Dolorosa* that thou must tread, there is the girding and the binding and the veritable cross. Follow Me! Yes, Peter, and here is this man John; but you do not need to know My arrangements for him. It is not necessary for you to know them. Follow Me! That is the Voice of supreme sovereignty.

Once again, and finally, as I look at these incidents, I see Our Lord's devotion to His own, His devotion to their physical necessities, and His devotion to whatever their spiritual obligation required. I see His devotion to His own in their suffering. I see His devotion to them in their weakness, in that He will make no peace with their folly, but will sharply rebuke it in order that they may realize the fulness of their fellowship with Him, and consequently with the Father.

As I close, I go back to the beginning of the chapter, to the things that immediately follow my text. For just a moment I want to look at the men. Who are these men round about our Lord? I see, first, Simon Peter, the impulsive, the great human; then Thomas, the magnificent, the skeptic—which simply means the man who looks hard, the man who by now was not only trustful, but trustworthy, having heard His Lord's words to him when they met on that eighth day after the resurrection. Then there is Nathanael, the man who was guileless, the man who would never have made a politician, the man who was so guileless that he admitted it. Observe that! Jesus said to him when he saw him: Behold, an Israelite indeed, in whom is no guile! Nathanael said:

"How knewest Thou me?" By now he had seen the angels ascending and descending on the Son of Man. James and John Boanerges were also there, the men who asked to sit on Jesus' right hand and on His left, and were admitted to the sacramental preparation of cup and baptism that they might do it. And who else? Two others. Thank God for these representatives of the anonymous multitude. No! no! not Andrew and Philip. Many an expositor has tried to prove to me that they were Andrew and Philip. Nothing of the kind. If it had been so, they would have been named. They were not of the twelve. They were two men of the outside crowd, of the anonymous multitude, the multitude which create the dynamic, in the force of which the named and prominent men go forward. I am perfectly honest in saying this. How could I preach except for the unnamed souls that pray for me? Two others! I like that group of men. That impulsive, hot, magnificent Peter; that critical, cautious, splendid, trustworthy Thomas; that guileless Nathanael; those Sons of Thunders, and two others. To these Jesus manifested Himself.

Jesus is the Lord of Life and Glory. He will be interested in the daily callings of His people to the end of time; He will sanctify all household duties so that they flash with the splendor of service heavenly; He will direct our spiritual campaign, and comfort us in all our sufferings. Think of the effect of these manifestations on subsequent days of fruitless toil. By His action we know that He overrules our failures, and makes them the processes of His successes. Think of what it meant afterwards to these men in days of weariness and hunger, when they were shepherding the sheep and feeding the lambs. Think of what it meant afterwards to these men when they had to confront death. Think of what it meant afterwards to these men in those days when they would be tempted to fussiness about other people.

I am not proposing to allow any man to take from me this twenty-first chapter of John. For *thus* He manifested Himself!

CHAPTER XV

LED OUT—LED IN

He led them out until they were over against Bethany: and He lifted up His hands, and blessed them.

LUKE 24:50.

AFTER HIS RESURRECTION FROM THE DEAD, OUR LORD AND Saviour Jesus Christ lingered on the earth for forty days, as though He were almost reluctant to leave it. He lingered, as we have no doubt, for very special purposes of revelation and manifestation, lingered in order to bridge over for His own first disciples the difficult period of the early days, when they would no longer have Him with them in bodily sight, and when it would be necessary, therefore, for the high faculty of the soul, faith, to be called into full play. He lingered for forty days, occasionally appearing and disappearing. The second part of the statement seems as though it were unnecessary, but, as a matter of fact, the disappearances were as important as the appearances, in both their manner and their purpose. He appeared to them sometimes when gathered together peculiarly as disciples, and sometimes to individuals. Coming suddenly and unexpectedly upon them, baffling them by the method of His coming, He yet always unveiled before their eyes some new wonder and glory of His own Personality and His own work. Then, with equal suddenness and strangeness of method, He vanished. This lasted, as I say, for forty days.

In the verse that I have taken as text we have the account of the very last act of Jesus before His Ascension. This was His last appearance, as the last disappearance was the Ascension itself. We are now to consider what these men saw in Him on this occasion: "He led them out as far as Bethany: and He lifted up His hands, and blessed them."

This Person, lifting His hands in blessing, is One who has been rejected in a threefold rejection: rejected by the priesthood of the time, rejected by the earthly government which was in the ascendancy at the time, rejected by the people on their own vote and claim. I am not now proposing to stay to discuss the reason of the priestly rejection, or the governmental rejection, or the democratic rejection. I simply face the fact as we look at this last appearing of Jesus. He was rejected.

Rejected, in the first place, by the priests of His time, and, consequently, by priestcraft. Here we pause for a moment to consider this question of priesthood in the light of Biblical revelation. In the divine economy as therein revealed, priesthood was really an accommodation to human weakness, and never a divine intention or provision. The history of the priesthood emerges in the most startling way. In the eighteenth chapter of Exodus we discover that when God emancipated a people from slavery and led them out with a high hand and outstretched arm into a large place, He brought them unto Himself, and the words that Moses was commissioned to speak to them were practically words of the New Testament, which came with greater meaning in the fulness of time: "I have chosen you to be unto Me, a kingdom of priests." In that declaration there is not the slightest suggestion of the creation of a caste of priests in the divine economy and purpose, but rather the creation of a nation in which every individual was to be a priest. I will make you unto Me a kingdom of priests, that was the divine original ideal for Israel. The people shrank from the high and awful function, were filled with fear in the presence of Jehovah, and naturally so: they were so filled with fear because of the consciousness of their sinfulness and inability. Then the principle obtained that runs through all the Divine dealings with men, accommodation to human weakness. Because the people were not able to rise to the high level of realizing their personal priesthood, a caste was created for a while to fulfil the function of priesthood on behalf of the people.

Through the centuries the story of priesthood runs on, and from beginning to end it is the story of failure, from beginning to end it is the story of corruption, of partial light eclipsed in darkness, of movement toward a higher forever falling to a lower, until the last act of priesthood was the inspiration that resulted in the murder of the Son of God. As I look at Him standing on Olivet's slope I see One Whom priesthood had cast out.

I also see here One Who had been cast out by government, by monarchy. Monarchy in Judea at that time was a poor and insignificant thing struggling to make its power great when, really, it was entirely paralyzed. Herod and those associated with him in the governing authority of the tetrarchies were under the mastery of Rome, that brutal bully in human history that for once subdued the world by brute force, and initiated the *Pax Romana*, which was but the pause of palsied inertia resulting from war. When Jesus was born, He was born into that peace, a peace not worth the name, and which happily was disturbed by war ere it had long continued.

But let me interpret this fact of government Biblically. What do we find concerning monarchy in the Bible? It was originally an accommodation to human weakness, just as was priesthood. I go back to this one nation that God chose, not in order that He might have a pet on whom to lavish His love, but to be the illustration of His Kingdom in the world for the uplifting of the nations. He said to them: "I have called you unto Myself." In the first glimpse of the history of the people, who were in many senses rude, almost barbaric, there shines a glory such as the world had never seen elsewhere. It is the glory of a theocracy, of a people governed by God, having no other king, and no other form of government. The history runs on for a little while, until there came a day in which this people said: "Give us a king like the nations." Then Samuel, brokenhearted by their failure, cried to God in complaint, and the answer of God, in the soul of Samuel, was this: "They have not rejected thee; they have rejected Me from being king. Therefore, go thou and anoint Saul, and give them what they ask." That was an accommodation to human weakness. Then followed the rapid exaltation and tragic fall of Saul, a king like the nations; the story of David, one gleam of light as to what kingship might be ending in black failure; then that of Solomon, the most disastrous failure in the Old Testament. Next, the kingdom was disrupted, and entered on a long period of conflict, until we see the people once again, a remnant weak and small, and Zerubbabel, Ezra, and Nehemiah setting them in order, after which they were locked up to law, until Christ. Thus government by monarchy in the Bible is marked as being a necessary accommodation to human weakness, a story of ghastly failure and loss which resulted in the crucifixion of the Lord of Life and Glory.

And what of the people? Christ was rejected by the people also. The people entirely failed; they submitted to the dominion of false rulership, so that they themselves caught up the cries of the false rulers, and hissed between closed teeth, "Crucify! Crucify!" The people! May God deliver us from a democracy which is not first a theocracy.

What is the history of the people according to the Bible? Their failure antedated that of priest or king. Babel is the first chapter of the federation of the people in order that they may manage themselves, and make themselves a great name in the world. From that first chapter the movement runs on through all your Biblical literature until, thank God, the day is coming, which is not yet come, when the supreme anthem of earth's emancipation will take the form: "Babylon the great is fallen, is fallen! The kingdom of this world is become the kingdom of our Lord, and of His Christ."

I look, then, at this Man, with the little group gathered about Him on the slopes of Olivet. Priesthood has rejected Him, government has flung Him out, the people have given their vote, consenting to the self-same rejection.

Then I look at Him again, and what do I see? I see the one Priest of humanity, the great High Priest of the race, fulfilling the function of priesthood by the mystery of His Person as it could not possibly be fulfilled in any human being. Jesus could never have been the High Priest of humanity merely in His human nature. By oneness with God, and identification with man, He can be that which Job in his agony sighed for—and in that cry the sigh for priesthood is found, perhaps as nowhere else. Would that there were a daysman who might lay his hand on God and on me. That was the great cry of a soul for the mediation of one who is in himself in true fellowship with God, and in himself in perfect identification with humanity.

As I look I see that Jesus as the One human Priest, the power of Whose Priesthood was created, as the Writer of the Letter to the Hebrews said, by the power of an endless life, which is more than a human life, but which is human in its qualification also. By His oneness with God and identification with man He is the One Priest of humanity.

I look again, and I see Him as the one and only Governor and King of humanity, the One on Whose shoulder the Government is to rest, the one King Whose kingship is based on His eternal authority and His temporal associations—I did not say, "temporary." I used my word with care. I referred to associations that have to do with time. We have to do with time, and we shall always have to do with time. There is a sense in which we are not eternal nor can be. We have eternal life. We come into an atmosphere that keeps, and sustains, and enlarges; but we are not without beginning. To be eternal there must be no beginning. God, as eternal King, is One Whose authority is eternal, Who comes out of eternity, out of the necessity of things, out of the infinite wisdom that lies at the back of everything; the One Who initiates a law for a race, a nation, a man; which is not a law resulting from the manipulation of things as they seem, but which is a law resulting from the perfect knowledge of things as they are. This King's authority is based on that. His authority is based also on temporal association. He Who is the Logos, the eternal, has been made flesh, has brought the eternal into the compass of the observation of the temporal. His Kingship is based now and forevermore, first, on that eternal authority, and, second, on the fact that He tabernacled in the flesh, and walked the ways of men. God came into no closer sympathy with man by incarnation; but by incarnation God did reveal Himself in the exquisite tenderness and eternal strength of His sympathy. God, apart from incarnation, is an abstract idea, vast, terrific; but there is no warmth in it, there is no life in it, there is no inspiration in it. But when I go to a King, and I know His word is the word of eternal authority, and yet hear it stated in the words that my mother taught me and that I lisped when I was a baby, lo, I have found my King! I see Him, outside of the government of the world, but God's appointed Governor.

I see Him again as the ensign of the people, according to the prophetic word concerning Him: "Unto Him shall the gathering of the people be." It was but a little group about Him on Olivet, but think how many are gathered about Him today. Yes, let us think of that sometimes even today, when, it may be, we are tempted almost to imagine that the whole Christian ideal is being blotted out in blood. He is still the rejected One, but He is also the Crowned. He is even yet cast out of the councils of the nations. Ah! but He is considered and obeyed by a vast sacramental host, a sacramental host the extent of which we cannot measure by our Church statistics. His sacramental host includes the membership of churches, but runs far out beyond that membership, gathering into its ranks all souls pledged to name the Name and live according to His law. He gathers the people to Himself, for the realization of a democracy under the reign of the one King, a democracy great because it is a theocracy. So He stands on Olivet's slopes, rejected by the priests, the governors, the people. There He stands, the One

Priest, the One King, the One to Whom the gathering of the peoples shall be.

Having thus looked at the principal matter, the Person, let us consider the statement, "He led them out." He took them towards Bethany. There were tender associations there. It was at Bethany that He found what was nearer to a home in His experience than any other place. There Lazarus lived, and Martha, and Mary, whom He loved. There He had often tarried; there He had spent those last tragic nights of the last terrific week. He led them that way. There was no temple there, no kingly palace. It was not the place where crowds ordinarily assembled. He led them out to Olivet, to some slope from which Bethany could be seen. He led them out from the temple, and the priests' ministrations. He led them out from the government, and its protection. He led them out from the people, and their permissions. They would have to run counter to all these things in the coming days, as He Himself had done. The priests would seek to destroy them and their testimony as they had sought to destroy Him. The governors would be against them, and would even declare that they were seditious; and ere very long a corrupt emperor-master of the world would amuse himself and his licentious profligate friends by watching them burn. All these things He knew, and that leading out signified that He appealed to none of these things to protect His disciples when He was gone. By that leading out, He suggested to His own disciples that they were not to look for help in their propaganda from priests or governors or people. He led them out into association with Himself, in testimony to all that which He had set up, and which He came to make possible in human history.

He led them out from the temple and the priests; He

led them into the true temple through a rent veil, where they might exercise their priesthood as appearing in the presence of God on behalf of humanity, and then passing out to appear in the presence of humanity on behalf of God.

He led them out from the protection of human governments; but He led them into the protection of His own Government, underneath His own sway and kingship and power.

He led them out from the promises and the voting of the populace; but He led them into association with the new democracy, consisting of all souls yielded to the Kingship of God, through Whom, at last, the Kingdom shall be established.

That leading out was thus, indeed, a leading in. As the writer of the letter to the Hebrews says: He went outside the camp to suffer, to die; we must go after Him, bearing His reproach. But the writer of the letter to the Hebrews also says: The veil was rent, and He opened the way into the holiest of all; we may go in with boldness. The people around Him are people led out to be led in, led out from the false into the true, led out from failure to the place of assured victory, led out from all the forces that disintegrate and break up humanity and into association with all the forces that construct and build up humanity. So He led them out, and so He led them in.

From that day to this, He has been leading out and leading in. In proportion as we understand the occasion of that last appearing, we shall discover that the Church of God must never depend on priesthood, or governments, or democracies for her strength or protection. Every form and fashion of religion, every form and fashion of government, and all the hopes of the peoples, are centered in Him to Whom we have come, and in Whose Name we go with gladness, and singing, and hope, back to every form of religion, not to destroy it, but to fulfil the essential truth within it, and purge it of its dross; back to governments, not to proclaim anarchy, but to declare that every form of government must be finally related to the government through Whom it may realize its high ideals; back to the people, not to descend to the devilish barbarity of men who speak of them as canaille, but to love them, serve them, giving our own life blood to lift them into the great Kingdom of our God. He led them out, not for their sakes alone, but, in the infinite mystery of His marvelous work, for the sake of the very things from which He led them out.

His last act was to give a blessing. He lifted up His hands and blessed them. In those Hands were arguments, scars of battle, stigmata of pain, the insignia of royalty. It was the High Priestly act. It declared that sin was atoned for, that death was vanquished, that sorrow was commandeered, captured, in order that, finally, it may do duty for the Kingdom of God. Henceforth sorrow is the most powerful agent in the sanctification of human life, in the deliverance of nations from their perils, and of individuals from their foolishness. That High Priestly act of blessing was the act of One Who had grappled with the darkness of sin, and mastered it, Who "death by dying slew"; and He had apprehended sorrow and taken it into His own control, that henceforth it might be the minister of His will in a gracious and infinite mystery. In the uplifting of those hands was no act of forgiveness, no act of intercession. Those acts also lie within the priestly function; but that was the uplifting of hands in blessing, and blessing means bestowment. He uplifted His hands on men whom He had led out from all the forces that seemed great in the world, denying to these men the protection of these forces, but He lifted up His hands, and blessed them; and as He did so He gave them fulness of life, He gave them fellowship with God, He gave them perfect confidence for all the service that He was about to appoint to them.

Christ is thus seen to be the fulfilment, and, therefore, the center of priesthood, of government, of humanity.

When He leads men out from things that seem so necessary it is always to lead them into the possession of the real things. No man loses anything in his individual life; no society loses anything in the true passion that creates it a society; no nation loses anything of the underlying nobility of its national life by being obedient to Christ. He fulfils. He is always leading out from things effete to Himself. Things effete are not necessarily things evil. They have become effete, but they were not in the first case things evil. Things effete are things that have done their work. He taketh away the first that He may establish the second. Yes, but He established the first. Yea, verily, but when it has done its work He takes it away that He might establish the second. Sacrifice and offerings Thou wouldst not! But He appointed sacrifices and He appointed offerings! Yea! verily; but when they had fulfilled their work, He destroyed them. That is the perpetual method of Christ. If, when they have done their work, we cling to things that were necessary, perchance for us in our individual lives as Christians at the beginning, they will destroy the life they helped to make. Grave clothes are necessary for a dead man; but when he lives, loose him, and let him go! The law written on tables of stone was necessary in the first period of religious revelation; but when the Spirit of God through the infinite mystery of the atoning work of Jesus comes into the life and writes with the Finger of God on the table of the heart, then I do not want tables of stone.

When I put myself in bondage to a table of stone written with the finger of God two to four millenniums ago, then I am in bondage to a thing effete.

Christ ever leads men out. One of the greatest troubles of the Christian Church has been that she so clings to things that were necessary yesterday, forgetting that Christ ever leads forward into something greater and grander. He led men out from things which in themselves had been necessary and had their place, a place made necessary by the bitter necessity of accommodation; but when these things had done their work He led the men out. The meaning of what He did that day had been revealed in His teaching previously. He said to a woman in Samaria: ". . . Woman, believe Me, the hour cometh, when neither in this mountain, nor in Jerusalem, shall ye worship the Father." The day is coming when you will not need a temple, but wherever the soul is in need it may find access to God.

Christ's last attitude, the last appearing, the last manifestation of Himself in these days of appearing and disappearing, was in the attitude of blessing, the attitude, not of the Aaronic priesthood, but of Melchizedec. He is a Priest forever, not after the order of Aaron, but after the order of Melchizedec. We find Melchizedec in the first book of the Bible. Melchizedec met Abram when Abram was weary from a warfare that he had conducted in answer to a demand for righteousness. Melchizedec brought forth bread and wine for Abram, and ministered to his need. Melchizedec blessed Abram, and then passed out of sight, and Abram confronted the king of Sodom. The king offered him part of the booty. In possession of that spiritual blessing which had come to new consciousness in his soul by the ministry of Melchizedec, Abram declined to take a hoof of anything that the king offered. Then God spoke to his soul: "I am thy shield, and thy exceeding great reward."

Jesus lifts up His hands in blessing on the souls who dare to follow Him without the camp, bearing His reproach. He is the High Priest Who brings bread and wine to refresh and renew us in our weariness. He is the High Priest who brings the consciousness, who steadies our faith in God, who enables us to say to every bribe that may be offered us: Not a hoof of anything. We have all we need in God.

CHAPTER XVI

THE FOURFOLD GLORY OF THE CHURCH

Who is she that looketh forth as the morning,
Fair as the moon,
Clear as the sun,
Terrible as an army with banners?
                              SONG OF SOLOMON 6:10.

THERE HAVE BEEN THREE METHODS OF INTERPRETING THE SONG of Songs, which, for the sake of brevity, I may describe as the material, the ethical, and the allegorical. There are those who treat it as being merely an Eastern love song. There are those who believe it was written in order to make a protest against polygamy, and to show the true ideal of marriage. There are those who believe that in the writing of it there were mystical intentions, that it was intended to convey spiritual truth.

My own view is that to lay undue emphasis on either of these is to miss the full value of the whole. It is an Eastern love song, but I think not finally. Even in that way it is the song of songs, for never was there a more wonderful unveiling of all the mystic wonder and beauty of love as the basis of marriage than is to be found in this song. In that sense, therefore, it has ethical values. I hold, however, that its chief value is spiritual.

It is an interesting fact, and a very suggestive one, that the Chaldee Targum contains a Jewish commentary on this Song of Songs, of which this is the title: "The Songs and Hymns which Solomon the Prophet King of Israel delivered by the spirit of prophecy before Jehovah, the Lord of the whole earth." That title at once reveals the fact that the Jewish commentator looked on it as being spiritual and mystic in application.

I think, moreover, that this view is warranted by the harmony of Old Testament literature, for the final relationship between Israel and Jehovah was repeatedly described by those who saw most deeply into the great truth under the figure of the marriage relationship. That creates the infinite pathos and beauty of the whole of the prophecy of Hosea. It is found also in the writings of Isaiah, Jeremiah, Ezekiel. When we turn from the Old Testament literature to the New, we find that the same figure obtained in the clearest thinking of New Testament writers concerning the relationship between Christ and His Church. If we think of the attitude of the Christian Church toward this Song in the past, we shall find that Hippolytus was its first Christian commentator, and he treated it throughout as allegorical. He was followed by Origen, who taught us that it was intended here to set forth the relationship between Christ and His Church, or between the soul and the Logos, between an individual and Christ. He was followed by Athanasius, Gregory of Nyasa, Jerome, Augustine, Chrysostom, all of them treating the Song in the same way. In the Middle Ages, those dark ages in which shone some of the brighest and most wonderful light that ever has shone in the history of the Christian Church concerning Christian experience, this Song of Solomon became the very textbook of the mystics. Bernard of Clairvaux preached eighty sermons on the first two chapters alone, and Aquinas made it perpetually the medium of teaching concerning the mystic relationship between Christ and His people.

I propose to employ the text in the allegorical sense. The Song of Solomon is not dramatic literature, but idyllic. There is not one consistent story running through, but certain phases of relationship are described. The opening chapters celebrate the marriage feast. At the center we have the matchless story of the betrothal. At the close we have pictures of the united state. If the writer was intending to suggest truth concerning the ideal relationship of Israel to God, then we have every right to take the Song and consider it as setting forth the relationship between Christ and His Church. Christ was the Revelation of Jehovah, the Church is the realization of the ideal of the Hebrew people. In that sense, therefore, I take this particular text, constituting as it does one of a series of interpolations running through the Song.

For the most part, the Song is made up of monologues and soliloquies by Solomon and the Shulamite, in which expression is given to all the deepest senses of the love and fellowship and communion existing between them. Ever and anon, between these soliloquies or monologues, the chorus is heard breaking out into inquiry. In the third chapter, sixth verse, we hear the inquiry of the chorus:

> Who is this that cometh up out of the wilderness like pillars of smoke,
> Perfumed with myrrh and frankincense,
> With all powders of the merchant?

Again, in the fifth chapter, ninth verse:

> What is thy beloved more than another beloved,
> O thou fairest among women?
> What is thy beloved more than another beloved,
> That thou dost so adjure us?

Again, in the sixth chapter, first verse:

> Whither is thy beloved gone,
> O thou fairest among women?
> Whither hath thy beloved turned him,
> That we may seek him with thee?

And then we come to our text, in the tenth verse of the chapter:

> Who is she that looketh forth as the morning,
> Fair as the moon,
> Clear as the sun,
> Terrible as an army with banners?

In the eighth chapter, fifth verse, we find two further inquiries:

> Who is this that cometh up from the wilderness,
> Leaning upon her beloved?

And in the end of the eighth verse:

> What shall we do for our sister
> In the day when she shall be spoken for?

The text is, first, an inquiry, which in itself constitutes a description of the bride in her glory and her beauty:

> Who is she that looketh forth as the morning,
> Fair as the moon,
> Clear as the sun,
> Terrible as an army with banners?

Lifting the literature on to its highest level of intention and suggestion, the text becomes a question concerning the Church as the Bride of Christ, in which we find a description of the Church. It is a comprehensive description of certain aspects of true Christian life, whether in the individual or in the corporate catholic Church. It is a text in which the glories of the Church are set forth ideally. It may be said, that the Church as we see and know her, never seems completely to have fulfilled the great ideal; nevertheless, there are senses in which these things describe exactly what the Church is, what she has been, and what she must continue to be, in her relationship to her Lord. Let us, therefore, first simply consider the fourfold figure, looking forth as the morning, fair as the moon, clear as the sun, terrible as an army with banners. We shall be aided, I think, if we can put ourselves imaginatively in some Eastern land at the break of day. First, we see the dawn, swift and sudden and beautiful, illuminating every thing. Then, sinking away to rest, we notice the moon, in the suggestive beauty of her whiteness. Then, as the flush of dawn spreads over the Eastern sky and the moon is lost to sight, the sun himself appears, clear as with burning heat. As he gradually rises to meridian glory he becomes "terrible as an army with banners." Inclusively, the idea is of daybreak and of the glory of day. It has night for its background, but night being driven away by light.

Looking forth as the morning. Here, for a moment, let us forget what the figure suggests. Let us see the thing quite naturally. Morning is the time of new life. Sleep and unconsciousness have passed away. There is the sense of renewal, of reinvigoration. It is the time of new light. Darkness is vanishing and hasting away, and in its passing becoming beautiful, for its deep, dense blackness grows to purple, and presently to saffron.

> Hail, smiling morn,
> That tips the hills with gold,
> Whose rosy fingers ope the gates of day.
> Who the gay face of nature doth unfold,
> At whose bright presence darkness flies away.

Morning suggests freshness. The dawn always comes with the moving of the wind. The night may have been dark, hot, sultry, and oppressive; and, perchance, the day presently will be hot and sultry and oppressive; but just when the first flush of the dawn is on the sky there is always a breath of wind. The dawn is the hour of true enthusiasm. Then the matin of the birds, then the opening petals of the flowers. The sun has not yet appeared, but he is creating the dawn.

"Fair as the moon," or literally, beautiful as the white one. The moon, which is being kissed into obscurity by the dawn, has been fulfilling her function in the night, reflecting the light of the hidden sun. She is perfectly prepared for the great and gracious ministry of reflection—having no light within herself, but catching on her otherwise darkened surface the glory of the hidden sun; then with gentle white beams she shines over the darkness, so that, while she shone there was no darkness, for the deep, dense darkness itself has been made silver until dead night gives way to living day.

At last, with magnificent willingness, the moon is hidden, for the sun has appeared, and so we get our third figure, "clear as the sun." The word *clear* is suggestive. It means clarified as with burning heat. The Hebrew word is the same as that occurring in the charge of Isaiah, "Be ye *clean*, ye that bear the vessels of the Lord." Be ye clear, clarified as by fire! It is a word never used of ceremonial cleanness, but always of moral and spiritual cleanness. It means that no evil thing remains; it partakes of the nature of fire; things destructible can never live in fire. Then is seen the day emerging under the dominance of the sun. It appears in all its strength, glory, and beauty. The figure is of an army, of hosts armed, and ready for conflict, keeping rank, with banners flying, the great attacking force of God. Men love darkness rather than light, because their deeds are evil. So at last the vision is of an

THE FOURFOLD GLORY OF THE CHURCH

army, terrible, with its banners flashing in the sun as it moves forward to the destruction of all the enemies of God.

Glancing again over the same line of perfect rhetoric and wonderful unveiling, considering the figures now as revealing truth concerning the Church, I suggest that each figure deals with a separate relationship. Looking forth as the morning, that is the figure which sets forth what the Church is within herself. Fair as the moon, that is the figure which sets forth what the Church is toward the world and its darkness. Clear as the sun, that is the figure which sets forth what the Church is toward her Lord. Terrible as an army with banners, that is the figure which sets forth what the Church is toward all the enemies of God and toward the things that are against the accomplishment of His high purposes.

"Looking forth as the morning." That is what the Church should be as within herself, not so much as to her effect on the world, to which we come presently—but what her own sense should be. It should ever be the sense of the morning, the sense of the dawning of the day; the sense of fire, the sense of light; the sense of freshness, the sense of enthusiasm, of music, and of motion. Her very consciousness should be a perpetual prophecy of the day that has not yet come, but which surely is coming. Yet, alas, how constantly the Church has sat down in sackcloth and ashes on a dark and dreary day. In the days of Isaiah there was a time when men were calling on God, and were saying to Him: "Awake, awake, put on strength, O arm of the Lord," to which God's answer was: "Awake, awake, put on thy strength, O Zion, put on thy beautiful garments, O Jerusalem." It was as though God said to them: I have never been asleep! It is you that have been asleep! Awake, put on thy beautiful garments! It is a picture of God's people, Israel, sitting in dust and ashes when they ought to have been shining in the darkness, for they were children of the day, even though the day had not yet appeared.

Alas, how constantly and perpetually the Church has sat in sackcloth and ashes, lamenting, crying out for God's help, when she should have been shining. Constantly the word of God to the Church is, "Arise, shine; for thy light is come, and the glory of the Lord is risen upon thee." Whenever the Church has realized herself, she has looked forth as the morning. "Watchman, what of the night? . . . The morning cometh, and also the night!" The morning is known when the night is darkest by those whose relationship to God is such that they catch the gleaming hidden glory, and reveal it in what they are themselves, in the freshness of their enthusiasm, in the evidence of their faith, in their determined loyalty to the great beliefs and convictions that have made them. That is the first aspect of the Church; but there can be no dawn save as the Church is conscious of morning within her own soul.

Then take the second of the figures: "fair as the moon." That is the Church toward the world, reflecting the glory of the hidden sun. That is not the final figure, for there is a sense in which the Church is called on to shine in the world, not merely as a reflector, but because, in relationship with her Lord, she herself is light. Yet, while not exhausting the truth, it suggests a matter of great importance concerning the Church. What is the light which shines as the dawn? In the midst of some hour of darkness, in the midst of some circumstance of terrible trial, there is one man, one woman, one youth, one maiden, on whose face there is light, by which other faces are irradiated. That light is the reflected glory of the face of Jesus Christ, of the One Who never fails, and is never discouraged, nor will be until He have set justice in the earth, for Whose law the isles are ever waiting. If we could but see things as they are we should see that amid the sad and awful darkness in Flanders, in Gallipoli, are men on whose faces is the light that never was on land or sea, and these men are helping their comrades. What is the light on the face of that lad as he stands where death stalks round him? It is light reflected from the face of Jesus! That ought to be true of all of us who bear the holy name. If we are a part of the bride of Christ, of the holy catholic Church, we should ever be beautiful as the white one, catching the glory that is otherwise hidden, and reflecting it on the age in which we live. "Fair as the moon."

Again, the poetic figure runs on, and we reach the next stage of exposition: "Clear as the sun." Now I seem to break down in the sequence when I declare that this suggests the Church's aspect toward the Lord rather than toward the world. Yet this is the mystery which only He understands. The Church is as the sun itself, clarified with burning heat, possessed with a passion which sustains her, and enables her to create day. The Church shines most gloriously, not in reflection of her absent Lord toward the world, but in her relationship with the Lord in that deep, mystic, inner life which in some senses never can be revealed to the world; for spiritual things can be discerned only spiritually, and there are essential strengths and glories and perfections within the Church that can be apprehended only of the Lord Himself. So it ever seems to me that the words, "clear as the sun"—clarified as with burning heat, all that is evil burned up by fire—tell the deep and profound secret of the Church's relationship to her Lord and of His understanding of the truth concerning her. Men look on the Church, and even at the best she seems to be beautiful only as the white one, reflecting a glory. They see much of the dark through the white, they see much of her failure; but the Lord Himself looks on His Church, and knows her perfectly, sees all her hidden purity, her aspirations after purity which in themselves are the guarantees of her ultimate victory and glory. There is a sense in which the true catholic Church of Jesus Christ in the world is affecting the world more by what she is in the seeing of Christ than by what she is in the seeing of the world. Involved in that view is the heartening deduction, the solemn declaration of obligation, that the Church's true passion is not to reveal anything to men, but to be true to her Lord, and to reveal herself to Him as answering the fire of His cleansing, and so sharing His enthusiasm and His emotion.

Finally, "terrible as an army with banners." That describes the Church in her attitude toward all the enemies of God, forever warlike, forever unconquerable, forever a terror. Do not let us soften the first word, for therein lies its force and beauty—*terrible:* the Church must be a terror to evildoers. The conception is microcosmically revealed in the history of Jesus. There was a day when, proceeding on His way, He found Himself confronted by a demon-possessed being, and the demon spoke, "What have we to do with Thee, Thou Son of God?" Then came the revealing answer of Christ: "Come forth, thou unclean spirit, out of the man." Evil is always saying to the Church of God, Let us alone. When the preacher is told he has nothing to do but to preach the Gospel, and must not interfere with any vested evil, the drink traffic for instance, the answer of the Church is this: We cannot let evil alone; we are bound to speak, and to say to every demon that damns humanity, Come out, thou unclean spirit! "Terrible as an army with banners." Add to the great poetic figure of this ancient, mystic song the words of Jesus Himself, "I will build My Church; *and the gates of*

Hades shall not prevail against it." That is the picture of an army terrible, marching against every form of evil, breaking through the very gates of Hades!

In conclusion, let us dwell on the first figure as expressing our responsibility. We must ever be looking forth as the morning. He Who walks amid the seven golden candlesticks, holding in His own right hand the stars of the seven Churches, said of the Church at Ephesus, "I have this against thee, that thou didst leave thy first love." The loss of first love is the loss of the quality of the morning. The freshness has gone, the enthusiasms have died out, the breath of the wind is no longer felt, the song of the birds is silenced, the flowers are not blossoming. For the Church and for the individual there is no tragedy more appalling than the loss of first love, the ending of the first upspringing of enthusiasm that inspired the song and created the light and brought the breath of the wind. Are these things lost? Have we lost them? Are we sighing and sobbing with Cowper,

> Where is the blessedness I had
> When first I found the Lord?

Then we are failing to reflect light on the world, we are failing to satisfy the heart of Christ in the cleanness of the fire nature, we are failing to be terrible as an army with banners.

What, then, shall the Church do, if she have lost her first love, if she is no longer looking forth as the morning? She must return to the source of her first love, she must go back to face Him Who came as the Dayspring from on high, visiting His people. Or, to utter again the eternal paradox, she must go back to the place of the Cross where the darkness was deepest, and where hatred seemed to have won its victory; there in the place of the Cross she will find light upspringing, and love outrunning, and life beginning. Being thus herself restored to her first love, she will look forth as the morning, and become fair as the white one, be clarified as with burning heat, and become terrible as an army with banners.

As are the units, so is the unity. As are the individual members of the Church, so is the catholic Church. Then let us aim high, individually. Let us attempt in our individual life to get back into the spirit of the Song of Songs. Let us earnestly pray and strive, that in the day of drought and darkness and desolation, and almost of despair, we may be fresh as the morning, fair with the reflection of the hidden light, clear as the fire nature in our intimate relationship with our Lord, and members of the host of God to whom He has given a banner for display, proceeding resolutely against all the enemies of God and the race.

> Behold the Bride. She, herald-like precedes
>   The royal sun, arrayed in dazzling light,
> As mild Aurora smiles away the night,
>   While all in dewy stillness shine the meads.
>
> Behold the Bride, fair as the moon outgleaming,
>   Melting dim shadows of the midnight skies;
> His grace, through her reflected, meets our eyes,
>   The light which she receives o'er others beaming.
>
> Behold the Bride, a terror to her foes;
>   As the vanguard of long embattled hosts,
> The power of heaven's Eternal King she boasts,
>   Renown to win, and glory, forth she goes.

CHAPTER XVII

WE HAVE THE MIND OF CHRIST

We have the mind of Christ.
I CORINTHIANS 2:16.

THIS IS ONE OF THE SUPERLATIVE APOSTOLIC CLAIMS FOR THE Church of God. It has nothing to say of organization, of polity, or of methods of service. It is concerned with its philosophy, or wisdom, with that whole of truth which is to express itself through the organization to be the criterion of its polity, and to govern the method of its service.

These words were written to "the Church of God which is at Corinth . . . them that are sanctified in Christ Jesus, called . . . saints, with all that call upon the Name of our Lord Jesus Christ in every place, their Lord and ours." Such were those of whom Paul thought when he wrote the words: "We have the mind of Christ." At the time, Corinth was one of the wealthiest of the Greek cities; it was also a center of learning, a haunt of the schoolmen. Its abounding wealth made it a seething center of corruption, while the professed leaders of thought were engaged in disputes over terms, and thus were contributing nothing of moral value to the civic life. This letter of the apostle shows that the Church had passed under the baneful influence of this false wisdom, and to correct this the letter was written. Paul declared that his preaching to them had nothing in common with these things. The wisdom of those scribes, those disputers, was a wisdom of the world, and its rulers were coming to naught.

Moreover, there was no need for the Christian Church to be thus influenced. It possessed its own wisdom. There was a Christian philosophy which was a mystery, which had been hidden in the past, but now was revealed through the Spirit.

Now, the whole truth as to the fact of this wisdom and its possession by the Church is contained in our text: "We have the mind of Christ." This is as true today as at the time when Paul wrote the words. Leaving, then, all the apostolic application to the then existing conditions, let us consider the statement in itself, that we may apply it to our own conditions.

And this we shall do by giving attention to three matters suggested by the text: first, the Mind of Christ as the sum total of Wisdom; second, the Church of Christ as the depository of that Mind; and, third, the consequent Responsibility of the Church.

We begin, then, with this phrase of Paul: "The mind of Christ." In writing to the Philippians, Paul charged them: "Have this mind in you, which was also in Christ Jesus." Now, the word of that Philippian letter and the word of this Corinthian letter are not the same. They have connections: there are vital relationships between the words both translated "mind"; but for the purpose of our present consideration we must keep them separate and not confuse the thoughts. The word in the Philippian letter which appears today as an abstract noun in our translation is, as many of you know full well, a verb. "Have this mind in you" might be rendered, Be thus minded, which means, Let your habit of mental activity be that of the Christ. The word there refers to an exercise of mind, an emotional exercise, and, consequently, an inspirational exercise, creating an activity: the mind of Christ, that emotional activity which was the inspiration of His self-emptying, His descent to the human level, and His final ascent to the throne of universal empire.

The word in our text is not this word. I say again that the underlying conceptions have close connection, but the word "mind" in our text refers to the understanding, the intelligence, and that not as capacity, but as consciousness. The mind of Christ here is not that instrument which enabled Him to apprehend, but the apprehension which resulted from the exercise of that instrument. The mind of Christ here refers to the whole knowledge of Christ as it produced emotion or feeling in Christ and resulted in definite choice of the will, not only the capacity for thinking, but the thought; not only the capacity for feeling, but the feeling resulting from the thought; not only the capacity for volition, but the definite choice made on the basis of emotion proceeding out of perfect knowledge. To summarize, the declaration here is that we have the knowledge of Christ, His consequent feeling, and His resultant will.

Passing, then, from that which is thus most technical, and yet most important, we will endeavor to understand the conception which is suggested by this pregnant phrase: "The mind of Christ."

Here we must first remind ourselves of the limitation of our consideration and of its unlimited inclusiveness.

First, its limitation. The conception is limited, and it was the limitation which caused the Greek philosopher to call the Christian philosophy "foolishness." That view of the Christian philosophy grew out of the fact that in all the presentation of that philosophy by apostles, evangelists, and prophets there was a clearly marked limitation. The limit of consideration is human failure. The knowledge of Christ, His emotion, His will, are seen only in relation to human failure; wisdom is conceived of only as it affects human failure. Consequently, the supreme sign and symbol of the Christian wisdom is the Cross of Jesus Christ. This is our limitation. When we quietly consider this phrase, and begin to think what the conception is, what is connoted by this wonderful bringing together of simple words, "The mind of Christ," we are compelled to remember that we can think only within this limited sphere of human failure.

Yet, finally, it is unlimited, for this central fact affects and includes all things, and the whole concept of Christian wisdom concerning human failure has at its heart a great belief that failure may be set right, and emerging out of that belief, we see the possibility of the full realization of the divine ideal, and so, at last, we discover that the Christian philosophy affects all the facts of the universe. Was it not that profound conviction which moved the apostle when he wrote to the Colossians words which I venture to say to this day are full of glorious mystery, suffused with suggestions we hardly dare believe—when he said that Christ is to reconcile all things to Himself, not only things on the earth, but things in the heavens?

What, then, was the mind of Christ as finally revealed by the Cross? If the consideration is limited in the way I have suggested, it is yet so vast that there is the greatest difficulty in speaking of it, as there is initial difficulty in thinking of it. I shall attempt to speak only from the standpoint of personal apprehension and realization, for there must inevitably be infinitely more in the suggestion of the phrase than I have yet understood.

As I think of the mind of Christ, I find three supreme facts therein. First, there was the unfailing and undying sense of the beauty of holiness; second, there was the forever undisturbed conviction of the possibilities of all lost things, and, finally, there was the supreme and always victorious conviction of the glory of the work of realizing lost things, even at infinite cost, in order to establish the beauty which is the outcome of holiness.

In the mind of Christ—His outlook on things, what He thought of things, His conception of them—I find, first, the fact of His consciousness—and I borrow the phrase from the old Hebrew Scriptures because of its exquisite delicacy —of "the beauty of holiness." First of all, Christ knew God, had perfect knowledge of Him. It was out of that knowledge that there came His tremendous word on one occasion: "This is life eternal, to know Thee, the only true God." He had that knowledge, and, consequently, all things were viewed in their relationship to God. He never thought of man as separate. He saw the whole universe related to God. He knew God, and He saw everything in its relation to God. Therefore, He knew that the secret of beauty in flower and bird and man was holiness, and that the issue of holiness is always beauty. In Himself, wherever He has been understood and yielded to, He has proved Himself to be the fountainhead and inspiration of everything that is truly beautiful, and that because He lived in perpetual relationship to the God of Whom a prophet in a high ecstatic moment of vision said, "How great is His goodness, how great is His beauty!" He realized through all His thinking, never forgetting it, always declaring it, that only holiness is beautiful, that beauty is always holy, that at the heart and center of everything fair and beautiful in the universe is God. From the grasses that deck the field with beauty to the souls of men that worship in the high and holy place the reason of beauty is holiness, adjustment to the Divine will, articulation with the Divine thought, correspondence with the Divine character. The mind of Christ was, first of all, the perfect understanding of the relation of beauty to holiness. That was evidenced in all His living, in all His teaching, but supremely in the Cross.

Everything of refinement today in human hearts and lives has come from that Cross, that Cross in which He first, amid its shame and vulgarity, did vindicate the holiness of God, and, consequently, that Cross through which He was able to give to men a life that permeates their thinking and their acting, and that through every succeeding age will blossom into beauty, the beauty of holiness.

All this may be described merely as Christ's high idealism, His acceptance of all the things that are highest and best; but when He came into the world, what did He find? Beauty everywhere spoiled, because everywhere holiness was violated. Now, I inquire, how will this Man of such high and wonderful ideals look on such a world as this? The answer is that of the New Testament. He looked on the world, believing always in the possibility of restoring, renewing, regenerating, re-creating everything on which His eyes rested. As I said concerning His vision of the beauty of Holiness, that He knew God, so now I say concerning His conviction of the possibility of lost things, that He knew men. In a moment of rare insight John the Evangelist and apostle, the lover of the Lord, wrote these words concerning our Lord: He needed not that any should tell Him what was in man, for He knew man. A great generic declaration, not merely that He knew individual men, though that also was true, but that He knew humanity. In all our Lord's relationship with men He treated man as supreme in the universe; according to the conception of our Lord and Master, everything was beneath man in the scale of being. He believed that man, in spite of all that He saw in man of failure and ugliness and depravity and ruin, was capable of being redeemed, was yet worth dying for. From that standpoint if from no other, the Cross of Jesus Christ forevermore flings the light of hope across all human darkness, and writes hope on the face of the most brutalized countenance that my eyes have ever seen. For such a man also Christ died, and His dying was the outcome of His conception of the possibility of lost things.

In which is involved what I state separately. The final thing here in this wonderful mind of Christ was that He not only knew the beauty of holiness and forever acted on it, not only believed in the salvability of humanity and the possible restoration of all lost things; but that He considered that a self-emptying, which involved in it the unutterable and unfathomable darkness of the Cross and Death, was, nevertheless, the highest glory that could be granted unto Him and unto all who will come into association with Him. The glory of reclaiming lost things was the master inspiration of His mind in all His pathway through this world of ours. He emptied Himself! Inevitably, the words must be quoted here. Why? It was an action of mind growing out of a mind which ever conceived the connection between beauty and holiness, which believed in the salvability of the lost, which considered no suffering too great that results in such saving. The master passion of His heart, then, was to glorify God in saving man, to realize the beauty that is conditioned by holiness, in the desert, in the barren soil, where the briars and weeds are, to realize the glory of the rose and the myrtle tree. In order to do this He counted it all glory to suffer. He was crowned with glory and honor, says the inspired apostolic writer, that He might taste death for every man. The crown of glory and honor was not that of His sinlessness, nor of His ideals; it was the high and holy authority which He received from His Father to lay down His life, that He might take it again on behalf of the lost.

Reverently we turn from that principal thought to the declaration of the text. The Church of God is the depository of the mind of Christ. "We have the mind of Christ." The statement gives us pause. We are a little afraid, and we begin to look around and wonder. I ask you to postpone all such halting and all such inquiry—perfectly right and proper and necessary presently—and to consider the declaration in itself. The Church of God has the mind of Christ; she thinks with Christ; the measure in which she does so is the measure in which she also feels with Christ; and the measure in which she is true to her thinking with Christ, and her feeling with Christ, is the measure in which she chooses with Christ. The Church of God has the capacity to see with Christ, to feel with Christ, to choose with Christ. This is true, not only as to capacity, but as to consciousness. The Church of God knows what Christ knows: the beauty of holiness. She feels what Christ feels: the possibility of the lost. She wills with Christ: to suffer in order to save.

The Church knows the beauty of holiness. Alas, and shame on us, that we do not always do the things we know. We know the beauty of holiness. The Church also feels the possibility of lost things. In spite of its theology, the whole Church knows and feels the possibility of lost things. And, again, the Church chooses, in the measure in which she really is true to her Lord, the glory of the Cross to rescue man, not His Cross only—His Cross supremely—but her own cross, in fellowship with His sufferings, in making up that which is behindhand in His suffering. The Church expresses the mind of Christ not when she asserts, I am rich and increased in goods and have need of nothing, but when she is out in the wilderness, seeking the lost, pouring out her life blood in the business of bringing the wounded and the bruised and the spiritually halt to spiritual life.

I am perfectly well aware that it may be objected today that all this is so ideally, but not actually. I reply it is actually so, if not actively; and it is actively so whenever the Church is truly loyal to her deepest life.

Disloyalty to these truths presently destroys the capacity for them, and there is such a thing as cutting out the fruitless branch that it may be burned with fire because it is fruitless. If we come from the catholic outlook to the individual, the question is, Have I the mind of Christ? Do I see the beauty of holiness as He saw it? Do I believe, as He believed, in the possibility of saving the lost? Am I ready, as He was ready, to pour out my life in sacrifice, that the great work may be done? That is the test of Church membership, and there is none other. It is the final one for the true Church, the mystic Church, the Church whose membership is known to God.

If this be a fact how are we to account for it? The Church shares the life of Christ. Now, what are the elements in the Christ life? Light first, love also, liberty consequently. The Life of Christ being Light, His thought is of the beauty of holiness; His Life being Love, His feeling is of the possibility of lost things; His Life being Liberty, His choice is being bound on the Cross by love, that He may be the Saviour. The Church shares that life. This is the condition of entrance to the Church. A man becomes a church member, not by being baptized either in infancy or in adult years, not by the vote of a church meeting, not by writing his name on a roll. He becomes a member of the Church by being born again, by receiving the new life, the very Life of Christ. Consequently, if I am a member of the Church, then in me is this Life: light, which reveals the beauty of holiness; love, that brings conviction of the possibility of lost things; liberty, in which I am free from bondage, that I may be bound with Christ to the altar of sacrifice on behalf of others.

This is so, moreover, because the Church, thus sharing the Life of Christ, is ever taught by the Spirit, by Whom her members are born into her most holy communion, by Whom she is always indwelt, and Whose one mission is to reveal and realize the things of Christ. So we have the mind of Christ.

Finally, I will indicate lines of consideration, rather than follow them, on the subject of the consequent responsibilities of the Church. These are threefold, and result from the facts we have been attempting to consider. The Church is responsible, first of all, for continuing to proclaim by her doctrine and her conduct Christ's ideal, the ideal of the beauty of holiness. The Church is responsible for continuing consistently to announce His confidence, and to act in accordance therewith in the salvability of lost things. The Church is responsible, finally, for being His instrument to express through her activity His activity, the activity of sacrificial service.

I say the Church is responsible, first, for proclaiming His ideal of truth as the foundation of all order, of justice as the law of life, of righteousness as the one strength of peace. The Church cannot neglect these fundamental matters. The Church can never consent that in the interest of freedom from suffering, in the interest of the cessation of conflict, these things should be denied. In proportion as she is true to the mind of her Lord, the Church of God stands for truth and justice and righteousness.

But the Church is also called on to announce our Lord's confidence in the salvability of the lost. She must declare the possibility of the emergence of a new order whenever humanity is plunged in such a cataclysm as that in which we are today involved. In the midst of an hour when it seems as if ideals were gone, hopes were lost, and all the progress of centuries was being destroyed in blood and fire and vapor of smoke, what is the Church to do? She is to declare that these very things, blood, and fire, and vapor of smoke, are the signs of the day of the Lord. She is to declare that out of chaos cosmos must come. By her sacred and solemn ministry she is called on to lift her anthem in the day of defeat to declare

> That cannot end worst which began best,
> Though a wide compass first be fetched.

She is called on to

> Argue not
> Against Heaven's hand or will, nor bate a jot
> Of heart or hope; but still bear up and steer
> Right onward.

That is the Christian message. The Christian Church is to declare anew the hopefulness of Christ, that out of the worst must come at last the realization of the highest and the best.

The Church is called on to express our Lord's activity. That activity is self-emptying, ceaseless service forevermore made intense and powerful by the element of sacrifice. The Lord was concerned not only about the salvation of a man's soul, He was also concerned about opening blind eyes, and giving steadiness to palsied limbs, and comforting broken hearts. The Church of God is called on supremely to fulfill that function. I thank God for the measure in which the Church is doing that work today, and for the measure in which the whole nation, as beyond the Church, is learning the lesson of the Church and is doing that work. For some of us just now the mind of Christ is revealed in bandages, and in visiting the fatherless and orphans. Oh, dear Christian woman, do not undervalue your service as, with smiling face and cheery words, you pass from bed to bed in a hospital. That is Christian service.

In conclusion, the supreme matter of the moment for those who have the mind of Christ is that they shall bear testimony to holiness as right relation to God, and of holiness as the one and only condition of beauty. Not by the victory won by the sword will beauty be re-established. That is for the moment necessary with a ghastly necessity; but unless spiritual idealism shall go beyond it, and men everywhere shall see that not by victories won over each other, not by policies arranged as between each other, but by restored relation to God, there can be no beauty. The new internationalism may be as ghastly as the old, unless it is the outcome of relating men to God. The work of the Church is to insist on that, and on the possibility of realization in spite of the darkest outlook. Therefore, the Church is to say that nothing which is salvable is to be destroyed, nothing that can be saved must be destroyed.

The Christian Church has also to teach men the glory of working toward the end of saving the things that may be saved. And because we want to see the saving of things that may be saved, peace must be on the basis of righteousness, and in its making the element of sacrifice must be included.

Finally, mark this word, this apostolic word—mark it well and consider it in all planning and arranging. The rulers of this world who know not this wisdom will come to nought; but the rulers of the world who learn this wisdom, this mind of Christ, will come to victory, and the victory shall be that of the beauty of holiness.

CHAPTER XVIII

THE CHURCH'S DEBT TO THE WORLD

I am debtor both to Greeks and to Barbarians, both to the wise and to the foolish.

ROMANS 1:14.

IT IS ALMOST CERTAIN THAT PAUL HAD NEVER BEEN TO ROME when he wrote these words. A question naturally arises therefore as to the reason why he wrote this letter and sent it to the Christians there. Other of his epistles were directed to churches that he had visited, some of which he had founded, to all of which he had ministered. But he had neither founded nor visited the Church in Rome when this epistle was written and sent.

Nevertheless, Paul was a Roman citizen. A Jew he certainly was—by birth; as he said of himself, he was a "Hebrew of the Hebrews," that is, a Hebrew born of Hebrew parents; he belonged to the economy of Hebraism to the last and minutest detail—but he was a Roman, not by accident, or even by personal choice, but by actual birth. When an officer of that nation said to him: "With a great sum obtained I this citizenship," Paul answered, "But I am a Roman born."

He was a Roman, having all the rights and privileges of Roman citizenship. It is perfectly evident in the study of his life and writings that this fact affected his thinking and teaching. While he was a Hebrew pre-eminently, and while he was not unconscious of the Greek thought and culture of his age, in some ways Rome seems to have affected him more than all. He was a Roman of imperial mold, a statesman with a keen sense of the value of strategic positions, and able to carry on great enterprises. In a recognition of this fact we begin to understand the reason for his writing this letter. When to this we add the supreme matter that Paul was a commissioned apostle of Jesus Christ we have the full and sufficient explanation. His supreme consciousness, that is, the consciousness that most constantly and consistently influenced him, was of his calling and commission by Jesus Christ. This did not make him unmindful of the other forces at work in his life. It rather sanctified them, and pressed them into the high and sacred service. There was no side of the apostle's life of which this inner fact did not take hold and make use. Paul the Apostle of Jesus Christ knew that Rome was the strategic center of the world. He was perfectly familiar with the fact that the world was borrowing Rome's language for commerce and learning, and culture from Greece. He was perfectly aware of the fact that the Hebrew system was the purest system of religion known to the world. But he also knew that from Rome the highways stretched out over the whole known world. Rome had flung out those long-reaching arms over all the lands in order that her cohorts and legions might ride along them. I think, then, that I can see Paul, the man of contemptible bodily appearance, who yet became so transfigured by his message that kings trembled as he preached—I see him looking at Rome, and saying: Oh, if I could but start the new enterprises of the Cross from Rome as a center. How that vast government, stretching out its scepter and taking hold of all things, would help me in prosecuting the great work of my life, to make the gospel known to the whole world. How well these great roads would do for the journeys of the missionaries!

When he said, "I must see Rome," he was not impelled by the curiosity of the tourist. It was the passion of the missionary. It was the statesmanship of a man whose mind was imperial in its grasp, whose heart and will were dominated by the Christ and by His Cross. And so, when for a time he was prevented from going, he felt he must write his letter. He must at least see to it that the Christians in Rome had a clear statement of the great Gospel, and its message put in such form as to make it plain to their understanding. It is as though he had said: I will write the Gospel that Rome may have it; because if Rome has it, and it has Rome, the world must inevitably be reached by its messengers and its power. Of course, all this is simply the statement of the human side. Behind all this was the Spirit of God, leading and inspiring. In our text we have found the deep, underlying impulse of the letter. And what is it? "I am debtor." To change the form slightly, the Apostle declared: "I am in debt both to Greeks and Barbarians, to the wise and to the foolish."

This leads us to some further inquiries. What did he owe to the Greeks? Something of their ideals of culture? Very little, as his writings show, for, while it is certain that he was always under the influence of his early training in Tarsus, it is also notorious that Paul's classical quotations are very few, and perhaps, always incorrect. What did he owe to Barbarians? Nothing, surely, but their attempts to murder him. What did he owe to the wise? Certain it is that he had sat at the feet of Gamaliel, but there is very little doubt that he had paid in kind for all that he gained from Gamaliel. What did he owe to the foolish? Surely this is a mistake. He could not be in debt to the foolish!

So far, we are quite consciously missing the whole heart of his meaning. Let us attempt to express that meaning in other language. He meant: The Gospel has been committed to me for men; and so long as there is a Greek or a Barbarian, a wise man or a fool, who has not heard it, I am in debt. The Gospel has been committed to me not merely in order that I may hear its message, and obey it, and become a saved man. All that is true, but it is only preliminary, initial. The Gospel has been given to me for others.

Now we begin to reach the underlying impulse of Paul's life. We begin to understand its passion, its movement, its enthusiasm, its terrific drive. We sometimes talk about the terrific strain made on ministers in this age. The fact of the matter is that we hardly begin to understand strenuous service as compared with Paul's. Sometimes we are taken severely to task by well-meaning friends if we travel easily by train and preach twice during the week. There were no trains for Paul; there were no resting places for Paul. He crossed tempest-tossed seas and mountain ranges, and knew real perils on land and sea. What, then, was the driving force? Why hurry, Paul, why hurry? And he would have replied: I am in debt, and I must pay. I have a Gospel, an evangel, a message. Let me go and tell the men for whom it is intended. "I am debtor." There is the ring of tremendous responsibility in this. "I must see Rome." I am in debt to Rome. I have a Gospel for Rome. I am ready to preach it in Rome.

This is the language of the true Christian man in every successive age of the Church, and therefore it is the true language of the whole Christian Church. In broad principles, that word of Paul declares the attitude and responsibility of the Church to the whole world of men, irrespective of differences of birth or of attainment. The Church of God is in debt

—in debt to the world. Not that the world has given the Church something for which she has to pay, but that God has given the Church something for the world.

But, you say, the world hates God. That is partly true; but it is yet more true that God loves the world. But, you say, the world will not have God. That is also partly true; but it is wholly true that God wants the world. And it is for that reason that He has given the Church something, not for herself, but for the world. If the Church appropriates this great evangel, and sings her songs about it, thanks God in her worship for what He has done for her, and stops there, she is playing the harlot, she is prostituting her very nature to base uses. I make no apology for these blunt and brutal figures of speech. They are the figures of the Old Testament prophet and of the New Testament apostles, and there is nothing I feel we need to have borne in on our hearts more than this, that until we take this Gospel and give it to the world we are dishonest—we are in debt.

Let us now take time to consider the nature of this deposit, which the Church has received for the world, in order that we may the better apprehend the character of our responsibility. Let me at once say that I am not using the word "deposit" at this point carelessly. In writing to Timothy, Paul said, "I know Him Whom I have believed, and I am persuaded that He is able to guard that which I have committed unto Him against that day." The words, "that which I have committed unto Him," are exposition rather than translation. To translate more literally what the apostle wrote we may render the statement thus: "I am persuaded that He is able to guard my deposit against that day." Now, it will be seen at once that this may mean that He is able to guard that which I have deposited with Him, or it may mean that He is able to guard that which He has deposited with me. Both in the Authorized and Revised Versions the idea of the translators was that the apostle meant that Jesus was able to guard what the apostle had deposited with Him. I do not so understand the statement. It is out of harmony with the whole reason and purpose of the letter. I have no doubt that he intended to declare, "He is able to guard the thing He has committed to me." The idea was that the Lord had deposited something with the apostle, and that the apostle held the deposit in trust for others. Referring to this deposit, Paul said, I have had to suffer for it. I am not ashamed of it. My joy, my comfort is that if God has given me this sacred deposit He is able to guard it. There is no need for me to be anxious to guard the deposit of truth. God can do that.

This, then, is the sense in which I have used the word deposit, the sense in which the apostle uses it in this case, as of something deposited with him.

What, then, we may now inquire, is the deposit? In order to find the answer, I look at the text in the light of the context. "For I am not ashamed of the Gospel, for it"—and there follows the description of the deposit of the great Gospel committed to him and the Church. First, there is a description in general terms—"It is the power of God unto salvation to every one that believeth." That is the heart and center of the whole matter. Power unto Salvation! That is what our Gospel is. Not education, not entertainment, not social organization, save as it is true that all these grow from this root. Salvation in the New Testament almost invariably means rescue rather than amelioration. Rescue and all that naturally grows out of rescue. It is salvation from evil, both moral and natural. Salvation from the penalty of evil, salvation from the power of evil, salvation from the presence of evil.

These are the tenses of salvation. A man is saved from

the penalty of evil in the moment in which he believes; he is saved from the power of evil by all the processes of sanctification; he will be saved from the presence of evil, finally, at the coming of the Lord Jesus. This, then, is our Gospel; it is a Gospel of salvation as justification, as sanctification, as glorification. It is the salvation of the spirit of a man, which is justification. It is the salvation of the mind of a man, which is sanctification. It is the salvation of the body of a man, which is glorification. It is a salvation which deals with the whole man: spirit, mind, and body. Thus the Gospel is essentially a message for such as are in need. It is the message of Christ, Who distinctly affirmed, "I came not to call the righteous, but sinners to repentance." If for the sake of argument it be granted that there may be human beings who have no need of moral cleansing and spiritual renewal—we by no means say that this is so, but suppose that it were so—then they have no need of a Gospel, and our Gospel has nothing to say to them. On the other hand, those who know themselves spoiled, mastered, depraved by evil, are in need of a Gospel, and it is for such that the Church holds the Gospel as a deposit.

It is, moreover, the Gospel of salvation through the power of God and not through the power of man. There is a kind of evangelism much in vogue in certain quarters at the present hour which speaks of the conflict in every man between angel and beast, and which declares that man's hope lies in his power to destroy the beast and cultivate the angel. Well, all I can say is that I know all about the beast in my own life, but not so much about the angel. But if this evangel says to me, All you have to do to be saved is to make the angel master the beast, then I declare it is no evangel, for I cannot do it. But if the evangel tells me that there is a power of God that destroys the beast by giving me a new life, which is the Christ life, then have I hope. The Gospel declares the possibility of salvation by the power of God. That is the deposit which creates our debt to the world.

Our context takes us a step further in the revelation of the nature of our deposit as it says: "For therein," that is, in this Gospel, "is revealed a righteousness of God by faith unto faith, as it is written, But the righteous shall live by faith. For the wrath of God is revealed from heaven against all ungodliness and unrighteousness of men."

The Gospel, then, is, first, the announcement that righteousness has been revealed. That is the fundamental and inclusive theme of the Roman epistle. The righteousness of God has been revealed in a person. We often speak of the righteousness of Christ. That is not incorrect in some senses, but it is at least a suggestive fact that the Bible never speaks of the righteousness of Christ. It speaks of the righteousness of God, and Christ is that righteousness. If men want to know what righteousness is they must know Christ. They cannot have a true idea of righteousness until they know Him. Every other conception of righteousness is faulty and false. In Him alone the righteousness of God is revealed.

But, further, the righteousness of God is revealed in Christ not as pattern only, but also as power. The Gospel declares that the righteousness of God revealed in Christ is at the disposal of the man who needs salvation. Such a man may be saved on his side by the activity of faith, and on God's side by the bestowal of righteousness, a righteousness which gives him the pattern of his life, a righteousness which, through the mystery of Christ's dying, being communicated to the man, becomes the dynamic of his new life.

That is the Gospel which the Church holds as a deposit for the world. Oh, the music there is in it for my heart! I cannot read this great doctrinal treatise, argumentative and logical as it is, without the song born of the experience begotten of its teaching finding expression. I was lost, but there came to me the Gospel of salvation, and that Gospel of God's salvation was, first, the revelation of God's righteousness in Christ. That was a revelation of surpassing beauty, yet the unveiling filled my heart with fear and a new sense of my own failure and unworthiness. Then, while I looked and was afraid, behold, I saw that the hands were wounded, and the side; and I discovered that the infinite mystery of death admitted me into the infinite dynamic of life.

But it may be well that we inquire again, Why is such a Gospel necessary? And again the context gives us a complete answer in the words: "For the wrath of God is revealed from heaven against all ungodliness." A revelation of righteousness was made necessary by the revelation of wrath. The revelation of righteousness by the law was in itself a revelation of wrath to the Jew, because the Jew had not obeyed the Law. The revelation of righteousness through conscience in the Gentile was a revelation of wrath to him, because he had not walked in the light of conscience. This Gentile application is most pertinent to ourselves. Let us consider it. Concerning the Gentiles the apostle declared —quoting the Authorized Version—that they were "men who hold the truth in unrighteousness." The Greek word means, to hold down, to imprison, to prevent its working. That was the reason of wrath. When is God angry with a man? When that man holds down the truth in unrighteousness. Let me attempt to express that in another way. God is angry with a man when he does not follow the dictates of his instructed conscience. In the case of the Jew the same principle obtained, but with another application. He was guilty of holding down, that is, of preventing the operation of the written law in his life. That to him was unrighteousness. The Gentile was held responsible for the measure of light which he had but did not follow. That was his unrighteousness. The Jew has sinned against law. The Gentile has imprisoned the truth in ungodliness and unrighteousness. Therefore the wrath of God is over both. Both Jew and Gentile need salvation in the sense of rescue.

The age has not changed—at least, if the age has, human nature has not. I have no care to argue with men whether they are sinners through Adam's fall. I hold that they are, but one note of the Gospel is that such race failure and pollution is accounted for, and atoned for, in the Cross. The point of human responsibility is that men have deliberately chosen darkness, even though the light, whether of law or of conscience, has been shining on them, because of which God's wrath is on them. Because of that they need salvation, and our Gospel deposit is the proclamation of the possibility of saving such. If wrath is revealed because of man's unrighteousness, righteousness is revealed as available for man by way of the infinite and superabounding grace of God. That is our deposit. It is committed to us. We are, therefore, committed to the work of proclaiming it to the world.

And now, finally, it must be remembered that this Gospel is for all men. In spite of all arguments to the contrary, that is the plain teaching of the New Testament. If I did not believe that I could never preach again. But there is no room for doubt or question. This Gospel is for all men, and for all men it is committed to us. This was made perfectly clear in the last command of Jesus to His first disciples. To them He said: "It is not for you to know time or seasons, . . . but ye shall be My witnesses." He then described the circles which bound the sphere of responsibility. Let us note them. "In Jerusalem"—that is the first circle, the city in which we dwell. "And in all Judea and Samaria" —this circle is wider, embracing our native land, and the country adjoining. The last circle is described in the words: "And unto the uttermost parts of the earth."

Jesus Christ, the Head of this church, is Head of the holy catholic Church. He stands in our midst, and He says to us: You are in debt to Westminster, to London, to England, to the uttermost part of the earth. So long as anywhere there is a man who has not heard that Gospel, we are in debt. So long as anywhere there is a soul underneath wrath for disobeying light, and we have joy and a glorious Gospel, we are in debt. For dealing with evil and all its issues this Gospel is sufficient. Every manifestation of evil is, therefore, a call to us. Personal evil, social evil, national evil, racial evil, are saying to us, Bring us your Gospel.

Oh, heart of mine, listen! Listen to the cry of the war. Listen to the cry of the woman on the streets. Listen to the cry of evil everywhere. What are these voices saying? You are in debt to us. You are in debt, for you have the Gospel. Bring it to us. The man of Macedonia is crying to us as clearly as he called to the apostle!

It is a great privilege to have such a deposit; but, oh it is a great responsibility! Debt is always dishonorable. A man is pitied when he is bankrupt; but if he has the money to pay, and he does not, then is he a rogue, and must be punished. We are not bankrupt. We have the Gospel that will meet the need of the age. If we hide it and keep it from this city, this land, this world, we are dishonorably in debt.

Suppose the Church fails to discharge this debt. Nay, let us close on a more personal note. Suppose I fail to discharge this debt. What then? Ah! what then? Have you ever asked yourself that question? Can any sin be greater than that of withholding a supreme remedy from supreme need? Have we ever asked ourselves which judgment is likely to be greater—judgment of the disobedient Church or judgment of the men who needed the Gospel and never had it because of her disobedience? If "holding down the truth in unrighteousness" brings the wrath of God, surely there is no sin so great as that of having this Gospel and not passing it on, telling it out. The Church's responsibility to the world is marked in these words. She is in debt to man because all her glorious evangel is hers for them. May God lay on us the burden of this duty, and send us out to discharge it. As the Church discharges this debt, she fulfils her mission in the world.

CHAPTER XIX

FAITH'S OUTLOOK

Lift up now thine eyes; and look from the place where thou art.

GENESIS 13:14.

THIS WAS THE WORD OF JEHOVAH TO ABRAM UNDER STRANGE circumstances. The point and the power of the particular words are found when they are placed in contrast with an earlier statement of the chapter, a statement found in the tenth verse. "Lot lifted up his eyes, and beheld all the plain of the Jordan that it was well watered everywhere, like the garden of the Lord, like the land of Egypt."

After that survey of the land, and after the choice he made, Lot moved east to the plain of the Jordan, to the circle of the five cities: Sodom, Gomorrah, Admah, Zeboim, Bela. Abram remained at Bethel, as it was subsequently called, the historian here using the later name, Luz, which, in all probability, was its name at the time. Abram remained in that neighborhood, where later Jacob arrived as an exile from home; it was a place that offered practically no hospitality to him in his wandering, a place where, after the long journeyings, it was necessary for him to pillow his head on a stone in order to rest, a neighborhood at that time undoubtedly characterized by its rocky fastnesses and its barrenness. Abram remained there, and there the word of the Lord came to him, introduced by the words of my text:

> Lift up now thine eyes; and look from the place where thou art.

Let us consider the story and attempt to deduce some of its values for ourselves. In the light of these particular words there are three matters of interest to me in this story: first, the command itself coming to this man to lift up his eyes and look from the place where he was; second, I am necessarily interested in what he saw when he obeyed the command, and, finally, I am interested, therefore, in the results which followed that uplifting of the eyes and the vision which greeted him when he obeyed the Divine order.

In regard to the command itself, you will at once see that it was perfectly simple. Abram was told to look north, and south, and east, and west. We immediately see that he was told to look in every direction. In imagination, we see him looking away to the north. His vision would not penetrate far, for the mountains would be in front of him; but they would suggest the things that lay beyond them. He looked to the south. There, perchance, he could see farther, and he knew that beyond what he could see lay Egypt. He looked to the east, the very direction in which Lot had traveled. He looked to the west to what remained of the land until it came to the uttermost confine, from where the great sea stretched beyond. Thus he looked north and south, and east and west.

But the command becomes more than simple; it becomes significant if we lay our emphasis on two points. First, on the little word "now"; and, second, on the final phrase: "from the place where thou art." These indicate a particular time and a particular situation. "Now!" And immediately we begin to remember the things behind the point at which this man had now arrived in his life. Away there in the back, how far none can tell, was that mystic experience in which at Ur of the Chaldees Abram had heard in exile the voice of God. In all probability the voice had first been a whispered suggestion. But we know certainly that there in Ur of the Chaldees Abram had become discontented, discontented with the conditions in the midst of which he found himself, discontented with the splendor and the glory of that city, discontented with it because he had discovered its hollowness, its emptiness; discontented because he had learned something of the infinite glory of a better order of things. This discovery was born of his knowledge, through mystic intercourse, of the one God. At last, that whisper in the soul, perchance, as I have said, long continued and persistent, became a clarion trumpet call commanding him to leave Ur of the Chaldees and to travel long, long distances across the desert lands until he arrived almost at the confines of things in this strip of land which we now call Palestine. He had arrived at Shechem, the valley between Ebal and Gerizim, from which, perhaps, the grandest views of the land can be obtained. There he had pitched a tent and built an altar.

Then there had come famine in the land, and the man who had dared to leave everything for God became fearful; there was deflection from faith, and hurriedly he passed south, and crossed the borderland into Egypt. The man who was able to trust God with his whole destiny when he left Ur of the Chaldees was not able to trust Him when there was famine in the land. There had been strange experiences in Egypt, in which even this great soul had descended to deception, but there had been restoration, and he had come back again, back to his own land, back to Bethel. So we come to the immediate circumstances.

A vulgar household quarrel had been an occasion for the manifestation of two men, Lot and Abram. To Lot, the man seeking his own, first choice had been given, for faith is ever able to be magnanimous in its dealings with men; and he departed to this well-watered plain, choosing it because it was well watered. Mark the significant word: *like* the Garden of the Lord, *like* the land of Egypt. Lot, pausing in that particular situation of possibility to compromise between his faith and his selfish desires, saw a region like the garden of the Lord, like the land of Egypt. The Garden was near to the cities, where he might seek for his own enrichment. He had pitched his tent toward Sodom, and Abram was left—a man declining to be progressive, a man having learned a lesson through past deflection from faith and his sojourn in Egypt. Now, said the Lord, look in this hour; from the place where thou art lift up thine eyes.

Lifting up his eyes that day, what did Abram see? In the first place he saw, north and south and east and west, lands which belonged to others. There on the east was the land which now, in some senses at least, belonged to Lot, for Lot had chosen it, and Abram had handed it over to him, so that he could not travel there, nor take his cattle through. He must keep away from the circle of the cities. The Canaanites were then in the land, says the historian. That place where Abram stood was in the center of territory that belonged to others. No foot of land belonged to him. That is what he saw by sight.

What did he see that day as he looked by faith? The whole land as belonging to him. It was all given to him, even the land that Lot had chosen for himself belonged to Abram; those lands stretching away to the north that were possessed by strange and strong and warlike tribes belonged to him. Those lands stretching away south, leading on to Egypt, from which he had traveled, were his. The rich and fertile borderlands, down to the margin of the sea, all belonged to him.

What were the effects produced in this man as the result of his obedience to the Divine command, as the result of the things on which his eyes looked that day?

The first result was the march from Bethel to Hebron. The Lord said to him: "Arise, walk through the land in the length of it and in the breadth of it"—a poetic way of saying walk through the central strategic points of this land—and walk through the land as its proprietor and possessor. Bethel was nearly as far north of the site of Jerusalem as Hebron was south thereof. Of course, Jerusalem was not there. The stronghold probably was there even then, the fortress of Jebus which presently became the City of the great King. But Abram walked from Bethel to Hebron through the strategic center of the land, and he walked through it as its proprietor.

Suppose that we could have communicated at the time with any of the possessors, and told them that the man walking from Bethel to Hebron was the owner of the whole land, they would hardly have taken the trouble to oppose him. Probably, they would have smiled at his unutterable folly. Yet this is the picture of a man marching over a land that he does possess because God ordains it so.

Arrived at Hebron, he settled down, so far as settlement can ever be consonant with loyalty. He pitched his tent and he erected an altar, the two abiding symbols of his relationship to the land and to his God, the tent forevermore a symbol of his readiness to obey the Divine command to remain or to move; the altar surely the symbol of his relationship to God through sacrifice, and the Divine grace. This man moving down through the land owned by others was the owner of it; this man journeying through a land that other people possessed was the possessor of it. He pitched his tent and erected his altar as the sign and symbol of the fact that he owned the land by the deed of God and the gift of the Almighty.

Then I glance on. I cannot go far. One page will suffice, half a page in the Bible, the next chapter. What is the next recorded activity of this man? There came news to him that the opposing kings had taken Lot captive with all his possessions, and had carried him and his possessions away to the far north. Immediately, this man, who by Divine deed possessed the whole land, went forth to restore the land, the things that really belonged to himself, to Lot. Struggling with the opposing kings, meeting them in battle, mastering them, he brought Lot back. He traveled over 150 miles in pursuit of those kings. He mastered them and came back. He restored to another man the things which God had given him. When he had done his work the king of Sodom offered to give him presents, and he declined. He would receive nothing from any other than the One by Whose deed he possessed everything.

But let us go a little further, and we will do so by turning to a New Testament letter and reading some sentences:

> By faith Abraham became a sojourner in the land of promise, as in a land not his own, dwelling in tents with Isaac and Jacob, the heirs with him of the same promise. . . .
> These all died in faith, not having received the promises, but having seen them and greeted them from afar, and having confessed that they were strangers and pilgrims on the earth.

So far, that was the end of it all. This man never possessed anything in the land except a grave. He heard the Divine covenant which set aside every other right of possession; he walked through the length and the breadth of the land, and pitched his tent and erected his altar; he greeted the ultimate realization from afar with a song in his heart and confidence in his soul; but he died never having possessed; and yet, by faith, he possessed from the moment of the Divine covenant until the day of his passing.

Such briefly is the story. Now, from that story I want to deduce some of its lessons as I see them. Here is a wonderful revelation of the true outlook of faith in an hour of darkness. I may condense the whole thing into a very simple phrase: when faith looks, things are seen to be not what they seem to be. Faith sees farther than man's sight can perceive. The vision of faith is a clearer and more penetrating vision into the very heart and essence and truth of things than is ever possible to sight and to calculation. When faith looked out on the land on this occasion, it was seen that the land did not belong to those who were in possession, but to God, and to whomsoever God chose to make it over in the covenant of His great and sacred will. I am not proposing to delay to make any detailed application of this. It is the great conception that I would fain pass on to you at this hour. If, however, I make any application, let it be along these lines.

This is an hour when civilization is at an end. This is an hour when the very props and foundations of order seem to be shaken, to be going down in catastrophe and clash. To faith this is an hour when true civilization is seen producing the shaking and the catastrophe, and the things that are true and abiding are seen deeper down than all the things that shake and tremble and totter and fall. The vision of sight fills the soul with fear. The vision of faith fills the soul with songs. I choose my words carefully. He giveth songs in the night. Because, even in this terrible hour, the men of faith see God, endure as seeing Him Who is invisible.

I will make the illustration somewhat more personal. Take the kind of experience into which we all come ever and anon in our pathway through life, a situation created in a thousand varied ways, and yet a situation in which we are inclined to say, looking at things as they are, The bottom is gone out of everything. I have heard that said more than once this week. Faith knows that it is not so. The foundations are unshakable. If we seem to have lost the sense of foundation, it is only that life may become better, profounder, and that we may pass down to the things that never shake, that cannot be moved.

Let us clearly understand that this outlook on life is created by the Word of the Lord, and by human confidence therein. This outlook is not created by our own desires. Again and again, our desires are in conflict with the things which by faith we see. Again and again, our desires, if they were granted to us, would ruin both ourselves and all those with whom we are associated. Not according to our desires. If I simply take up an outlook on life which is inspired by my desire, then I have no peace, and no sense of rest, no quietness, no assurance, no authority. Neither does this confidence spring from our own conclusions. This man did not move with quiet, kingly dignity through the length and breadth of the land and pitch his tent and sustain his heroic soul in patience because he had concluded thus and so, and knew presently what the issue was likely to be and was assured that things would work out all right. By no means. This man heard the Word of God in his own soul clearly in spite of all appearances, and so he knew the final abiding truth concerning the things in the midst of which he lived. That is always the secret of quietness and peace.

I want to emphasize at this point the duty of this outlook to the man of faith. This was a command which God laid on Abram, "Lift up now thine eyes from the place where thou art." It was Abraham's duty thus to look, and his duty to look in the light of the word that God spoke in his soul. Here faith might have halted, here faith might have wandered from its right relationship to God. Had this been so, then there had been no quiet triumphant march through the neighborhood, no pitching of the tent and the altar, and no conflict presently to restore the possession to another, no travail, no holy prayer after a while that Sodom might be saved. The great nation would have failed if faith had failed at this moment. Of course, this is our difficulty. There are days when faith is a march with banner and song and joy; there are days when faith is a march into the mists, into the darkness, with no glimmering light except the assurance within the soul that God is right and God is truth.

In the second place, observe what this story suggests as to the activity suggested by the outlook thus inspired. Life will now be conformable with the truth which it receives. In all the attitudes of the life there will be evidences of the conviction that possesses and masters the soul. Here perhaps is the point when faith becomes most difficult. I have referred more than once to this man moving down from Bethel to Hebron along that central tract of the land now given to him. Look at him again. It was the march of proprietorship. I think there is a word that we often have need of: "Strengthen the hands that hang down, confirm the feeble knees." There should be to the man of faith no trembling, no feeble knees, no yielding to the pressure of circumstances, but the courageous definite positive authoritative triumphant march that is conformable with the inner, sacred, deep conviction between the soul and God.

But if the activity is that of conformity to the truth it is that also of submission to the Revealer. There must be a pitching of the tent, and it must be a tent of submission, an erection of the altar, and it must always be the altar of sacrifice. Finally, here must be an activity which is the activity of co-operation with the patience of God, getting things ready for others, the ability to do without things. This is the picture of Abram to the end. Further on in the story, Lot is dwelling in the city, and, more, he is raised to a position of eminence, he is the chief magistrate, for that is the meaning of the Hebrew phrase, "sitting in the gate of the city." What influence had he in the city of which he was chief magistrate? None morally, none spiritually; in the day of Divine wrath not ten souls could be found that he had influenced. Yonder was the man who had pitched his tent and built his altar and walked, a lonely pilgrim, in the unfathomable comfort of the comradeship of God. He very nearly saved Sodom by his prayer, and would have, if Lot had created just one vantage ground from which God could move. So we see a man co-operating in the patience of God, enabled to wait, without ever possessing the things which were his own, and content to be without them, because of his comradeship with God Himself.

The last thing I learn from that story, coming naturally and simply out of the things already said, is a lesson concerning the results which we may expect when we obey the Divine command and lift our eyes and see, not the things which are seen, but the things which are not seen. What may we expect for ourselves? Nothing! Everything! Nothing of the land of promise, nothing of the success desired, nothing of the business which we toiled to do. Yet everything of the land and the fulfilment of high desire, and the ultimate glory, and the work accomplished in the God with Whom we work, and Who, when our pilgrimage is over and our day of toil is spent, will take our little things and link them with His eternal might, until the final goal is reached and the ultimate glory is obtained.

So, then, for the future we are to expect victory and realization, and for today the honor and the joy of co-operation with God.

Therefore we may draw these simple conclusions of faith. It is never important that we should get anything we desire. It is supremely important that God should get what He purposes. It is glorious to do without, and still to have by sharing in the process that moves toward God's final victory:

> Others shall sing the song,
> Others shall right the wrong,—
> Finish what I begin,
> And all I fail to win.
>
> What matter, I or they,
> Mine or another's day,
> So the right word be said,
> And life the sweeter made?
>
> Hail to the Coming Singers!
> Hail to the brave light-bringers!
> Forward I reach and share
> All that they sing and dare.
>
> Ring, bells in unreared steeples,
> The joy of unborn peoples!
> Sound, trumpets far off blown,
> Your triumph is my own!

FAITH'S OUTLOOK

I feel the earth move sunward,
I join the great march onward,
And take, by faith, while living,
My freehold of thanksgiving.

CHAPTER XX

THE FIXED HEART IN THE DAY OF FRIGHTFULNESS

*He shall not be afraid of evil tidings:
His heart is fixed, trusting in the Lord.*
PSALM 112:7.

THE FIRST PART OF THE TEXT DESCRIBES A MOST DESIRABLE state of mind, that of being able to hear evil tidings without trembling and without panic. The second part of the text reveals the secret of such fearlessness. It is that of the fixed heart, and of the heart fixed because it has confidence in God.

This is supremely a day of evil tidings. Our newspapers are full of them. They contain nothing else. Their good news, the good news for which we look, and which comes to us ever and anon, is always laden with anguish. Battles won mean hearts broken. The tide of sorrow is rising higher and higher in the national life, and its dark waters are overflowing into every hamlet and every home. But they are especially emphatic, these newspapers of ours, about the tidings which are wholly evil. They tell us that the Government is incapable and weak, that politicians are blind, that generals are incapable, or, to summarize, that all the wise men are out

THE FIXED HEART IN THE DAY OF FRIGHTFULNESS 251

of office. These are evil tidings, because for the most part they are untrue.

But there are other tidings coming to us day by day. The situation in the Balkans is critical, the position in Mesopotamia is uncertain, the peril of the sea is not over—perchance Germany is arming every ship in her fleet with seventeen-inch guns, and building submarine monitors; and the summer is to bring the Zeppelins perpetually! Well, these tidings are evil, because there is an element of truth, perchance, in the whole of them. These are the tidings that assault the soul, the mind, the heart, day by day.

Is it possible under such circumstances to be free from panic? Can broken hearts still be courageous? Can minds assaulted by panic-stricken rumor still be fearless? Can wills be dauntless in the presence of great perils? The answer of the text to these inquiries is that there is a man who is unafraid of evil tidings, and that the secret of that man's quietness is that "his heart is fixed, trusting in the Lord." Let us, first, look at his man; and then let us consider the secret of his fearlessness in the midst of circumstances that make for fear.

The whole of the psalm from which the text is taken is in celebration of this man; and it is closely related to the preceding one. Both are acrostic psalms in the Hebrew Bible; each has twenty-two lines, and each line in every case commences with a letter of the Hebrew alphabet.

Their relationship is patent. Psalm 111 celebrates Jehovah. Psalm 112 celebrates the man who trusteth in Jehovah. A most interesting exercise is to read them together, that is, to read verse one of Psalm 111, then verse one in 112, and so on throughout. Such a reading will reveal that all the things of excellence and glory and beauty celebrated in Jehovah are found also in the man who trusts in Him, and is obedient to Him. Observe the closing of the first of these psalms and the opening of the second, for there we have an immediate indication of relationship. The psalm that celebrates the glory of Jehovah ends in these words:

> The fear of the Lord is the beginning of wisdom;
> A good understanding have all they that do thereafter;
> His praise endureth forever.

And the next psalm opens:

> Praise ye the Lord.
> Blessed is the man that feareth the Lord,
> That delighteth greatly in His commandments.

Psalm 112, then, is a character sketch; it is the revelation of a man. It is as beautiful as anything in literature. One wonders whether the writer knew some one man of whom he was thinking. Be that as it may, a man is in view, whether actual or ideal, and it is of this man that the words of our text are employed:

> He shall not be afraid of evil tidings;
> His heart is fixed, trusting in the Lord.

Now, we must see this man. Let me try to describe him as he is here described by the psalmist, but in other words.

The first thing I notice about him is the fact with which the singer opens. He is a God-fearing man.

> Blessed is the man that feareth the Lord,
> That delighteth greatly in His commandments.

So reads the first verse of the psalm. My phrase is a much more modern one: he is a God-fearing man. He is a man whose first thought is Godward, a man whose whole life is

THE FIXED HEART IN THE DAY OF FRIGHTFULNESS 253

lived under the mastery of the supreme and fundamental fact that he believes in God. This man may regularly, once or twice a week, or more often, say: "I believe in God the Father Almighty"; or he may hardly ever recite the creed in that particular form, but that is the truth about him. He is a God-fearing man.

The next thing I observe about him is that he is a home-making man.

> His children shall be mighty upon earth:
> The generation of the upright shall be blessed.
> Wealth and riches are in his house,

(Remember these qualities are often found, in the high sense of the words, in the cottage as well as in the castle.)

> And his righteousness endureth forever.

His seed mighty in the earth, his generation blessed among the sons of men—wealth and riches in his house are set in relationship to righteousness. He is the home-making man, the man who, first believing in God, has realized, in the deepest of life, though it may be that he does not often talk about it, that God's first circle of human society is the home and the family. He is a home-making man.

The next thing I observe is that he is a helping man:

> Unto the upright there ariseth light in the darkness.

Let me say at once that this translation misses the point of the declaration, which really is that this man ariseth unto the upright as light in the darkness. He is a center from which light flashes out on the way of other men. Notice what follows: "He is gracious, and full of compassion, and righteous." "He dealeth graciously and lendeth"; and yet again, presently,

> He hath dispersed, he hath given to the needy;
> His righteousness endureth forever.

He is a man who is helping other men.

Finally, I observe one other thing about him. He is a hated man:

> The wicked shall see it, and be grieved;
> He shall gnash with his teeth, and melt away.

This, then, is the man; he is a God-fearing man, a home-making man, a man who is always helping other people, a man who is hated by wicked men. Of that man the psalmist says:

> He shall not be afraid of evil tidings,
> His heart is fixed, trusting in the Lord.

Let us watch him in the day of evil tidings. What will he do? He gets the news of battle and of death! His heart is stricken, but he does not tremble. He reads his newspaper, and then puts it down, and goes on with his duty. If that man should be destroyed in an air raid, it will be at his post, and he will meet death cheerfully. "He shall not be afraid of evil tidings; his heart is fixed."

Whether this man was a man in the olden time on whom the psalmist looked, or whether he is the man you know, your father, perchance, he is a strong man, and all men know it. How is his strength to be accounted for?

And so we pass to consider the second part of the text, the revelation of the secret of this man's fearlessness:

> His heart is fixed, trusting in the Lord.

First, "His heart is fixed." Men who are strong are always men who are fixed somewhere, who have a conviction from which they cannot be separated by argument, which cannot be changed, whatever the circumstances in the midst of which they live. Sometimes these men are very narrow, but they are wonderfully strong; they are singularly obstinate, but they are splendidly dependable. Sometimes their convictions resolve themselves into two or three great fundamental truths, and they are never moved from them. Consequently, we always know where to find those men. The fixed heart is the secret of courage. Courage is an affair of the heart; courage is the consciousness of the heart that is fixed. The positive is sometimes best illuminated by the negative. Therefore, let me say that men not so fixed are weak men, however strong they may be. I cannot better illustrate here than by a quotation from old Jacob. When Jacob was dying, he looked out on all his sons, and described them. Mark particularly his description of Reuben, and do not begin where people generally begin, "Unstable as water, thou shalt not excel." We must go further back. "Reuben, thou art my firstborn, my might, and the beginning of my strength; the excellency of dignity, and the excellency of power. Unstable as water, thou shalt not have the excellency." Was there ever a more graphic picture of the failure of a strong man than that? Reuben, thou art the excellency of dignity, thou art the excellency of power, thou art the beginning of my strength; thou shalt not have the excellency, thou shalt not enter into the inheritance of thine own possession! Why? Thou art unstable as water! The man, who potentially was a great man, was weak, vacillating, because his heart was not fixed, he had laid hold on nothing that was eternal and positive! Such a man drifts, is moved by every wind that sweeps over the surface of the sea, is unstable as water. That man is afraid in the day of evil tidings; that man leaves his post of duty when he expects an air raid; that man talks in the railway train, and everywhere, about the failure of the Government and the failure of the politicians and the failure of the generals! Such a man is a menace to the State, and a hindrance to the purposes of God. His heart is not fixed; he has no central secret of power. He is dynamic, he is kinetic, but he is not static. He is full of power, full of activity in certain directions, but he lacks that secret strength that enables his power to operate to purpose and to victory, and that keeps him strong in the shock of battle, in tempest and hurricane.

We leave him, and by the contrast we see more clearly this old-fashioned man, this God-fearing man, this home-making man, this man who is always willing to help someone else, this man who is hated by evil men, and so is highly complimented. This man is not afraid of evil tidings, because his heart is fixed.

The supreme value of this declaration, however, is that the psalmist has defined the fixity, "His heart is fixed, trusting in the Lord." This man finds his strength in the fact that at all times he maintains in his thinking the central and fundamental relationships of his life; he is trusting in the Lord. Again, to use the negative method of illustration, his heart is not fixed, trusting in himself, but is fixed, trusting in the God Who explains what he is within himself, the God to Whom he himself is related. In a certain way this man has no confidence in himself at all. In another way this man is perfectly confident of his ability to do the thing that God has appointed he should do; and he will do it, whatever storms may sweep, yea, though the mountains be removed and cast into the midst of the sea. He will not go on tour to watch them falling in the sea. He will stay where he is, and do his duty in the midst of the clash. He is trusting in the Lord, not in himself. And yet again, the fixity that characterizes the man described by the psalmist is not of confidence in circumstances. A man who is not confident in circumstances is careless about them. If a man sees only the things that are happening, then, if they are not going according to his idea, he is perturbed, filled with fear—evil tidings render him hopeless. But if a man sees that there is a God controlling all circumstances, then, if circumstances are characterized by turmoil, so that nothing seems in place or in order, he is still unafraid, because he knows that circumstances are the arrangement of God. Therefore this man, trusting in God, knows that while he abides at his post, in the midst of the turmoil, the last word is not the word *turmoil*, but the word of the God Who is presiding over it. "His heart is fixed, trusting in the Lord."

And so one is driven to inquire: Who is this Lord in Whom this man trusts? Who is the God Whom this man fears, and in the fear of Whom he makes strong his own home, holds out helping hands to all who need his help, and because of these things is hated of wickedness? We go back again to Psalm 111, and there we find no doctrine of God, so far as a declaration of the mystery of His Being is concerned, but He is celebrated in the things He does, and by these things He is made known. The psalmist says of Him, "The works of the Lord are great," and "His work is honor and majesty." Here are two words, the light and shadow of which we miss in our reading. Great are the things done! Majestic and honorable is the thing made! The psalmist says of Him that He "is gracious and full of compassion," that He is faithful to His covenants with His people; that He is true and just in all His deeds. Evil tidings come to the man who trusts in his God, tidings of death, tidings of disaster, tidings of difficulty; but the man knows by what he knows of God, not so much in character as in history, that God is overruling. The man knows that God is great in His doing, that He is majestic and stately in the things that He makes to be, that He is in Himself gracious and compassionate, that He is faithful to His covenants, that He is true and just in His deeds, and, therefore, the man is not afraid.

Come back again to the second of these psalms, and observe the effect of this knowledge on the character of the man. This fixity of heart results in fixity of character, and that fixity may be expressed in the two simplest phrases possible. This man is a man in whom there burns persistently a passion for righteousness and a pity for all need. "Holy and reverend is His name," sings the psalmist of the God in Whom the man trusts, and when he comes to write of the man who trusts in the Lord, the references to the righteousness of the man run throughout. The God in Whom this man believes is the God of unsullied and undeviating holiness, and, therefore, the passion of this man's life is a passion for truth, for righteousness. But the God in Whom this man believes is also a God full of compassion and tender mercy, and, therefore, the man who believes in Him becomes God's distributing center: he scattereth, distributeth, helpeth. His own heart fixed in the God of holiness, he stands for righteousness in human affairs. His own heart homed in the infinite compassion of Deity, he stands for pity and grace and tenderness in the sons of men. Consequently, he is not afraid of evil tidings.

Mark the reasonableness of his quietness, and observe the expression of it. There comes to that man the tidings of death. His own boy is gone! He is not callous. The wound is full of pain, but there is no panic, there is no trembling, there is no whining. He is not afraid, because he knows that death is not the final news, that beyond death, even in that tragic form, all the meaning of life is discovered. He will fold his arms for a moment, perchance ceasing his work while his bosom heaves, but he will say, "He shall not return to me, but I shall go to him." His heart is not afraid of evil tidings.

He also knows that the tidings of incompetence is not the last word. God has always had to deal with human incompetence, and he overrules it in order to arrive at His own goal, to realize the destiny He purposes for humanity. Where have we as a nation ever arrived as the result of our own competence, tell me? We have arrived at wonderful places of power, and influence, and responsibility. What marvels our eyes have seen through these past nineteen months of the sons of the far-flung places of our empire coming to us in the hour of our anguish and travail! Have we won them by our competence? I hear that it is so, that we are a wonderful people for colonizing purposes. Yes, but if the Lord had not been on our side, now may Israel say we should have failed! If we will but read our history aright, we shall find it to be a story of the overruling of incompetence by God; and that it is this that has brought us to the position of power and influence we have occupied in the world, and shall still occupy if our feet are but turned back to the way of His commandments, and our heart becomes fixed, trusting in the Lord. This man says, there may be much incompetence, but the last word is God. His heart is not afraid of evil tidings.

And so, finally, to this man the tidings of danger is not the only tidings. Like the ancient prophet, he has heard other tidings. Do you remember how Obadiah began that weird prophecy of the doom of Edom, the doom of the nation that trusted in its might and its frightfulness? Listen to this: "We have heard tidings from the Lord." Tidings from the Lord! These are the tidings which this man hears every morning. He read something before he read his newspaper—he has read his Bible. The man who is reading his newspaper and listening to the clamor of the voices speaking of failure and disaster and incapacity, and is not afraid is the man who listens in the morning for another Voice, and goes to his work in the halls of legislature, in the mine, in the training camp drilling, in the home toiling, in the battle fighting, and as he goes he says, "We have heard tidings from the Lord."

What are the tidings from the Lord? Well, this is what God said concerning Edom:

> Behold, I have made thee small among the nations: thou art greatly despised. The pride of thine heart hath deceived thee, O thou that dwellest in the cleft of the rock, whose habitation is high; that saith in his heart, Who shall bring me down to the ground? Though thou mount on high as the eagle, and though thy nest be set among the stars, I will bring thee down from thence, saith the Lord.

The man who has heard those tidings from the Lord goes out and does his work, and is not afraid of evil tidings; his heart is fixed, trusting in the Lord.

Now, let us take up our newspapers again, and what do we see? We see a combination of words that I hardly know how to read! The Casualty List. By a wonderful spiritual instinct, hardly conscious, but coming up out of the subconsciousness of our national life, even our newspapers are putting something else; instead of Casualty List, we read Roll of Honor. They fall, our sons, our brothers, our lovers, our friends! We mourn, we grieve, we sorrow. We read these evil rumors, but we have heard tidings from the Lord, and, consequently, we are not afraid. We hear of grave situations, of peoples still halted, not knowing whether to pass to the right or to the left, to take this side or that side. We hear of diplomacies attempting to capture them for one side or the other. But, in spite of all, we are not afraid. And why not? We can best express it in the language of Julia Ward Howe:

> Mine eyes have seen the glory of the coming of the Lord. . . .
> He is sifting out the hearts of men before His judgment seat.

That, verily, is what He is doing. I am no prophet or the son of a prophet in the sense of predicting things to come; but I declare that when presently the war is over, and the conflict is done, we shall sit down quietly and see how these nations dropped into line, howsoever they may go, by virtue of what they were in their own heart and soul. God is compelling them to express themselves, and will do so to the end. If the only thing I see is what the diplomatists are doing, or not doing, then my heart is filled with fear; but when I see God sifting out the hearts of men before His judgment seat, then I continue with Julia Ward Howe, and I say:

> Oh, be swift, my soul, to answer Him!
> Be jubilant my feet!
> Our God is marching on.

What, then, shall we do in the day of frightfulness? We will do our duty, the thing that lies nearest, the thing we have to do tomorrow morning. We will do that, and do it well, and do it cheerfully. We will leave the rest to God, the sorrow, the suffering, and the issues. What this nation needs just now as much as, and perhaps more than, anything else is the multiplication of strong, quiet souls who are not afraid of evil tidings, who will go quietly to rest, even though the Zeppelins may be coming, and will not add to the panic that demoralizes, but will do their work. The men and women who can do that on such a day are the men and women who have hearts fixed, trusting in Jehovah. May God make us such men and such women.

CHAPTER XXI

"AS AN EAGLE . . . THE LORD . . . DID LEAD."

As an eagle that stirreth up her nest,
That fluttereth over her young,
He spread abroad his wings, he took them,
He bare them on his pinions:
The Lord alone did lead him.
                    DEUTERONOMY 32:11, 12a.

THESE WORDS ARE TAKEN FROM THE SWAN SONG OF MOSES. IN that song there is a remarkable alternation between praise and blame. It celebrates the goodness and faithfulness of God; it chronicles the wickedness and unfaithfulness of His people.

Calling to mind how God had found the people in a desert land, in the waste howling wilderness, and given them among the nations the place of prosperity and privilege, the singer employed this pictorial method of setting forth the way of the Divine government. It is peculiarly a figure of the wilderness, where for forty years Moses had kept his flocks. Probably he had often watched the eagles with their brood on some rocky height or sweeping over the broad and silent expanses. It was a daring figure, but he was warranted in using it, for forty years before he sang this song God Himself had employed it in speaking to him: "I bare you on eagles' wings, and brought you unto Myself."

The Bible is full of fine figures of speech and parabolic illustrations of the various aspects of the Divine government; but in all that it is intended to teach, none is more simple and sublime than this. It thrills with tenderness and with strength. It makes us conscious of the passion and power and purpose of God in all His dealings with those whom He loves.

First, let us observe the comparison broadly. In the eleventh verse we have a picture of the eagles in their activities, the mother stirring up her young, fluttering over them, the father spreading abroad his wings, taking the young and bearing them on his pinions. These words reveal to us the activities of the eagles, but they do not suggest their purpose. In the first phrase of the next verse we have a revelation of God's purpose—"The Lord . . . did lead him"—but there is no suggestion as to His activities, as to His methods. In the figure we discover the activities of the eagles: in the declaration we find the purpose of God. When we allow the first part of the text to be illuminated by the second, and the second by the first, we have the figure in its completeness. The purpose of the eagles is revealed by what is said concerning the purpose of the Lord. Why is this eagle stirring up her nest, fluttering over her young? Why is this eagle spreading abroad his wings, taking them, bearing them on his pinions? In order that they may lead the eaglets, in order that they may guide them. The activities of the Lord are revealed by what is said concerning the activities of the eagles. How does He lead His people? He stirs up their nests, He broods over them, He spreads His wings before them, He catches them on His wings, and carries them.

In the text, then, in its entirety, we have a revelation of God, a revelation of His activities in government, and a revelation of His purpose through those activities.

First, let us consider the revelation of God. There is a touch of genuine Eastern color about this. In the Bible, the eagle is more than once employed as the symbol of Deity. When Ezekiel was in captivity on the banks of the river Chebar he had a vision of God, and in the midst of the flashing glory of the light, and amid the turning of the mystic wheels, he saw faces: the face of the lion, the face of the ox, the face of a man, and the face of an eagle, all being manifestations of life proceeding from God, having its origin in God. Authority was suggested by the face of the lion; service, by that of the ox; the highest form of creation, by that of the man; while the eagle, with unflinching eyes, and wings spread for flight into the abysmal depths of mysteries that are beyond human ken, was the symbol of Deity. When, long after, the seer of the Galilean lake was imprisoned in Patmos, washed by the waters of the sea, he saw a door open in heaven, and round about the throne four living ones having the same faces that Ezekiel saw, the faces of the lion, the ox, the man, and the eagle. The Fathers of the Church interpreted the Gospel narratives by this symbolism, not always agreeing in their placing of the signs, but all making the eagle the symbol of John. For myself, I find in Matthew the face of the lion of the tribe of Judah, the King; in Mark, the face of the ox, pointing to service, priesthood, sacrifice; in Luke, the face of a man, the highest glory in God's creation; and in John, the face of the eagle, the symbol of Deity.

In our text, all the mystic wonder of the symbolism is brought down to simplest terms. Let us watch the scene as therein described. First, the mother eagle is seen doing a strange thing, stirring up the nest, the nest in which the eaglets, having been fed, are sleeping, and will sleep on until they are hungry again. The word "stirreth" is, undoubtedly, an accurate one here, but its root meaning is suggestive: the mother is awakening the birds, disturbing them in their slumber. Next, she is seen fluttering over her young, and the word "fluttering" means—and I prefer to use it—brooding. She is brooding over the birds she has disturbed. Then the father bird is seen spreading his wings in the air. The mother has wakened the eaglets, she has made them conscious of her mother heart as she brooded over them; and now the father spreads his wings, and the eaglets try to do the same thing—they flutter and stumble, and fall. Now the last phase is seen, the father is beneath them, has caught them on his wings, and is bearing them back.

That is God, said the singer of the olden time, and that is how God deals with His people. What, then, does this figure reveal to us of God? It is, first of all, a revelation of His Parenthood, that is, of the Motherhood of God and of the Fatherhood of God. The personal pronoun "He" is capitalized at the beginning of the third and fourth lines of this eleventh verse simply to conform to the rules of poetry, and not to suggest that the figure merges into a direct description of the activity of God at that point. The masculine pronoun is undoubtedly accurate, and thus we see the mother and father, the mother bird disturbing the eaglets and brooding over them, while the father bird spreads his wings, and presently bears them on his pinions. As an eagle stirreth up her nest, the feminine; fluttereth over her young, the feminine; he, the masculine, spread abroad his wings, and he, the masculine, bare them on his pinions. Thus we have a revelation of that supreme and glorious fact, that in God fatherhood and motherhood merge. We have never grasped the fullest fact concerning God until we have recognized the double truth.

Look at the eagles again as they are seen with their young, and mark them well. The eaglets are of the very being and nature of the eagles, and therefore are the supreme objects of the love of the mother bird as she broods over them, and of the father bird as he spreads his great wings before them. Here also the figure holds good. Man is of the very being and nature of God, and therefore he is the supreme object of God's love. This is the poetic and beautiful suggestion of this picture of the eagles with the eaglets. As the eagles love the eaglets because they are of their very nature and being, so God loves man because he is of God's very nature, of His very Being. This is fundamental. It is only in proportion as we grasp this underlying truth that all the beauty of that which follows will be apprehended. All that we see in the picture, the disturbing of the young birds, the brooding over them, the spreading of the wings, and the carrying on the pinions, all must be interpreted by motherhood and fatherhood.

But, again, as I watch the eagles at their work I am impressed with their strength and the consequent security of the eaglets. Watch the eagles' wings in the storm. They seem to beat back the rushing of the wind and master it, or travel with it in excellency of strength. Watch the eagles' wings in the hour of conflict, and see with what skill they beat down the foe that would harm the eaglets. Watch the wings as they brood over the eaglets, and mark their gentleness. Gentleness is not weakness; gentleness is strength held in restraint. We talk, said George Matheson, of the gentleness of the brook. The brook has no gentleness. It rushes and roars down its way over the pebbles. If we would speak of gentleness let us stand on the beach and see the mighty ocean with silver foam kiss the feet of the little child that plays on the shore. That is gentleness.

That is the true picture of God. Listen to some of the ancient singers:

> Hide me under the shadow of Thy wings.
> The children of men take refuge under the shadow of Thy wings.
> I will take refuge under the covert of Thy wings.
> Under the shadow of Thy wings will I rejoice.

Or listen to another, who employs the same figure, but in another way. Singing of God, he said:

> He flew swiftly upon the wings of the wind.

The wings of the eagle seem stronger than the wind, but when this singer used the figure he magnificently modified it, and made the wind itself the wings of God:

> He flew swiftly upon the wings of the wind.

When, then, did He fly swiftly on the wings of the wind? This is what the singer said:

> In my distress I called upon the Lord.

That was when "He flew swiftly upon the wings of the wind."

The glorious strength of God is such that the figure breaks down, and the metaphor fails, and we are left face to face with the naked fact, and of the consequent security of all those who are underneath His wings as they brood, or over His wings as He carries them.

In the figure there is, at least, a suggestion of the nature of God. What is the nature of the eagle? It dwells on high, and it takes its flight sunward, with eyes that never flinch as they are fixed on the light. But here supremely the figure suggests, and then breaks down; and whenever a figure thus breaks down it is fulfilling its highest function, for it is leading us beyond itself to the fact which it is intended to suggest. The eagle is the mystic sign of Deity because of its flight to the heights; but there the figure halts, for God is the ultimate height. The eagle is the symbol of Deity, because with unflinching gaze it beholds the light of the sun and soars into it, until human eyes can no longer follow it; but there the figure breaks down, for God is the light.

But now let us consider the activities of the eagles as representing the activities of God in His government. The first activity is suggested by the words: "As an eagle that stirreth up her nest"; that is disturbance. The next, by the words: "That broodeth over her young"; that is love assuring the disturbed ones that it is still active. The next, by the words: "He spread abroad his wings"; that is inspiration and illustration in order that those disturbed should be taught to fly. The last, by the words: "He took them, he bare them on his pinions"; that is protection that comes when, essaying to obey inspiration and illustration, the eaglets flutter and fall.

These are the elements of the Divine government of human lives. The first is ever that of disturbance. The life that is never disturbed by God is dying and withering and falling. God is forever more stirring up the nest, rousing us from our lethargy, lest, perchance, we also should become like Jeshurun, who waxed fat and kicked in his sleekness, forgetting not God only, but his own manhood. God disturbs the place of our abode; the home is stricken, and we are flung out. Our plans, so carefully and so prayerfully made, are broken down. Our very conceptions, the highest and the best, have to be reconsidered, and we discover that somewhere in our highest thinking we were wrong. God plunges us into a maelstrom in order that we may know how wrong we were. Our very service, the highest service we can render, service which He has appointed, is suddenly interfered with by the changing of our strength to weakness, or by a command that we relinquish it for another that seems less important. God is always disturbing us.

There is nothing more perilous than forming a false estimate of the meaning of disturbed life, that we should say of some soul who, through long years has always been tempest-tossed, buffeted, hurled hither and thither by storms, that there must be something wrong with him. It may be that God is preparing that soul for larger vision, clearer seeing of the light, and upward movement toward heights to which we have never mounted. As the eagle stirs up the nest, and will not allow the eaglets to settle into the lethargy of a sleep that follows feeding, so God stirs up the nest, takes away the loved one, brings into the midst of life the pain and shadow of suffering, contradicts our highest plans, hurls us out from the place where we love to be, makes us feel the sweeping of the storm, and so prevents the fatal lethargies that destroy.

But that is not all. The eagle also "broodeth over her young." The figure is the more striking in that it so closely follows the other. Probably, if I had been writing this, I should have put it the other way: first, the brooding, and then the disturbing, and this because I know neither the eagle nor God as perfectly as did Moses. He knew both. He had watched the eagle, and he knew God. The first thing is disturbance, and then the brooding over the young. Here we cannot be too realistic in our imagination. Look carefully at that eyrie on the rocky height. There are the eaglets and the mother bird, and she disturbs them who fain would sleep in the quietness that follows feeding; she will not have it so, she wakes them, she pushes them with her wings to the very edge of the nest, and presently will push them out. Then, as they are puzzled and fearful, she flutters over them, she broods over them, she says to them, in effect: Yes, I have disturbed you, but I am your mother! She broodeth over her young. That, also, is a picture of God. He disturbs, but He gives to the soul an immediate qualification of the disturbance, not by explaining its meaning, but by assuring the heart concerning Himself. Nothing is more wonderful than this. Souls that are struggling, but who, nevertheless, believe in God, are constantly made conscious of this brooding love of God. Again and again, during these months of desolation and disturbance, when some loved one has been taken away, plans have been broken up, and all that looked so fair has become desolate, have we heard it said: "I cannot understand it; but I am perfectly sure of His love. It is the Lord, let Him do what seemeth to Him good!" What has inspired the word? God—God brooding over the heart, giving the heart that knowledge of Himself, offering no explanation of the meaning of the disturbance, but assuring the troubled soul that there is a meaning in it, that there is wisdom in it. "The Lord gave, and the Lord hath taken away." Why has He taken away? I do not know, I cannot tell, I cannot see the meaning of it; it seems to have no meaning! But "blessed be the name of the Lord." When the soul says that, it is because God, like a mother, broods over the heart, and whispers the sweet secret into the soul: "As one whom his mother comforteth, so will I comfort you."

But the figure moves on in its revelation of the Divine activity. The mother eagle who has disturbed, and who has fluttered broodingly over the young, now watches; and the father spreads abroad his wings. By this act he is insisting on the fulfilment of the purpose of the disturbance and the brooding of the mother. He spreads his wings in front of them, they being now fully awake, and fully comforted. She waked them when she disturbed them, comforted them when she brooded over them. Now, in effect, he says: This is what we mean. He spreads his wings, and by inherent instinct, the eaglets begin to spread their wings. As in imagination, we watch them, we cannot help laughing at them, their movements are so grotesque. I am sure the mother and the father laugh at them with that tender sympathetic laughter that is always in the heart of parents for the follies of child life.

All that also is a true picture of God, Who is always going before us, and yet is ever near enough to show us how to do the things He demands if we are but looking at Him. Too often the trouble with us is that we are not watching our God. If we were doing so we should find that when He has disturbed us, comforted us, He will show us what He means, and so help us to spread our wings.

I watch the eaglets doing it, fearful as they find themselves flung out of the nest; in the element of the air, so strange to them, they begin to beat with their wings, but they are going down, they are falling. Now comes the last phase of the revelation. The father swoops beneath them, catches them on his broad pinions. They try and fail, but they never fall! In their trying and their failing he is nigh, and when they fail and would fall, he is beneath them, bearing them on his pinions. That process is repeated until the day comes when the eaglets will not want the father underneath; their own wings will find their strength, and they will fly. So with us. We shall fail, but we shall not fall. Our attempts will seem grotesque to us, and to others who watch us, but our Father will always catch us on His wings, and bear us up.

Finally, let us consider the purpose revealed by the figure. What are the eagles doing with the eaglets? The eagles are developing the eaglets' natural powers. They are eagles too. What is God doing in His government of our lives? He is developing our natural powers. Man is made for God; he is in the Divine image and likeness. By all God's government, by His disturbing of us, by His brooding over us, by

His guidance of us, when on His wings He is catching us when we fail and flutter and fall; by all these things He is bringing us to the fulfilment of our own destiny, to the realization of our own manhood. The supreme tragedy of human life is that man thinks so much less of himself than God thinks of him.

> Man is not flesh, man is not flesh, but fire!
> His senses cheat him, and his vision lies.
> Swifter and keener than his soul's desire,
> The flame that mothers him eludes his eyes.

That is why God disturbs him. God wakes man from the lethargy which oftentimes comes from overfeeding, from the attempt to satisfy the life with the things of dust. The purpose of the Divine government is to end weakness. Only by flight can eagles fly, only by struggle can strength be gained. That is an illuminative story of the boy who came to his mother with the chrysalis of a glorious butterfly. He knew something of the beauty that was hidden there; he had been told about it. He watched the chrysalis until he saw it beginning to burst; he observed the struggle, and a mistaken pity in his heart said, Oh, let me help it! Then with scissors he snipped the chrysalis, and made it easy! With what result? Those gorgeous wings were never spread! You cannot help the butterfly; from the chrysalis it must struggle to the glory of its final beauty.

So also man can come to the final dignity of his own being and the fulness of the meaning of his own life only as God disturbs him, rouses him from the lethargy which means death. By all the processes of strain and stress and disturbance, by His brooding love, by the inspiration of His outspread wings as He lures us toward flight, by the great strength with which He swoops beneath us and catches us on His pinions, by all this He is perfecting our strength and leading us to the heights as He develops within us His own thought for us.

In its first application, the word of the singer is national. It was to a nation that this thing was said. Oh the peril, the ghastly peril of failing to fulfil national destiny by reason of prosperity! No nation ever failed to fulfil its destiny because of adversity. It is prosperity that blasts a nation. Jeshurun waxed fat and kicked. He became sleek and forgot God. That was the trouble threatening our own nation, and therefore I say it with great solemnity, we thank God when He disturbs us. He is waking us from our lethargy that we may find our wings and reach the heights.

But if the first application is to the nation, the application of the song is also personal. Let it sing to us the sacred story of our own dignity. Let it argue His meaning as He disturbs us, and broods over us. Let us trust and obey, knowing that if we fail and fall, His pinions will be underneath; and if we wake with the horror of the disturbance His wings will be over us. The day will come when we shall spread our wings and find the meaning of God and the meaning of our own lives.

CHAPTER XXII

THE ACCOMPLISHED MYSTERY

It is finished.
JOHN 19:30.

WHEN I APPROACH THE CROSS OF OUR LORD I FEEL INCREASingly that I am beaten, baffled; its mystery is so vast, so wonderful that it is impossible to understand it. With that increased consciousness of its mystery there grows in the heart an increased sense of its necessity, its perfection, and its glory.

"It is finished," was the last but one of the sayings which Jesus uttered on the Cross. The previous saying, "I thirst," was supremely the word of His physical agony, the only such word that escaped Him through all the period of His travail. The next and last word was pre-eminently one of rest and triumph and quietness, "Father, into Thy hands I commend My spirit."

John does not record for us the fact of the three hours' darkness, and consequently he omits the central cry of the Cross, "My God, My God, why hast Thou forsaken Me." In view of the purpose and motive of John's narrative, this is perfectly natural; but for our understanding of these words, "It is finished," we must include the fact of that darkness and the cry that escaped Jesus therein, for it was, indeed, the central word, the word of the darkness, the word of the mystery.

Let us, then, recall the sequence of the seven words. Our Lord uttered three before the noonday darkness: the first, "Father, forgive them, for they know not what they do"; the second, to the thief, "Today shalt thou be with Me in Paradise"; the third, with infinite tenderness to His mother, "Woman, behold, thy son," and to John, "Behold, thy mother." Then from noon until three o'clock darkness covered the land. At the close of that period of darkness that central cry passed the lips of the Son of God, "My God, My God, why hast Thou forsaken Me?" Beyond the darkness three other words passed His lips: "I thirst"; "It is finished"; "Father, into Thy hands I commend My spirit."

Let us observe carefully, even if rapidly, the relation of the last four of these words. In the darkness, toward its close, Jesus said, "My God, My God, why hast Thou forsaken Me?" That is translation. In the saying, our Lord fell into His mother speech, crying, "Eloi, Eloi, lama sabachthani?" John tells us what followed: "After this, Jesus, knowing that all things are now finished, that the Scripture might be accomplished, said, I thirst." They immediately brought the sponge or hyssop dipped in vinegar and put it to His lips, which, having received, He said, "It is finished." Then He said, "Father, into Thy hands I commend My spirit," and, bowing His head, He gave up the ghost.

Thus our text is the record of an exclamation. In the Greek New Testament there is but one word, "finished!" In that exclamation, Jesus openly declared what John tells us He knew before He said, "I thirst."

"Finished" is an arresting word. It means completed, not merely ended, not merely done, but perfectly done, rounded out, absolutely and actually accomplished. Jesus knew, not merely that He was at the end of the process, but that the process was perfect in its operation, its purpose absolutely achieved.

Something was completed. What was it? Let us endeavor to consider that which was then completed, first in itself, and then in its bearings on the whole work of our Lord, and on the experience of human souls.

First, then, the fact in itself. Here, indeed, we must proceed with all reverence and all caution, conscious from the first that the deepest and profoundest meaning must remain a mystery, eluding the grasp of the intellect, but not eluding the confidence of the heart. It is well to remember that no man is made a Christian by intellectual belief. With the heart man believeth unto righteousness. While the mystery of the Cross will elude the wisest of us to the end of time, souls, instructed so far as earthly wisdom is concerned, will grasp with the heart the inner message of the Cross, and find life.

What, then, we inquire, was completed when Jesus said, "It is finished"? First, it is evident that what was completed was the work which had been Jesus' set purpose in all His journeyings toward the Cross. That was completed for which He went to the Cross. That was completed which He had declared, against the opinion of His dearest friends, could be completed only by the Cross. For at least three months Jesus' face had been resolutely set toward Jerusalem. Over and over again, He had tried to tell His disciples about His coming sorrows and triumphs, and always they had shrunk from the Cross. It is perfectly evident that what Jesus now declared to be completed was that which He had declared He must go to the Cross to do; that which He could not do in any other way than by going to the Cross.

Again, it is quite evident that when He said, "It is finished," He was referring to the one thing which He was authorized to do in order to complete every part of His doing, and so to fulfil the Divine purpose of His coming. I use the word "authorized" with all carefulness, for in this gospel of John we have the record of the fact that Jesus had declared in the hearing of the people in Jerusalem, "I lay down My life, that I may take it again. No one taketh it away from Me, but I lay it down of Myself. I have power to lay it down and I have power to take it again. This commandment received I from My Father." He persistently spoke of Himself as the Sent of God for a certain purpose. He declared that He was authorized by God to do one specific work; and so definitely was it in the mind of the Lord, that it was the will of God that the work should be done, that in the discourse already referred to He added, "Therefore doth the Father love Me, because I lay down My life, that I may take it again. . . . I lay down My life for the sheep." It is evident that He was referring to the one thing which He was authorized to do, and the one thing which constituted the perpetual passion of His life. Underneath all His teaching, underneath all His miracles, this one thing was ever present to His mind. He referred to it, not clearly, not definitely, but quite certainly, in the early days of His ministry. Reading things which He said in the light of subsequent events, we see how perpetually it was with Him.

When the disciples came back and found Him talking to the Samaritan woman, and they thought He would be hungry and offered Him food, He said this strangely mystic and wonderful thing to them, "My meat is to do the will of Him that sent Me, and to accomplish His work." Later on in the same connection He referred to "the works which the Father hath given Me to accomplish." At last, in the quiet seclusion and solemnity of the intercessory prayer, He declared to His Father this same passion for the accomplishment and finish-

THE ACCOMPLISHED MYSTERY

ing of the work that had been given Him to do. What was this work? The answer is found in the words already recited. It was the work of laying down His life, of dying.

Now we approach both the mystery and the light. Jesus said, "This commandment received I from My Father"—that I lay down My life. "Therefore doth the Father love Me, because I lay down My life, that I may take it again." Now on the Cross, He said, "It is finished!" But physically He was not dead. How, then, could the reference have been to His death? Here let me pause to refer to at least an interesting, and, as I believe, a most suggestive and significant fact. None of the evangelists calls Jesus' physical dissolution His death, not one of them speaks of that ultimate fact or act as death. Matthew says, "He yielded up His spirit"; Mark, "Jesus gave up the ghost"; Luke, "He gave up the spirit"; John, "He gave up His spirit." The death of Christ by which men are saved, the laying down of His life, out of which comes the possibility of our renewed life, was finished before the physical death occurred. That dying whereby we live, that dying or laying down of life in which Christ made possible the taking of it again for its communication, was finished before the physical dying. That dying was experienced when He said, "My God, My God, why hast Thou forsaken Me?" That is the experience and the inquiry of the human soul in its lost condition. Whatever hell may be, or wherever hell may be, that is hell—the soul conscious of its lack of God. There are men and women living today, living without God and without hope in the world, who are not yet conscious of the loss, the ultimate unutterable agony of missing God and knowing that He is absent. "My God, My God, why hast Thou forsaken Me?" Let us pass, so far as we reverently may, into the state of mind that made that question possible. It was a quotation from one of those old Hebrew psalms, which pulsate and throb with the agony of the human soul. In the book of Psalms the human soul sobs or sings itself out in its agony or its joy. In the psalm from which the word is taken, a pilgrim of the night woke to find himself without God, and he cried out, "My God, My God, why hast thou forsaken me?" The Word of God incarnate, the One Who was also the incarnation of ideal humanity in all its essential, universal values, entered voluntarily and vicariously into that experience, in its profundity and fulness. The language of the singer of long ago became the language of this One on His Cross: "My God, My God, why hast Thou forsaken Me?"

Let us place beside that sigh of the dying One another psalm quotation: "The pains of hell gat hold upon me." That is a far more pregnant saying than appears on the surface. The word "pains" might be rendered distress. Sheol was the underworld of departed spirits. The root of the word "sheol" is to request, to demand; sheol is the land of darkness, where perpetual demands are made and never answered. That is the distress of sheol, of death, not physical death, but the death of the spirit, the separation of the spirit from God, the inquiry, the request, the demand, the agony of the insatiable longing which has no answer! That is the experience expressed in the cry, "My God, My God, why hast Thou forsaken Me?" There we stand aside. We have come only to the confines of the great sea of sorrow; its waters fill the soul with fear, surging with the horror of the ultimate night. Who shall follow the goings or interpret their sighings of those condemned to this endless night? Presently Jesus said, "I thirst." When did He say it? When He knew that all things were accomplished. Then He said, "It is finished."

We follow Him to the Cross and stand before it in the darkness until He says, "It is finished." After that He died physically, and the physical death of Jesus bore the same relation to the spiritual death by which He redeems as His physical birth bore to the essential fact of His being. He emptied Himself before He was born in time; He died in all spiritual significance before He died in time. But the birth in time was necessary, that we might have some grasp on the eternal mystery. So also the physical death was necessary, that we might have some grasp on the spiritual mystery. These spiritual mysteries are wholly within Deity; it is the passion of God, whereby humanity is redeemed.

Our certainty, as we hear this word of Christ, is that however dark was the night that the Lord passed through ere He found His sheep that were lost, the darkness passed, and the light dawned; however deep was the pit out of which He must dig and lift the souls of men, He fathomed its black profundity, and emerged victorious over sin and death; for He Himself did say, ere He gave up His spirit, that the work was accomplished, that the work was done.

So, passing from the fact itself, let us attempt to see something of the fact in its bearing on the whole of Jesus' work and on human experience.

This whole of His work is so great and so vast that we must find some method of reducing it to simple terms in what must necessarily be a brief meditation. Therefore I shall employ the threefold official designation of the Lord with which we are familiar. I think of Him as Priest, as Prophet, and as King. I think of Him as Priest mediating between God and men. I think of Him as Prophet revealing to men the truth concerning God. I think of Him as King establishing the broad, beneficent Kingdom of God over men. I think of Him as Priest dealing with sin in its relation to the human soul. I think of Him as Prophet dealing with sin in its relation to the knowledge of God. I think of Him as King dealing with sin in its relation to the rule of God. He came to be a

Priest. Sin had alienated man from God, divided man from God, shut him off from the very life of God; consequently, sin had destroyed humanity. The Priest must deal with that sin if He is to be a true Mediator. This Christ did by His death. We cannot go beyond the word of Scripture, "Who Himself bear our sins." We may employ figures in attempting to illustrate it, but they all break down. We may endeavor to interpret the Cross from the ethical viewpoint, and there will always be a measure of truth in the interpretation, but the infinite mystery will elude us. If we are inclined to ask, How can this One bear the sin of the race? we must remember that we must not separate between that One on Whom we look and the God He is, "For in Him dwelleth all the pleroma of the Godhead corporeally." The uttermost reaches of that Personality include all the facts of Deity. He bore sin in His own body on the tree, and so He canceled sin; and by this means He restores man to God. His work as Priest could be completed only by that Cross, with its infinite and unfathomable mystery.

In His work as Prophet Christ dealt with sin in relation to the knowledge of God. Why is it that men are against God? It is certain that they are against Him. There would have been no war if men had not been against God. That is a broad, brutal illustration that we cannot escape. The human heart is naturally against God. Why? Because men do not know God. There is blindness and consequent ignorance of God. This Prophet of the Most High, this Man Whose work it was to speak to men and to humanity, and to all ages the supreme truth about God, could not say the final thing except by the way of the Cross. It was by the Cross that He said the last thing concerning God. He was the Word of God, the Word of God incarnate; but where and when did the Word incarnate utter the deepest truth? In the Logos of the

Cross, the Word of the Cross, by the truth concerning God there uttered. By that unveiling He gave to men knowledge of God. All true knowledge of God must begin in the Cross, and be conditioned by the Cross. Men say that they find God in nature! They cannot! No man ever yet found God in nature. Men have sought the truth in nature, and they have found evidences of a "double-faced somewhat," a strange union of intelligence and power, and that is all that men can find of God in nature. To know God we must begin with the Cross. "The Son Who is in the bosom of the Father hath declared Him"—hath given an exegesis of Him, to be quite literal in our translation. We never find the bosom of the Father in nature. Reverently, but without hesitation, I say that we never find the bosom of the Father ultimately even in the Son until we hear Him speaking by the way of the Cross. He completed the work of uttering His prophetic word concerning God which is to condition all human knowledge of God by the Cross.

Once again, and last, in this connection, Christ's work was the work of the King. Here it was necessary that He should deal with sin in relation to the rule of God. Because of his ignorance of God, man is hostile to the government of God, and will not yield to God's control. By this death, when its mediating quality has restored the soul to knowledge of God, all sense of hostility passes out of the human heart, and the human soul, having come to God through the Cross, then dares to lift itself up and look into God's face, and say,

> O God, of good the unfathomed sea,
> Who would not give himself to Thee?

This yielding to God's Kingship in love of Him makes possible the establishment of His Kingdom in the heart, and contributes to the final establishment of the Kingdom for the world. This King cannot establish the Kingdom save by the Cross. When Christ said, "It is finished," He spoke of the central mystery of His mission, and included therein His work as Priest, as Prophet, and as King.

What bearing, then, has this fact on human experience? I need do no more than attempt to name in the simplest way the effect produced by this fact in the human soul. First, sin is overcome as pollution, as paralysis, and as penalty. I name penalty last because it seems to me that forgiveness of sins, insofar as it means escape from the penalty for sin, is a poor and paltry thing if there is nothing more in it than that. I believe that when the human soul wakes up to know its own vice, its own unutterable pollution, it would prefer hell to escape from hell with pollution still clinging to it. The first thing is that God overcomes the pollution and poison of sin, that principle in the life which makes the fever rise and masters all capacity. He overcomes the paralysis of sin so that the man who said, I cannot overcome this evil thing, stands with his foot on it, master of it. Here we are getting into the realm where there is very little mystery except as to the method. These are the credentials of our religion: living men emancipated from the power of sin and standing erect who once were in its awful grasp and grip. Sin is overcome by way of the Cross.

The next thing is most marvelous! Shame is transmuted by the Cross. In enduring that Cross Jesus despised the shame, and even the shame of sin and the past becomes the occasion for glorying in the Lord, Who cancels its pollution, paralysis, and power.

Finally, by the Cross sorrow is transfigured. Sorrow becomes the very way of life, the very method of perfecting, the very furnace of purifying. The hour is electric with problems and perplexities. Out of these overwhelming sorrows something finer is yet to come. I try to look out on the world sorrows of today from the height of the green hill. That is the central sorrow, that is the central death. That is at the heart of all our agonies and pains. Because we trust there, we trust everywhere; and we know by that sacred token that it is by sorrow that life is to be perfected and fulfilled at last.

Some troubled heart burdened with sin is saying, What, then, shall I do to inherit eternal life? What, then, shall I do to be saved if the inner purpose which took Jesus to the Cross was that of saving? I will answer that question by repeating a simple hymn of a generation ago:

> Nothing either great or small—
>   Nothing, sinner, no;
> Jesus did it, did it all
>   Long, long ago.
> When He from His lofty throne
>   Stooped to do and die,
> Everything was fully done:
>   Hearken to His cry—
>   It is finished! Yes, indeed,
>   Finished every jot;
>   Sinner, this is all you need—
>   Tell me, is it not?
> Weary, working, burdened one,
>   Wherefore toil you so?
> Cease your doing, all was done
>   Long, long ago.
> Till to Jesu's work you cling
>   By a simple faith,
> "Doing" is a deadly thing,
>   Doing ends in death.
>   Cast your deadly doing down,
>   Down at Jesu's feet;
>   Stand in Him, in Him alone,
>   Gloriously complete.

Or let me recite other words yet more familiar, and let the inquiring soul use them meaningly, for as the soul uses them all the infinite values of the Cross are appropriated:

> Just as I am, without one plea,
> But that Thy blood was shed for me,
> And that Thou bid'st me come to Thee,
> O Lamb of God, I come.

CHAPTER XXIII

THE WELL-DOING THAT BRINGS HARVEST

Let us not be weary in well doing; for in due season we shall reap if we faint not.
GALATIANS 6:9.

THIS APOSTOLIC INJUNCTION HAS A MUCH WIDER APPLICATION than its context. There the reference is to the fellowship which they that are taught in the Word have with their teachers. The apostle, writing to these Galatian Christians, charged them that they were to communicate unto their teachers in all good things—which, I may say in passing, means much more than that they were to pay their teachers' salary. The phrase, "good things," includes sympathy, prayer, co-operation, as well as the very necessary supply of material necessities. The injunction in itself may, and indeed must, be applied to the whole area of life and service.

The figure in the mind of the apostle throughout the paragraph was clearly agriculture. Having said, "Let him that is taught in the word communicate unto him that teacheth in all good things," he immediately adopted this figure: "Be not deceived, God is not mocked, for whatsoever a man soweth, that shall he also reap." Again he wrote: "He that soweth unto his own flesh shall of the flesh reap corruption; but he that soweth unto the Spirit shall of the Spirit reap eternal life." In our text the word "reap" shows that the same figure was in the apostle's mind. Thus the thought of the text is that the harvest is the issue of well-doing. Therefore, well-doing must be interpreted in the light of that figure. It is the activity which leads to harvest. This central idea of the text is introduced and followed by words that reveal the special perils which threaten such well-doing: weariness and fainting. The whole text is an injunction to guard against these perils. Let this, then, be the line of our thought: first, the harvest; second, the well-doing that ensures it; and, third, the perils that threaten well-doing.

First, the harvest. Here, as so often, we are in danger of taking a great word and interpreting it very narrowly, and perhaps very selfishly. It has been altogether too much the habit of our thinking to interpret the big things in the New Testament in the narrow circle of our own personality. What is the harvest? To what was Paul looking forward when he said we shall reap? I do not for a moment believe that uppermost in his mind was the conception that presently we shall reach heaven. I do not think the idea was a personal one at all. I believe, rather, that in harmony with all his writings, with all New Testament revelation, with all the unveiling of what Christianity is in the supreme and central Person of Christ—that when Paul wrote, "We shall reap," he was thinking of something much larger than his own winning of heaven. No one will suppose for a moment that I am undervaluing that grand hope. I think we are sometimes in danger of failing to do what Rutherford charged us to do—climb to the City of God, and walk its streets, and gaze on its beauties, and talk with its inhabitants, and so prepare ourselves for the day of our arrival. Yet this is not the biggest outlook. What, then, is harvest?

I turn from Paul's writings for a moment to borrow

some words of another New Testament writer in which the same general idea was in mind. I refer to James. He wrote:

> Be patient therefore, brethren, until the coming of the Lord. Behold, the husbandman waiteth for the precious fruit of the earth, being patient over it, until it receive the early and latter rain. Be ye also patient; establish your hearts.

James was using the same figure. The picture he suggests is the husbandman waiting for the precious fruit of the earth. It is a common, everyday picture, but one that perfectly reveals God's attitude toward the whole earth. God is waiting for the precious fruit of the earth, patiently waiting for it. James was urging men to come into fellowship with God's patience.

In that phrase, "the precious fruit of the earth," there is a rich and wonderful suggestiveness. It describes the very harvest for which God is waiting, the very harvest to bring in which there must be the well-doing referred to in the text, the very harvest to reap which we must fight against weariness and fainting. The words, "the precious fruit of the earth," might with equal accuracy be rendered, "the costly and valuable harvest of the earth." That is what God is waiting for. This is the reaping for which we are looking. Here emerges a vital principle of Christian experience. Our real hope, our true hope, is not a selfish hope. The real inspiration of the Christian, that which buoys him up, and prevents weariness and fainting, is not the idea that some day he will gain something. When the Christian soul is most truly in fellowship with Jesus Christ he is prepared to lose everything, even his own soul: "I could wish that I were accursed from Christ for my brethren." Do not let any expositor or preacher persuade us that Paul did not mean that. He meant exactly that, and never was he nearer to the heart of his Lord than when he penned those words. I go further and declare that his passion was not so much for saving his brethren as for the glory of God and the realization of the Divine purpose, for the healing of the wound in the Divine heart, and the satisfaction of the infinite and immeasurable and unfathomable love of God. True Christian hope is not selfish. The harvest we look for is not gaining things that we shall enjoy in our own personal life, but God's victory, God's triumph. This was the meaning of what Paul wrote in his Roman letter when he charged the saints to rejoice in hope of the glory of God. Not for a single moment does it mean that we are to rejoice that one day we shall reach the glory land, but rather that we are to rejoice in the assurance that one day God will win this earth, and the prayer that Jesus taught us will be answered, His Kingdom will come on earth as it is in heaven. The harvest will be the golden era when God's victory is won. This is the reaping for which we are to look.

Let us return to the phrase of James, "the precious fruit of the earth," the costly and valuable harvest of the earth. The idea of that phrase is that the harvest will be the realization of the Divine purpose and the victory of the Divine travail. The harvest toward which we are looking is that time when the whole meaning of the earth will be realized and manifested. In God's temple they perpetually sing of His glory, and the whole burden of their singing is that the whole earth is full of His glory. This earth of ours is surcharged with the potentialities of the Divine glory. When, at last, all that is realized, when those hidden things have been finally led out to manifestation, when out of the old there shall come the new, the new being the full realization of the first Divine intention, the precious fruit of the earth—that will be harvest. That includes, and is dependent on, bringing man to his true end, the realization of what was in the heart of God when, according to the poetic and accurate account of Genesis, He said, "Let us make man." That harvest will come when man, who is the offspring of God, shall be the offspring of God, understanding God, co-operating with God, revealing God. This "far-off Divine event toward which the whole creation moves"—this is the harvest, this is the reaping.

All that will be the realization of the Divine purpose, but it will be the victory of the Divine travail. Harvest will be that hour in which He shall see of the travail of His soul and shall be satisfied, that hour in which the ransom and renewal of man and the earth shall be perfected, completed. That will be the hour in which the Divine grace, as it was involved in creation but now shown therein, shall have its perfect and final outshining in the whole universe. I still think of this little earth of ours as central to the universe in some senses. Its material smallness matters nothing. I honestly believe that here on this earth of ours God is working out the infinite plans and purposes of a revelation and unveiling which are not for this earth alone, but for all the vast and splendid majesty of the universe of which we know so little. The morning stars sang together over creation; but the singing of the morning stars over creation was not so wonderful, nor could be, as shall be the singing in the universe of God of a people who were not a people, of a people who had not obtained mercy, but who have obtained mercy, and who, to borrow Mrs. Elizabeth Barrett Browning's wonderful phrase, shall sing "their passion song of blood." I do not know, I dare not say, that therein is the solution of the mystery of evil. Yet sometimes I dream my dreams, and think and wonder whether, at last, the vast problem of evil may not prove to have some value, in that through its long processes to the ultimate harvest God's heart by breaking has been revealed.

In the light of all that, I look again at this little paragraph in Galatians, and I see in it an illustration of the fact that in Christianity, as interpreted by these apostolic writings, every little thing becomes vast. People who have been taught in the Word are to communicate to the men who teach them in all good things. The really arresting phrase in that instruction is the phrase, "the word." We do not capitalize it in our printing, and we are in danger of thinking of what is preached, and of the people who listen, as being very small. As a matter of fact, the whole thing is big with the bigness of the Logos. The Word preached is the creative Word, the redemptive Word. The teacher of the Word, and those who are taught, are those who are brought into fellowship with God's vastest enterprise. When the teacher is doing his work, and when men and women are being taught, what is happening? Something is being done toward the day when God shall see of the travail of His soul and be satisfied.

And then we go on with the paragraph, and we read, "He that soweth to his own flesh." The man who does that is the man who takes the good things, whatsoever they may be, and makes them minister to his own selfish desires and appetites. Of the flesh such a man will reap corruption. On the other hand, he that of these good things, whatsoever they may be, soweth to the Spirit shall of the Spirit reap eternal life, the ultimate age-abiding life, God's great victory, the harvest, and the full harvest. So the apparently little things are found to be big indeed when they are set in relation to the harvest, wherein the old creation delivered from its bondage of corruption and death will rise into the new life, and God will be satisfied in His creation, in His redemption, in the gathering of the precious fruit of the earth.

It immediately becomes manifest that the word "well-doing" describes and covers the activities apart from which this harvest cannot be. The husbandman's expectations are always based on his work. The husbandman has not patience for the precious fruit of the earth unless he has put into the earth his toil. God's expectations in creation are based on the work of the six days that preceded the rest of the seventh, and God's expectations in redemption are based on the travail that abandoned rest. When men charged His Son with making a man break the Sabbath, the son answered in those exquisite and wonderful words: "My Father worketh hitherto, and I work." God cannot rest while man is restless and wounded. God cannot rest while a man lies in the grip of an infirmity thirty and eight years, and there is none to help and deliver. "My Father worketh hitherto, and I work." God's expectation of the ultimate realization of His own purpose is based on the infinite mystery of His travail! The measure of our right to expect the issue of harvest is our participation in the labor. The activities which demand patience are the activities of putting toil and seed into the earth in dull days, with no immediate sign of result. There I think is the point at which this figure proves itself to be of such value. Think of the autumnal days, and the days of winter—cold, bleak, dark days, often with no sun, when everything seems to be dead. Those are the days in which the well-doing is practiced that prepares for the harvest. Broadly and simply, then, well-doing is putting things into life when everything is dark, and apparently dead. It is the persistent going on, doing the thing on the day when there seems to be no use in doing it. That is well-doing. This is the whole story of our Lord's earthly ministry. If you and I had been called on to fix the date of the Advent we would not have fixed it when it was fixed. There was never a more hopeless hour than that in the history of the world. The hour in which we are living today is not half so deadly and dark and desolate as the hour in which Jesus was born into the world. There were no signs of life! Then God sent His Son. That was well-doing. Follow Him through the days of His public ministry: all His great ideals were implanted in human thinking in the day of philosophic decadence and deadness. There had been a great period in philosophy before Christ came, those first three centuries of philosophy, but He came when it was dead, He came when men were amusing themselves, and thought they were learned when they were discussing the difference between words and views. It was a barren hour. Jesus came, and taught, using words, parables, pictures. His words were so few that if you gather up them all they will not fill a penny exercise book, yet they are so wonderful that when he had done, the writer of the last Gospel said that if all the truth about Jesus should be written the world itself would not contain the books that should be written. Sometimes, after reading that, we close our New Testament and say, That is a very beautiful, a wonderful piece of hyperbole! It is nothing of the kind. John was right. If all the meaning of all Jesus said and did were written, the world could not contain the books, for the universe would be included. Yet all was of the nature of well-doing; it was patient continuance in doing things that brought forth no immediate result. The immediate result of our Lord's teaching, what was it? Not one single human soul to stand by Him in the hour of His catastrophe; they all forsook Him and fled!

What, then, is well-doing for us? Preaching when there seems to be no result, and yet continuing to preach. Teaching in the Sunday school, keeping on when it seems as though nothing were being done. Living by truth, living by grace, when a lie is on the throne and hate is the master movement of an age. Making the whole life the simple doing, putting toil and seed into the soil that seems to be barren, in a day when there is no light anywhere, and the birds have ceased their singing. That is well-doing.

Now, what are the perils that threaten us? We have seen them as we have tried to speak of well-doing. What are they? Weariness and faintness. What is weariness? Not tiredness. That is not the meaning of the word. We cannot do these things without getting tired. Tiredness is a sacrament that compels rest and prepares for new endeavor. Jesus was tired again and again. "And being thus tired, He sat by the well." What, then, is weariness? It is losing heart. It is losing interest. It is the sense of dullness that comes when the keen edge has gone off, when the thing does not seem to be worth doing. Weariness! We might translate the words thus: Let us not be worthless in well-doing. This word is the revelation of a subtle peril. It is the word of an inevitable danger which may be—I think it ought to be—overcome. We cannot, however, escape from the peril of it. It is the natural result of doing things that do not immediately realize themselves. It gets us before we know it. Its symptom is the sigh that escapes us when the thing has to be done. The preacher says, This is Monday morning! I must get ready for next Sunday. And he says it with a sigh. That is it. The teachers says, It is Wednesday. There is that Normal Class I have to go to again! And she says it with a sigh. That is it. We must guard against it. That dulling of the edge is weariness.

Fainting? What is that? That is quite another word, a stronger word. It is the issue of weariness. If weariness is losing heart, losing interest, fainting is that loosening carried to its ultimate, until there is dissolution. Fainting is failure of co-ordination, so that the thing we attempt is not done because we have lost the power to do it. Fainting is the outcome of weariness, the last issue.

How are we to escape these things? You say to me, You

have admitted that these things get us before we know. It certainly is so, and perhaps the sermon is born of the fact that I am at the end of three months' preaching here, very probably so. How are we to escape it, how are we to miss it, how are we to be delivered from it? This vision of the harvest must never be lost. I pray you make a careful note of that. This is nothing new to say. It has been said again and again, but it needs to be said. I need to say it to my own soul. Man, lift thine eyes from the dull earth where no blade of grass is springing and look to the golden harvest. But that vision of harvest can be maintained only by maintaining fellowship with God. I shall doubt the harvest altogether if I look simply on things as they are. Does it seem as if God's great harvest can ever be gathered in Europe? What the answer will be depends on where you live and where I live. It is only as we live in the realization of fellowship with God, pressing ever farther into the secret place, beholding His face, listening for His voice, that we shall see the harvest and see it perpetually.

Yet once more. The relation of sowing and reaping must always be remembered. That dull piece of earth and those leaden clods with no song bird or sign of life! Yes, but these make the harvest, and there is no harvest without them. There never will be the fruitage of autumn and the golden sheaves unless there has been first the cold of the previous autumn merging into the snows and the desolation of winter. Through these things harvest comes to us. When we next face the well-doing, which is doing a thing that seems as though nothing were being done, let us say, Everything is now being done. It is by this travail that the triumph comes. By this sweat and labor and agony and continuity the great glad day shall come.

There is one other thing I would like to suggest to my

own soul and to others. If we are to escape these perils it will be more than ever necessary as the days run on to exclude from our lives all things that deflect strength into false channels. In proportion as we can find the one thing God wants us to do and do it, and refuse to do anything else, in the very concentration of our attention on the well-doing that seems to be monotonous, that very thing will be transmuted, and there will be light and glory in it, and we shall begin to feel the throb of the life that triumphantly moves through the tyranny of death toward the final harvest of the world. These are days surely when we supremely need to hear these apostolic words, "Be not weary in well doing." The strain of darkness and death is on us, the terrible temptation to relax is powerful! Therefore these are the days when we need as never before to practice our fellowship with God, that we may see the harvest through the light of that communion, and that the doing of the apparently small things may be transfigured by the self-same light. So we shall not be weary in well-doing, nor shall we faint.

CHAPTER XXIV

THE SPELL WHICH JESUS CASTS ON MEN

And He called unto Him the multitude with His disciples, and said unto them, If any man would come after Me, let him deny himself, and take up his cross, and follow Me.

MARK 8:34.

THIS IS A VERY OLD TEXT, BUT IT IS BY NO MEANS EXHAUSTED. It is central to Christianity, being the inclusive message of Christ, having universal as well as individual application. According to Matthew and Mark, these particular words were spoken at that hour of crisis in Christ's own ministry when He inquired of His immediate disciples what the result of His preaching and teaching and living had been. At Cæsarea Philippi He asked them: "Who do men say that I am?" One of their number made the great confession that He was infinitely more than a prophet, being the Messiah, the One to Whom all the prophets had given witness. It was then that Christ uttered the words of our text.

It is evident that these words were based on the supposition that some men desired to follow Him. That is the first arresting note of the text.

Immediately following it, we have our Lord's clear enunciation of the condition on which such a man may follow him. "Let him deny himself." He then indicated a pro-

THE SPELL WHICH JESUS CASTS ON MEN

gram of life to the soul who would fulfil that condition and so follow Him. Let him take up his cross and accompany Me.

Three lines of thought are suggested by these words. The first is of the spell of Jesus. I resolutely use the word "Jesus," because that is where we must begin. That is where these men began. They had no theory of His Deity, did not know anything about it, in the early days of His mission. They began with the Man Jesus, and that is where we begin. There was in Him something which cast a spell on men, which made them want to follow Him, an attraction which created in the souls of men that desire to which He made His appeal when He uttered these words: "If any man would come after Me . . ." That is the subject of our present consideration.

We shall consider on subsequent occasions the sense which that spell produces in the human soul. It is the sense of surprise, of shock, of upheaval. Directly a man comes face to face with Jesus this is the result. In the days of His flesh, when men really knew Him, really reached Him, it was so; and directly men come face to face with Him today, really get to Him beyond all the things that hinder, they are staggered and shocked and frightened.

When the soul is shuddering with fear in the presence of the infinite glory and beauty of the One Who has thus attracted, He calls that trembling, frightened soul to come with Him. Let him take up his cross and travel My way.

Let us now consider that which is suggested by the words: "If any man would come after Me." Amid the myriad marvels merging in the mystery of the Person of Christ one of the most patent and persistent is His attractiveness. It is safe to say that without exception He casts the spell of His personality on all who come face to face with Him. That is the revelation of these Gospel narratives. They show how irresistibly He attracted men. I am not saying that they yielded to Him, that they obeyed Him, but that they were attracted by Him. There was something about Him which drew men after Him. They could not leave Him alone. Someone once said, and it was at least an illuminative suggestion, that probably more days of work were lost in the three years of Jesus' public ministry by men running after Him from place to place than had ever been lost in that neighborhood before.

The same sense of attractiveness exercises its spell on all those who read these records, if they read the records simply and naturally. They are the records of a Person Who irresistibly drew men after Him. Read them, and the very attractiveness that drew the men of His own age after Jesus comes through the reading and produces exactly the same effect on men today. Of course, the spell of the Lord is not felt if He be veiled or in any wise changed. If this Person of the Gospel narratives passes under the influence of merely ecclesiastical organization, they retire Him behind veils into some realm of mystery, and men are not attracted. Also, over and over again this Person of the Gospels has been hidden from men by discussions of schoolmen who have dissipated Him by theorizing. I am inclined to go further and say that very often the spell of Jesus has been destroyed by systematic theology, which at least tends to harden Him into formulas and rob Him of that vital principle that drew men in the days of His flesh and that draws men still if only they can get near Him. If we would consider Him we must do so directly, through the only medium provided. In these four brief pamphlets (gospels) we find Him, and we find Him nowhere else. Whatever method we may adopt in our attempt to understand this Person, we must correct our method by these pamphlets, or we lose Him. That is in itself a mystic test of every method that men have employed in approaching Christ.

Any departure from these pamphlets ends in changing the Person or veiling Him so that He ceases to attract.

I am not going to attempt to describe Jesus in detail. Realizing the fact of the spell which He evidently cast on the men of His age, and which He still casts on men, I want to speak of the nature of that attraction as I apprehend it. Let us, then, go back and see Him as these men saw Him in order that we may discover what it was in Him that created a spell that irresistibly drew men after Him in the days of His flesh. It seems to me that there were three things about this Man that created that attraction:

First, men felt that He lived, that, somehow, He had the secret of life.

Second, men felt that He knew, that when He spoke it was with authority.

Finally, men felt that He cared, that He was not merely interesting Himself in examining social conditions, that He was not merely occupied in the academic work of collecting specimens, but that He cared.

The men who gathered about Him in Galilee, in Judea, in Perea, in Nazareth, in Jerusalem, in the metropolis and in the village, in the great crowds assembled at the feasts, in the little groups that met Him by the wayside—these men who looked at Him, listened to Him, became familiar with Him, felt, first, that He was a Man Who lived, and a Man Who knew, and a Man Who cared. In these things I find the secret of the attractiveness of the Lord.

First, they felt that He was a Man Who lived. I am well aware how very commonplace a statement that sounds. It may at once be said that we are all living. That, however, is exactly the point. Were not all these men living who saw Him? It is evident that the impression He produced on them was that they were not living, and that He was living. He had a secret that they lacked. In reading the New Testament, all of us have observed how perpetually that great word "life" was on the lips of our Lord, and I think that nothing is more interesting than the fact that over and over again His use of the word, His reference to it, was in answer to men who asked Him questions. Men constantly broke in on His teaching to ask Him a question about life. The lawyer said to Him: "Master, what shall I do to inherit eternal life?" The young ruler came to Him and said: "Good Master, what shall I do to inherit eternal life?" Peter, in one of those great outbursts of understanding, said to Him: "Lord, to whom shall we go? Thou hast the words [sayings] of eternal life." All these recognized, somehow, that Jesus had the secret of life.

Now, our trouble in reading these stories often is that we read them evangelically. We get our theological values presently. We shall be driven there. But if we take up the story, and see a young man coming to Jesus and saying to Him, "Good Master, what shall I do to inherit eternal life?" and think of this young man as going to a mission service and asking what he must do to be saved, in the full evangelical sense of the inquiry, we are wrong. This young man did not understand things as you and I understand them. It was the question of one man, who saw another Man live. In effect, he said, Tell me how you live. You have the secret I lack. What lack I yet?

Now, the arresting fact was that Jesus lived, apparently without possessing the keys of life. The very keys that men thought were necessary to admit to life He lacked. He had none of them. He was without wealth, He was without possessions. He was without worldly advantage. Nevertheless, the supreme impression He made on men who went after Him and listened to Him was that He was living a full-orbed life, a life that was rich and glorious and satisfying. The rich young ruler had all the supposed keys of life hanging on his girdle. He had wealth. He was a ruler among his people. He had social and worldly advantages. Yet he came to Jesus and said, in effect, You have the key of life and I have not; you are alive, and I am not. Tell me the secret of the life you are living. Through those fields and along those roads of Palestine there walked a Man alive, and as they watched Him men said, What is the secret of it? Here is a Man Who seems to be excluded from everything, Who is limited in every way, but Who is living. I am going to make all this superlative by saying that I think sometimes we are wrong when we speak of the poverty of our Lord as though it was something that we should be sorry for, or that He was sorry about. I do not think Jesus needs pity for being poor in the measure in which He was poor. Do we not sometimes recite great words of the Bible in such a tone as to make them utterly wrong?

"Foxes have holes and the birds of the air have nests; but the Son of Man hath not where to lay His head."

I have quoted these words over and over again with a touch of sorrow in my voice. I do not think now that there was any touch of sorrow in Jesus' voice when He uttered them. It was the declaration of One Who was independent even of those very things which men count to be necessary if they are to live. It is possible to live, without nine hundred and ninety-nine out of the thousand things which we have counted necessary.

Men looked at Jesus, and saw that He was excluded from no realm of life. He lived and talked, always with reverence, but always as One Who was admitted into the very inner secret of the Presence of Deity, and as One Who knew no veil between Himself and God. He spoke of angels as though He knew much about them, and said things about them that we do not understand today, which yet seemed to be commonplaces in His own life and experience. Then remember that in all the illustrations that I have given we find that He answered questions by giving the secret of life. Said the lawyer, How am I going to live? Said Jesus in answer, If you want My secret of life, this is it: Love God and love your neighbor. That is life.

Said the young ruler, What shall I do to live? Jesus said, Follow Me. Put your life under control. Human life is altogether too big to manage itself. It must find its master.

Said Peter, speaking for the disciples, To whom shall we go? Thou hast the sayings of eternal life. Later on, in the hearing of the disciples, Jesus gave the ultimate key to life: This is life, age-abiding, to know God. Thus He solved the problem. We, however, are supremely interested for the moment in the experience itself and the effect it produced on men. Jesus lived, and men, rich and poor, went after Him, and said, Tell us the secret. You are alive and we are not. How do You live?

That sense abides until this moment. If we could rescue this living Personality from behind the veils of ecclesiastical organization, from the discussions of the schoolmen, from the hardening of theological formulas, so that men could see Him as He is, they would still say: What does this mean? This is life! What is its secret?

Again, men felt that Jesus knew. There are some things in these narratives that really are amusing in a holy sense. One day the Pharisees sent officers to arrest Jesus when He was teaching in Jerusalem. The officers were not prejudiced, but were under orders, and they went. By and by, they came back without their man. The rulers said, Why have you not brought Him? The officers replied, Never man spake like this Man! They forgot all about arresting Him. He had arrested them, and that simply by His teaching, by what He was saying.

Matthew tells us how after the great Manifesto to the multitudes, the people were astonished because Jesus taught them as One having authority. That is not a remarkable statement. So far, the marvel of the statement has not emerged. Jesus taught them as One having authority! Certainly, that is natural. But let us hear the statement to the end. And not as their scribes. That is what makes the story remarkable. The scribes were the men who had authority, but the multitude said, This is not like the teaching to which we have been listening all our lives. We have had authority, official authority, dogmatic authority, but this is different. This is Authority itself! What then was the nature of Jesus' authority? It was not a sense of authority created by anything in the personal appearance of our Lord. Artists never can express all the truth about Him, so they give Him a halo. But He had no halo visible to the men who were impressed with His authority. He had not the insignia of the scribes. There were no signs on Him that spoke of official position. Wherein, then, lay His authority? It was the authority of what He said. It was the authority of the truth. The arresting fact to men was that there was no gainsaying Him, no contradicting Him. Prejudice was ever angry with Him, will was constantly rebellious against Him, but conscience was ever agreeing with Him. I need not speak in the past tense. I can employ the present tense. Take any words that are recorded in either of these Gospels as having fallen from the lips of Jesus, and listen to them carefully. I declare that, finally, you cannot gainsay them. Though prejudice may be against Him, though will may be rebellious, the human soul will always say of His teaching: Yes, that is so; it is authoritative truth. The only criticism of the teaching of Jesus that is at all reasonable, the only thing that can be said, that ever has been said truthfully against the teaching of Jesus, is that His ideals are not practicable. That has been said.

I make no apology for repeating an illustration I have used more than once in this pulpit. A generation ago, full thirty years ago, a man said to me, "You know, my quarrel with your Christ is that He is unreasonable." I said, "Tell me what you mean by that." And he gave me this illustration, and it is a perfectly fair one. He said, "Confucius said to his followers, Be just to your enemies. I can do that; it is reasonable. Your Master said, Love your enemies. I cannot do that. That is unreasonable." Don't you agree with that man? Where are you living today? Are you finding it easy to love your enemies today? As I said, I was thirty years younger then. I did not quite know how to answer him. I felt the force of what he said. I shall always believe that I was led and helped. What I did say to him was this: "I see your point, but suppose that men could learn to love their enemies!" His answer came sharp as the crack of a pistol. "Why, then," he said, "there would be no enemies in the world." Exactly. Therein is the greatness of the ideal. Not practicable, we may say of the teaching of Jesus, but we must admit immediately afterward that if it could be done, then we would have solved all our problems, social, political, and economic. Herein was, and is, the marvel of Jesus. He taught, and men were very angry because what He said ran counter to their desires, their prejudices; but they knew He was right. He spake as One having authority. Again, to quote the words of Peter with another emphasis, "Thou hast the words [sayings] of eternal life." Jesus had not only the life itself, but the interpretation of it. He interpreted this authority also. He was perfectly willing to tell men exactly how He knew. He said,

My teaching is not Mine but His that sent Me. He claimed to be in direct communication with the eternal Wisdom. He gave men only the Word of God. I think on this point there is almost startling light in something John tells us. On one occasion our Lord said: "If any man hear My sayings, and keep them not, I judge him not; for I came not to judge the world, but to save the world. He that rejecteth Me, and receiveth not My sayings, hath one that judgeth him; the word that I spake, the same shall judge him in the last day." This is most arresting, differentiating as it does between personal authority and the eternal authority of truth. Christ said distinctly, a man is to be judged at last by His word. Men knew it, and they went after Him. Here was a Man Who never said: It is reasonable to suppose; a Man Who never said: In all probability it is so; a Man Who talked quietly and simply, and as we ponder the matchless words, so full of simplicity that all the children can understand them up to a point, and we know we are hearing the last wisdom of eternity, and we have no appeal. We are often angry! We will not obey! We will crucify Him, silence His voice! But as we do it, we still know that what He said was the truth.

And last, men not only felt that Jesus lived, and that He knew; they felt also that He cared, and that He cared about them. He proved His interest by all the facts of His life. Some of the little sentences of the Gospel narratives reveal simply the exquisite beauty of the fact. Listen to this: "He could not be hidden." Why not? I put over against it another Scriptural quotation which contradicts it: "He hid Himself." Put them together. "He could not be hidden. . . . He hid Himself." They do not contradict. The paradox is the revelation of truth. Why could He not be hidden? Because out there in the street was a woman in trouble about her child, trying to get help. Ah! He could not be hidden then. The agony of that woman drew Him forth from hiding. He cannot be hidden there. He hid Himself. When? When unbelief and the pride of ignorance were refusing His message and were about to do Him harm, then He hid Himself. But men irresistibly drew Him. If I have said that He attracted men, let me now add that was the deep reason that men attracted Him. He could not let them alone. That ultimately is the meaning of the Incarnation. God could not abandon the sinning world. It brought Him out of His heaven. All that found expression in the manner of life of this Man. Men knew that He cared. The appeal that He made to humanity was not due to His curiosity. You may be curious about men, but that will not attract men to you. His interest, I say, was not academic. He was not studying specimens. His interest in men was not artistic merely. What is art? It is the expression of a truth. But He shared human experience rather than sought to express it. He lived in man. His own consciousness was a self-emptied one, and therefore through it He received the consciousness of others. He felt all the agony of the widow of Nain whose boy, her only son, lay dead on the bier. He felt all the withering paralyzing pain of two women who had buried their brother, and He wept. There is a supreme illustration of this very sympathy. I confess that it is to me a most amazing story and I can understand the expositor and the commentator trying to account in some other way for those tears of Jesus. Suppose I came to see you in the presence of your dead and found you in agony and in tears, and suppose, just for the sake of argument, that I knew that in half an hour I could give you your dead back again, I do not think I could weep with you. But He did. My inability is the result of the comparative coarseness of the texture of my personality. The very fineness of His soul was such that although He knew that within half an hour the light would shine on the tears and make the rainbow, yet He wept in keen sympathy with the sorrow of their heart. Men knew that He cared.

So I see Jesus, living, knowing the deep secrets of life, and caring. Now, this is not the Gospel. I am not preaching the Gospel. But this creates the conviction that a Gospel is needed, and that we shall see more clearly in our next consideration. For the present it suffices me to say, and here I end for now, that the man who is not conscious of personal failure either has not seen Jesus, or has deliberately decided to be content with less than the best. To see Jesus is to say before He says it, If this is life, then I must be done with all my ideals, I must deny myself; everything is changed. The spell of Christ brings the soul to the shuddering, staggering sense of its own failure, of its own poverty.

CHAPTER XXV

THE SHOCK WHICH THE SPELL OF JESUS BRINGS TO THE SOUL

And He called unto Him the multitude with His disciples, and said unto them, If any man would come after Me, let him deny himself, and take up his cross, and follow Me.

MARK 8:34.

OUR TEXT FOR THE MORNING CONSISTS OF THE FOUR WORDS AT the heart of that saying of Jesus, "Let him deny himself." That presupposes our previous meditation on the assumption of the first words of the text: "If any man will, or would, or should desire, to come after Me," namely, our meditation on the attractiveness of our Lord. That attractiveness is as powerful today as ever. Whenever men really come face to face with Him they feel the spell of His Person and character. In these central words, then, we have our Lord's statement of the condition on which those desiring to follow Him may do so: "If any man would come after Me, let him deny himself."

I want to remark, in the first place, that these words of our Lord express the sense of the soul concerning itself in His presence. When our Lord said these words in His time on earth, when He still says them, He but voices what the soul itself feels.

The sense of the glory and beauty of His character is inevitably also that of the meanness and deformity of self. Really to get near to this Christ of the Gospels is to be conscious of the most staggering, shattering shock that has ever been experienced. Of course, we may hear a great deal about Jesus and never have this sense of shock. It may be that we are made familiar with facts concerning Him from our childhood, and yet it may be a long while before we arrive at this sense. I am referring to the sense of the soul when it really meets Him, apprehends anything of the glory of His Person. Really to know this Man Jesus, to see Him as One Who has the secret of life, and is living a full life while lacking all the things on which men ordinarily depend, to listen to Him, and to be assured that He is speaking the word of truth by the appeal that what He says makes to our deepest souls, to come face to face with Him, and to pass under that matchless influence of the keen, quick sympathy of His heart, is to come to the sense of His perfection; and then invariably that sense reacts on the soul as a revelation of its own imperfection and failure. I see Him, I listen to Him, I follow Him, I become more and more acquainted with Him, and as I do so I am more and more convinced of the beauty and the glory of His character and of his Person, and I start after Him, desiring to be like Him. In that very hour of starting I am halted, because I become conscious of my own unlikeness and of my inability to be what He is. He lived, and I have not the secret of living. He knew, and I lack certainty about anything. He cared, and so gathered to Himself all human souls in the comradeship of a great fellowship, and I find myself excluded from it, and the poverty of my isolation surges on my soul. I behold Him, and I say already to myself, Yea, verily, this is glory, this is beauty, this is life, this is perfection! But I am not that, I cannot be that. Therefore am I filled with fear, and the fear is generated by the apprehension of the glory and the beauty of Christ.

Now, this is exactly what Christ says. He recognizes that fear. If you desire to come after Me, you must recognize that you are not what I am. Would you be, you must deny self. All the ideals of the past, the purposes of the past, and the passions of the past are to be denied. You are to be at the end of everything if you are coming after Me.

Let us observe very carefully that these words reveal in a flash the difference between the Lord and all others. He was supremely the One Who denied Himself. That is the whole story of His human life. Therefore He says to men, If you will come after Me, you must do what I have done. You must deny yourself. That is the story of Jesus. He was the most self-emptied soul that ever trod the earth, and therefore the most self-possessed. Of other men, the story of life is that of being self-centered, and therefore self-destroyed.

This very spell which Jesus casts on men, then, is a revelation of the malady which affects humanity, and it is a proclamation of the only way by which that malady may be cured. The spell of Jesus is the dawning sense of sickness in the soul, and the word of Jesus is the indication of the way of cure. Let us think, then, along these two lines, the human malady, and its cure, dealing first with the malady.

What is the matter with humanity? The hour in which we live makes the question very vital, very pertinent. The hour is characterized by a vastness altogether too great to be apprehended. I need not stay to argue that. Is not that the difficulty in all our thinking? Is not that the difficulty that statesmen have to confront today? I shall carry you with me, however, when I say that we may sum up the story in a very blunt and brutal word by declaring that humanity today is tossed with a raging and destructive fever. What is the nature of the malady? How are we to diagnose this sickness which, at the moment, has its expression in blood, brutality, and death?

The individual is always microcosmic. If we can understand the human soul, we understand humanity. Our Lord here addresses Himself to the human soul, to one man. If any man, seeing the glory and the beauty of the ideal, feels moving within him some desire to realize it, let that man deny himself. The malady in its vastness is thus diagnosed in a human soul. Yet for a few moments let us take the general outlook as we press this question.

I begin with some negative considerations. Man's intellect is not at fault. Man's emotional nature is not at fault. Man's will power is not at fault. Never in the history of the world were these things more manifestly strong and mighty than they are today. Never have we seen the manifestation of the strength of intellect, the strength of emotion, and the strength of will, as we are seeing it today. These are all essential faculties of human personality, and the essential faculties of humanity as God created it; and today they are all mighty in their operations, and yet we are in this terrible fever.

I say that man's intellect is not at fault. His scientific achievements prove this. Never was the intellect of man so successful along every line as it is today. Man's capacity for visualizing a better order was never keener than it is today. Is there anything more interesting, more arresting, to the thoughtful soul today than this fact, that wherever we turn, whatever newspaper, or magazine, or new book we read, we find that men are seeing through the darkness to a new order? As to what it is to be, there are different opinions; as to how it is to be brought about, there are varied and conflicting opinions; but man is everywhere talking about the new order.

Man is visualizing for himself some order of life from which this dire and disastrous fever shall be shut out. The intellect of man was never more active, never stronger.

Man's emotional nature is not at fault. Man still loves unto death; and, thank God, man still hates with the fierceness of the wrath of God everything that is unholy and unlovely. The emotional nature of humanity today is being stirred and is manifesting its power as it never has before.

Man's will power is not at fault, and that is being proved in both camps of this great strife. Whether will power, and the will to power, are the same things I am not now discussing; or, at least, I may say, in passing, they are by no means the same thing. I am not now speaking of the will to power, but of the power of will. The war did not end before Christmas, 1914, and it is not over yet! The will power of our enemy is still strong, and our own is mighty. Moreover, that will power will not be broken by material defeat, however unpalatable a truth that may be. That is one of the truths we have to face. If we look back through the history of mankind we shall find that it is the defeated nation that is often victorious in the long issue. One of the greatest perils that threatens a nation is the peril that is born in the hours of its victory. Unless the victory be consecrated to useful and holy purpose, the very victory generates the evil thing that undermines the life of a nation.

If, then, these things are still stronger, what is the matter with humanity? The malady lies deeper. The malady is something the effect of which, whatever the something may be, is to make all the God-given and God-like powers of intellect, emotion, and will, forces of destruction instead of forces of construction. Now, there is some reason for it. What is the matter with humanity?

Now I return to the text and I say that here we have a

perfect diagnosis of the disease. Let us get back to one soul, and not to the soul of the one man to whom Christ spoke, but to the soul of Christ Himself. The very charm of His personality, the very spell He has cast on me, demands that I should understand the profound secret of that life that lived, that knew, that cared, the life that lures me by its beauty. What is the secret of life? When I have discovered that, I have discovered the nature of man's malady.

In the light of that revelation we discover that no man can control himself, and therefore humanity cannot govern itself. All its blunders, all its raging fevers, all the unutterable and unfathomable agony of this hour, all these things are the result of humanity's attempts to govern itself, to manage its own affairs—or bluntly, yet truthfully, let us say it, the result of humanity's attempts to do without God. Look again at the glory of the Man we have been considering. The secret of His greatness was that He denied Himself. I quote from the great passage in Philippians, beginning resolutely right in the middle of it rather than at its commencement: "Being found in fashion as a Man, He humbled Himself, becoming obedient." What humanity needs is to understand that the word "obedient" is a very different word from what humanity really has imagined it to be. We had better return to the individual soul again. The human soul has to understand that the word "obedient" is the greatest and most beautiful word that can be used to describe its attitude. *Obedient!* How we fight against it! How we struggle against it! Account for it as you will, and I am now at the business of accounting for it, from childhood upward it is the one word we have hated most. *Obedient!* Yet this is the one great word that reveals the secret of the perfection of Jesus. Being found in fashion as a Man, He humbled Himself, and became obedient. I go a little further back in the same passage and I read concerning Him that He was in the form of God, but did not consider that equality with God was a prize to be snatched at and held for Himself, and that therefore He emptied Himself and took the form of a servant. He was the servant of God. All the story of His life as Man is the story of obedience to the one central perfect will, the will of God. Multiply that Man by the new race of newborn souls—I am now speaking in the realm of the ideal—and what have you? A race of souls obedient, mastered, a race of souls who have learned this as the supreme and fundamental thing, that no man can control himself, that he is too big to manage himself, that he was not constructed to run by his own design, his own willing and his own planning, that he must be under the control of the God from Whom he came. Humanity cannot govern itself. The attempt at self-control is the root of the malady. Intellect is there, but it lacks the true light. Emotion is there, but it has not the true inspiration. Will is there, but it is not mastered by the true principle.

In a recent article in *The Nation*, headed "Minerva at the Cross Roads," a very remarkable article in many ways, the writer describes the present condition of humanity, and speaks of the passion for power prevalent throughout the whole world. Among other things, he writes:

> Power over man, over nature, over land and sea and sky; power we seek everywhere in size and speed and treasure, power over everything but ourselves.

I have nothing to do now with the context of the article. That was the writer's diagnosis of the situation. I have quoted the passage for one reason: says this writer, "power over everything but ourselves." That is true, but it is not our fault, it is our nature. That is the exact point that we are trying to see. Humanity cannot have power over itself. Humanity can master the land and the sea; humanity can have power in size and speed and treasure, but it cannot have power over itself. Humanity is not capable of governing itself. This is the lesson that humanity has yet to learn. Whether it will learn it from this war or not, I will not predict. Whether it will even learn it until He shall come, the flaming of Whose advent feet will usher in the final revelation of God's will for men, I will not now pause to argue. When Jesus said that day at Cæsarea Philippi to that multitude, mainly of Jewish men, "If any man would come after Me, let him deny himself," He was uttering no mere superficial words that affected only the passing hour. The final character of them has not yet dawned on humanity, for humanity has been running on its way, trying to manage for itself by its cleverness, by its policies, by its armaments, which it cannot do. The ultimate issue of such attempts is this appalling and wicked waste of human life and the welter of the present war. Humanity cannot manage itself. My God! Are we going to learn it or not? That is where repentance must begin if ever hope is to be possible. The doctrine of self-control is a doctrine of unfathomable nonsense as well as hopelessness.

I pass back once more from the larger outlook to the individual soul. If I tell this young man that he must control himself, I am talking nonsense. He cannot control himself. He is too big, he is too vast for his own apprehension. He may not believe it, that young man! Some of us who are a little older are finding out that the things we thought were so easy are not easy. Where we thought we had controlled ourselves we were mastered by wrong forces which would have destroyed us but for the grace of God. How can anybody control himself in any way? I am sure you are ready to have patience with me if I take a personal illustration. In the days of my youth my favorite athletic sport was wrestling. Now, how can a man wrestle with himself? The whole art of wrestling is to get your opponent down and put him on his back. Try that with yourself. You cannot put yourself on your back and hold yourself there. When you are there, who is on top? That is the whole business. A man says, I will manage myself. He may sign pledges, and give up, or he may decide to give up without any pledge. He is just cutting off here, and lopping off there, and he thinks he is self-controlled. The fact is that he is more self-confident in all the foolish pride of his nature than before he began to lop off his branches.

Humanity thinks it is able to govern itself. Government of the people by the people for the people is a ghastly failure unless you preface your idea with some other word, or follow it up with some other word. Government of the people by the people for the people under God. Yes, verily. But if we attempt it without God, the last and worst tyranny of this world will not be the tyranny of monarchy or the tyranny of wealth—it will be the tyranny of democracy. A democracy is hell unless it be also a theocracy.

Thus we see the human malady. We have been trying to do without God, and without control, and to manage; and there is no ideal we held, high or low, but that at this moment lies in ruins on the plains of Flanders! High or low, the ideal is broken, and the will to power is defeated. The ideal that we can deal with humanity by treaties and conferences at The Hague is broken into a thousand fragments.

Jesus Christ still stands, His head lifted above the smoke of battle, His eyes still lit with the vision of the eternal truth, and He is saying to men: If you will come after Me, deny yourselves, confess your folly, repent, not first of your drunkenness, and your gambling, and your lust: these are symptoms of that deeper wickedness, the underlying imagination of the nation that God is out of date, and that we can do without Him.

And there also is revealed the cure. To see the malady is to know the cure. The cure is radical and revolutionary. I have chosen my words with care.

It is radical. By that I mean it goes to the very root of the business. Let man deny himself. The word "deny," as it is usually translated, means, as many of you at once recognize, to disown, to abdicate, to put self off the throne entirely. To deny self is a great deal more than to practice self-denial in our modern sense of the phrase. We are all being urged to practice self-denial now, and a few people are doing it! But that is not the call of the text. The word of Jesus is a profounder word than that. Let man deny himself. Jesus calls men to central readjustment. To deny self is to make room for God. And that is what our governments are afraid to do. It is also to believe in God. It is, therefore, to hand the keys over to God. It is to confess folly, and to confess weakness, and to wait for God.

The call is also revolutionary; it demands the readjustment of every other relationship. Through the denial of self in the individual home is revolutionized. Given a home in which those who constitute it know this principle of denying self, and you have music and harmony and love, and all those subtle but marvelous forces that make Home.

Self being denied, the Christian Church is revolutionized. When we in the Christian Church learn the secret, and submit to it; when self is denied, and the living Lord is enthroned actually, then we shall have done with our conflicts. Not with our differences of opinion. But then we shall be able to sit down, and talk with the men who do not agree with us, and with whom we do not agree, and so we shall feel our way nearer to the truth. It is bitterness of heart that makes schism, and paralyzes power. The Church of Christ itself never has fully realized the importance of the call of Christ to deny self.

It is so also in the national life. It is so in all international relationships. In proportion as man is at the end of himself, and humanity recognizes the necessity for the wisdom from on high, and the strength of God, in that proportion the malady will be healed.

Now let me end by stating that in nothing I have said so far have I been preaching the Gospel. But the Gospel is involved. I have already quoted some words concerning Jesus, and I stopped short. Now is the time to complete the quotation. "He became obedient unto death, even the death of the Cross." There was no need for the Cross in the life of One Who was always self-emptied. It was an improper thing for Him, unless there was some larger purpose in it than that of His own Personality. He was always self-emptied. Why, then, the Cross? The Cross created the way of denying self for man who had been self-centered, self-governed, and self-ruined. The Cross is the place where we receive life as a gift of grace. At the Cross of Christ we confess that we cannot lift ourselves or save ourselves out of the depths into which we have fallen, and we take all that is provided in the Cross as His free gift.

That is why the Cross is unpopular, and that is why the Cross is powerful. The real reason in human thinking for attempting to get rid of the Cross is that it denies man; it tells man that he cannot save himself, that he can never govern himself; but that having ruined himself, it can restore that which he has ruined. Christ comes with His Cross to human cleverness, and to human might, and declares the folly of that cleverness and the wickedness of that might. He says to men:

You can be made new, you can climb to the height of the ideal; but you must begin here, by the way of the Cross, taking your life from God as a gift of His infinite compassion and His infinite grace. That is where we begin to deny ourselves, not by taking up our own crosses. That comes after. No man takes up his cross in order to be saved. From that other Cross, which is outside us, in the mysterious transactions of which we had no part, there comes to us the gift of life and power and healing. It is a gift of love that keeps us forevermore sensible of our own weakness, a gift of power that keeps us forevermore sensible of our need of control from without, a gift, having received which, we shall walk every foot of the way with the sense of dependence on God.

CHAPTER XXVI

THE FAITH THAT CANCELS FEAR

*The eternal God is thy dwelling place,
And underneath are the everlasting arms.*
                    DEUTERONOMY 33:27.

THERE ARE TWO REALMS OF MYSTERY WHICH PERSISTENTLY assault the soul of man and produce in it a sense of fear. They are the unknown future, and the unfathomable present. It is a little difficult to know which of these is more provocative of fear. We look ahead; we think of tomorrow with fear. We look on to the inevitable days which will multiply into years. Sometimes, when we dare, we think of the persistent years which are running relentlessly on and completing the period of our earthly sojourn. For all of these we have our hopes, we have our ideals; but we see the perils, and the question that perpetually comes to us concerns what will happen tomorrow, in the coming years, and how life will end and how it will be rounded out; whether at eventide there shall be light, or whether the end shall be darkness.

Or at other times we stand still and think, attempting to grasp the present, the present of life itself, of suffering, of weakness, and of that which is always present with us, death. In all these things, life and suffering and weakness and death, there are profound and unfathomable mysteries. We have grappled with the surface of them all; but ever and anon we have become sensible of the deeps, the deeps of life itself at its highest and its best. We are related to these things, and cannot escape them. We lift our eyes and look to tomorrow and say, What will happen? We look within, and attempt to fathom the infinite mystery of the moment, and cry out, What shall we do?

Now, the answer to both these inquiries is found in the text. Of the first, the fear of the future, the text declares, "The eternal God is thy dwelling place." Of the present, with its sense of depth and profundity and unfathomable mystery, the declaration of the text is, "Underneath are the everlasting arms."

Let us, then, consider the declaration, and then take counsel with our fears in the light of our faith.

First, then, as to the declaration in itself. It occurs in the blessing which Moses pronounced ere he left the people whom he had led for forty years. This was almost the last thing he said:

> The eternal God is thy dwelling place,
> And underneath are the everlasting arms.

Here we have that great name of God by which He is introduced to us in the Biblical revelation, and which we so constantly find: this name Elohim, standing, as it does, for the unfathomable and immeasurable might of the Most High. That is the one thought suggested by the word. In this particular name of God there is really no revelation of His character, nothing that tells us of the motive that inspires Him in His activity, nothing that reveals to us the purpose of all His doings. It is the intensive Hebrew plural, Elohim, speaking of might, and consequently of majesty.

The arresting word in the text is not the name of God,

though, of course, that is necessary to our understanding of the declaration. The arresting word is the word which we have translated eternal. It does not mean, for instance, what the word "everlasting" means: "Underneath are the everlasting arms." That word "everlasting" is the greatest of all the words that attempt to express for us what is beyond our calendars and our almanacs—the timelessness of Deity. But the word here translated eternal has another meaning and another thought. Let me say quite simply that the word really has no reference to tomorrow. It has to do with yesterday. It is a word that bids us look on. It is a word that compels us to look back.

Now, immediately we may say, What comfort, then, can there be in that declaration in the presence of the fear of tomorrow? That is the very genius of the text. The word means literally the front, whether of place or of time. Absolutely, it means the forepart. Relatively, it means the east, the place of the sunrise, the place where the day began. The great thought concerning God which this particular word suggests is that He is the God of the beginning. We would do no violence to the Hebrew if we translated the passage, The God of old is thy dwelling place. That would lack the poetry of the word eternal, but it would come nearer to the thought of the singer. The God of old, the God of the beginning, is thy dwelling place. All that was involved in the beginning is persistent through processes to the consummation. The eternal God, the God of the morning, the God of the morning when the stars sang together over the initiation of a new mystery in the universe on which they had never looked before—that God of the beginning is thy dwelling place.

Out of that interpretation arise suggestions, which, in some senses, are paradoxical and startling. We are ever prone in our thinking of tomorrow to think of it as being in front of us. Tomorrow is not in front of us. Tomorrow is behind us. These are the later days. The earlier days are gone. Tomorrow is still later. In other words, the whole underlying suggestion is that of a great procession. Fasten your attention for a moment on some great procession you have seen pass along the highway. The beginning of the procession is always in front; the end of it is always behind. Yesterday is in front; tomorrow is behind. The whole history of humanity is a procession, and in the beginning is God, leading the procession. We are not moving away from those who went before us, as though we dropped them somewhere behind, and left them. We are moving after them, we are following them. The generation that shall be born will not be in advance of us. They will be behind us. God leads, and accompanies; He is the God of the morning, of the beginning, and He is thy dwelling place.

The description of God, the eternal God, thus interpreted may seem to suggest that every succeeding generation is further away from Him than the first. We may gather the comfort of the fact that He leads, that all those early movements were closely associated with His power and His wisdom and His love, as the Biblical revelation declares to us; but they are far away from us; and even though we follow in their train, we are far distant. But the text answers the inquiry at once. The God Who was at the beginning is our refuge, our dwelling place. God is no further removed from me than He was from the first man in the procession. God is no further distant from His creation after the long ages of its development and continuation than He was from the first propulsion from the night. The eternal God, the God of the beginning, the God of old time, the God of the morning is our dwelling place.

Then immediately the deduction is patent. The future which is behind us is not our care. We have nothing to do with that which follows. We have two things about which we must forever be concerned; those, namely, of yesterdays which are in front of us, and of the today in which we set our faces toward the things that have gone before. We follow God, in company with God. "The eternal God is thy dwelling place."

All that prepares for, and leads to, the second part of the declaration, "And underneath are the everlasting arms," which really is a large interpretation of the truth declared in the first. The great suggestion is made to us that God is the God of the beginning. It is declared that He is our dwelling place on all the march, and then we are told what that really means: "Underneath are the everlasting arms." That is the only place in the English Bible where we find that word underneath. The Hebrew word is found in other places. If we would understand it, we cannot be too absolute in our simplicity. The Hebrew word means the bottom. The root idea is that of depressing, and humbling, and beating down. Underneath is the uttermost limit of the depressing and the humbling and the beating down. How far down can your imagination or your experience carry you? Those depths, those profundities of life are suffering and weakness and death—how far do you know them? How deep have you been into life? How profound has been your experience of sorrow? How far have you sunk in some hour of weakness? How nigh have you come unto death? When you have reminded yourselves of that lowest level—and some soul may say, I was never deeper down than now—then listen, "Underneath," lower than that, "are the everlasting arms."

"Everlasting arms." Arms in the Bible always constitute

the figure of strength, and the idea is always qualified by the root meaning of sowing, fructifying, bearing. Motherhood lies in the figurative use of this word in the Bible, as well as Fatherhood. "Everlasting" is the word to which I have already made reference. The Hebrew word is full of poetic suggestion. It means the vanishing point, the ultimate reach of imagination and thought, and that which lies beyond the ultimate reach of imagination and thought, the concealed. There is no exact equivalent in the Bible really for all we mean when we say eternal or everlasting. We are attempting to grasp the infinite, and to express it in a word. The Bible never makes that attempt. The Hebrew and the Greek, by figures of speech, pile suggestion upon suggestion, and leave us with a sense of mystery, of the unfathomable and unreachable, and of the fact that we have not said the last thing. So it is with this great word "everlasting." The everlasting is the vanishing point, the concealed, that which lies behind and beyond the uttermost effort of imagination and thinking. The everlasting arms are arms that reach to, and exist in, that realm of darkling mystery that baffles the soul and assaults it with fear. All the mysteries of the deeps have beneath them the strength, the enclosing power, the infinite tenderness of God. "Underneath are the everlasting arms." Whatever the abyss, however much it seems to be a darkling void, dare it, dive into it deeply enough, and you will find you are falling on the arms of God. "Underneath are the everlasting arms."

Now, let us consult our fears in the presence of this declaration of our faith, fears for the future, and fears in the presence of present mysteries. What fears for the future we have today! Am I not rightly interpreting the mood of all our minds today, when I say that they are ever with us, fears about the future, fears for the world at large, fears for the

Church of God, fears for the very Christ of God, and fears for our own souls?

Fears about the future. When we look out on the world, one word tells the story just now, and that word is the word "chaos." The apparent hopelessness of it all is patent. We cheer our hearts ever and anon because we think we see some gleam of light in the sky, and it goes out again, and storms sweep up, and the darkness is deeper than ever. We are wondering about the future of the world. Is all the history of the running centuries and the world to end in cruelty, and the victory of wrong, and the destruction of ideals, and the plunge back of a race into a barbarism more devilish than has been known, or the world has ever seen, because wrong is better equipped?

Fears for the future of the Church are with us every day. The hopeless confusion of the Church at the present moment, her inability to realize herself, or the unity of her life, and the catholicity of that life; her inability to deal with the present situation, her poverty as an organized institution on the field of battle and among our soldiers—all these things oppress us, and we wonder what is going to happen presently when the war is over.

And right in the heart of all this, fight against it as we will, protest against it as we may in our higher and nobler moments, there is a haunting fear about our Christ. Not that we doubt Him, but we see Him refused, we see Him put to open shame; and the question comes to us again and again, What next?

Then, to narrow the circle, and we cannot omit this, how perpetually, as we look on to tomorrow, fear assaults us about our own souls; our failures yesterday and in the past, in spite of all our highest aspirations and our most ardent desires after the things that are of God, we know too well. There is the dark way we have come, with its failure, its paralysis, and its folly, and there is the growing sense of weakness, and we are afraid. The future is always fearful, and never more so than today.

In the presence of all these fears, I go back to this old song, and I read: "The God of the beginning is thy dwelling place," and in that declaration I find the one and only answer that silences our fears, our fears for the world. That answer is the God of the beginning. He created this world in its present state of order out of chaos. The earth was waste and void. God did not so create it at the beginning, in that remote beginning which is merely named, and of which we have no detail. Catastrophe had somehow overtaken it. It was waste and void, a turmoil; darkness was everywhere. Then the Spirit of God brooded over the face of the waters, and the voice of God spake, and there came up out of the darkness, light; and out of the chaos, order; and from the desert, roses. The God of the beginning is thy dwelling place. That cannot end worst which began best, though a wide compass first be fetched. The eternal God, the God of the morning, is the God of the advancing hours; the God Who led is accompanying all pilgrims on the march. If there be a repetition of chaos, a recrudescence of evil that threatens to devastate all order, then He is the God of a new beginning. The very last words of prophetic utterance which I find in my Bible are these: "Behold, I make all things new."

And what of the Church? God created it, and He created it a new order and pattern of life out of the old. Make that perfectly simple by thinking of the material with which He dealt at the beginning to constitute His Church. Think of those twelve men, men of like passions with ourselves in very deed; and yet those men constituted the beginning of His Church. Read with great care the book of the Acts of the Apostles, read with great care this little handful of letters that were sent out to the early churches, and mark, not merely the brightness of the glory shining, but the darkness of the shadows gathering. See how right away, at the beginning of the history of the Church, the heresies that are called new were powerfully operating, the schisms that we mourn today rending the body asunder. All the things that fill our hearts with foreboding were there then. Then remember that He Who created that Church has led that Church through all the centuries and the millenniums; and in spite of her failure, in spite of her recurring powerlessness, in spite of the fact that over and over again she has seemed to miss the moment of opportunity, she has been God's witness through the ages, and her testimony has never failed. Again, I go to the end of my New Testament, and I read a prophetic word concerning the Church, and it is this, He, the Son of God, the Christ of God, God manifest, He shall present her faultless "before the presence of His glory."

When I turn to that third realm of fear that I hardly like to mention, our fears concerning the Christ, it is well that we let Him speak to us again, for His own words are the only words we need to hear, the only words that can be powerful: "I am . . . the Living One; and I was dead, and behold, I am alive forevermore, and I have the keys of death and of Hades." Does He seem to be dead again? Does it seem as though this age, with all its vaunted progress, has nailed Him to the Cross anew? Does it seem as though we have wrapped Him in grave clothes, and placed Him in a tomb, and rolled a stone to the door? He is saying, I am alive, I am alive forevermore. . . . So surely as He came forth from the Syrian tomb in Joseph of Arimathea's garden He will emerge in new light and glory from the hour when we think Him dead.

And what about my soul? The God of the beginning is thy dwelling place, Oh, soul of mine. He Who began a good work in thee will complete it. He is the God of Jacob. He will perfect that which concerneth me. So my fears are silenced. Let us hear Paul once again, and perhaps with an entirely new sense: "Forgetting the things which are behind" (that is, the future), "and stretching forward to the things which are before" (that is, God and all He has done), "let us press toward the goal." I am to forget my yesterday, and remember tomorrow; but that yesterday is in front, and my back should be on tomorrow.

> E'en let the unknown morrow
> Bring with it what it may.

Turn your back on tomorrow, face the yesterday, look to the glory of the sunrise, and have no thought for that which is following on, no fear about tomorrow. That is in God's keeping. March, my soul, with strength today, thy face toward the beginning where the glory of God was manifested, knowing that the God of the beginning is with thee now on the pathway.

So we turn to the second realm of fear, fears of the deeps. I said at the beginning that I sometimes wonder which realm of mystery is more provocative of fear, the mystery of the future, or the mystery of the present. I am inclined to think that the present life itself is more terrible, when a man dare face it. And here for the moment I do not mean its weakness, suffering, and death. I mean life, the mystic elements of being, the surprises that come up from within, good and bad and mixed; the sudden breaking out as from within of high aspirations, and sense of ability that I had never dreamed I had, the sudden upspringing from some deep, low level of being of that which is slimy and devilish and hateful. Of these mysteries we become more and more conscious as the years run on. In the dawning, in youth, golden, glorious, beautiful, glad, we are not conscious of life at all. Youth touches only the surface of things.

In later years we are faced also with the mystery of sorrow and of suffering, its reason, and its value; our own suffering, and, principally, the suffering of others. The problem of suffering is created in the human mind in the presence of suffering other than that which is personal. It is not your own pain that causes you so much conflict as the pain of others.

Or, again, there are the depths of weakness, physical, spiritual, moral. So far as I may speak experimentally, I say that there is no experience more poignant in its agony than weakness. In the physical realm I can conceive of nothing more truly hopeless and helpless than the last extremity of utter weakness. As in the spiritual, so in the moral—these deep, deep things of weakness, how they fill the soul with fear!

Finally, there are the depths of death, death which we have observed, but never known. We have watched death, we have seen it, but we have not known it. Death is the admitted enemy. Christianity never calls it a friend. That is Sadducean paganism which affects to call death a friend. Christianity says the last enemy that shall be destroyed is death.

The answer to all these fears is found in the words: "Underneath are the everlasting arms." Oh for some master of music who shall set that one word underneath to melodies and harmonies that swell and grow, vibrant with tenderness, and mighty with thunder! Underneath life, this mystery of my own life that baffles me, and fills me with fear, and drives me hopelessly along the pathway—underneath it all are the everlasting arms. There is nothing in my life unknown to God. There is nothing in my life outside the compass of that embrace of eternal strength and tenderness. "Underneath are the everlasting arms."

Underneath all suffering. He encircles our sorrows with His own; but in His sorrows there is nothing of despair, there is nothing of weakness. They are greater than mine by virtue of the strength of God, but there is nothing in them of despair, and nothing of weakness. In the depth of suffering I presently find the arms of God underneath.

Weakness? Oh, yes, that is where some of us found the arms as we had never known them before. In the last reach of the descent we found the arms of God, we fall, and fall, all supports giving way; we sink, sink, sink, until, when no finger can be lifted and no glance of the eye tell the agony of our weakness, we suddenly find we are cradled in the arms of God. "Underneath are the everlasting arms."

By these signs and tokens, by these experiences of the soul, we know how it shall be in death. "Underneath are the everlasting arms." Death will be the gate of life. Through it we shall find God.

Here, then, is the answer to our fears. We still admit the mystery of tomorrow and of today; but we find our rest in God. He is the beginning. He is always the beginning. He began this day, this very day. This is the day that the Lord hath made. He will begin every tomorrow that shall come, until the cycle of the running days has completed the story of humanity, and it finds itself at the goal, at the destination. He is the God of the everlasting arms. It is impossible to sink beneath them, for they are always underneath. "The God of the morning is thy dwelling place, and underneath are the everlasting arms."

TOPICAL INDEX

(The number of the volume in which the sermon appears is listed immediately following each title. Please note that the titles are cross-indexed, and that many of them appear both in alphabetical order and in group listings as well.)

A

Ability for Disability, Vol. I, 284
Accomplished Mystery, The, Vol. X, 275
Advent, The Purpose of the:
    To Destroy the Works of the Devil, Vol. I, 298
    To Take Away Sins, Vol. I, 312
    To Reveal the Father, Vol. I, 326
    To Prepare for a Second Advent, Vol. I, 339
All-Sufficient Solution, The, Vol. III, 264
Amazing Love, Vol. I, 125
Ambitions, Vol. IX, 23
"As an Eagle . . . the Lord . . . Did Lead," Vol. X, 263
Ascension, The, Vol. IX, 281
Atonement, The, Vol. V, 48
Authority of Jesus, The, Vol. I, 71

B

Backsliding, Vol. I, 97
Beginning of Sin, The, Vol. V, 338
Be Strong—and Work, Vol. VIII, 310
Building of the City, The, Vol. V, 167
Burdens: False and True, Vol. VII, 233
Burning of Heart, The, Vol. I, 85
But! Vol. IV, 162

C

Can a Just God Forgive Sins? Vol. III, 157
Center and Circumference, Vol. II, 332
Children:
    The Training of Our Children, Vol. II, 111
    The Children's Playground in the City of God, Vol. I, 256
    Suffer the Children, Vol. III, 63
Christ and Sinners, Identified and Separate, Vol. IX, 232
Christ in You the Hope of Glory, Vol. I, 24
Christ Jesus, the Lord, Vol. IX, 217
Christian Citizenship:
    No Abiding City, Vol. V, 140
    Search for the City, The, Vol. V, 153
    Building of the City, The, Vol. V, 167
    Cooperation in the Building, Vol. V, 179
Christ's Call to Courage, Vol. VII, 9
Christ's Knowledge of Men, Vol. II, 319
Christ's Next of Kin, Vol. VII, 22
Christ's Vision of Jerusalem, Vol. II, 177
Church, The:
    The Church's Debt to the World, Vol. X, 226
    The Church, The Pillar and Ground of the Truth, Vol. VIII, 9
    Church Ideals:
        The Church Instituted, Vol. V, 191
        The Church Governed, Vol. V, 205
        The Church Disciplined, Vol. V, 219
        The Church at Work, Vol. V, 233
    The Fourfold Glory of the Church, Vol. X, 201
Cities of Men and the City of God, The, Vol. III, 116
Clean for Service, Vol. III, 341
Coming of the Word, The, Vol. VI, 9
Conditions of Coming to God, The, Vol. X, 139
Conditions of Renewal, The, Vol. VIII, 114
Conditions (Holiness), Vol. III, 303
Conscience, Vol. X, 37
Cooperation in the Building (of Christian Citizenship), Vol. V, 179

Crippling That Crowns, The, Vol. VII, 313
Cross, The:
  The Stumbling-Block of the Cross, Vol. II, 217
  Pardon by the Cross, Vol. VI, 61
  Purity by the Cross, Vol. VI, 75
  Peace by the Cross, Vol. VI, 86
  Power by the Cross, Vol. VI, 100
  Promise at the Cross, Vol. VI, 113

D

Daniel: A Man of Excellent Spirit, Vol. VIII, 221
Darkness of Golgotha, The, Vol. VII, 195
Death Abolished, Vol. V, 100
Definition (of Holiness), Vol. III, 276
Deity of Jesus, The, Vol. II, 243
Divine Selection, Vol. IV, 256
Divine Worker, The, Vol. VI, 48
Dwellers in Fire, Vol. I, 58

E

Easter Meditation, An, Vol. VIII, 100
Eternal Life, Vol. VI, 181
Ethic and Evangel of Jesus, The, Vol. X, 127
Ethical Perfection, Vol. VI, 314
Evangel of Grace, The, Vol. VII, 129
Exaltation and Humbling, Vol. V, 36
Exalted Christ, The, Vol. VI, 192

F

Faith:
  Faith's Outlook, Vol. X, 238
  The Faith That Cancels Fear, Vol. X, 322
  The Fight of Faith, Vol. II, 11
  The Optimism of Faith, Vol. IV, 294
  The Supreme Inspiration of Faith, Vol. IX, 203

The Touch of Faith, Vol. VIII, 233
The Tragedy of Life Without Faith, Vol. IX, 175
False Fire, Vol. VIII, 35
Famine for the Word of God, The, Vol. II, 206
Fellowship With God, Vol. V, 60
Filling of the Spirit, The, Vol. VIII, 181
Final Words, Vol. IV, 269
First-Born, The, Vol. VIII, 337
First Message of Jesus, The, Vol. VI, 154
Fixed Heart in the Day of Frightfulness, The, Vol. X, 250
Follow Me, Vol. VI, 220
Forgiveness, Vol. IX, 120
Fourfold Glory of the Church, The:
  How the Wall is Built, Vol. X, 103
  How Can a Man Walk With God? Vol. X, 49
  How God Has Made Possible What He Requires, Vol. X, 63
  Individuality in Religion, Vol. X, 91
Four Mistakes about Christ, Vol. IX, 51
Fruit-Bearing Friends of Jesus, The, Vol. VIII, 270
Fruit of the Spirit, The, Vol. I, 166

G

Gethsemane: The Garden of Spices, Vol. VII, 182
God:
  Can a Just God Forgive Sins? Vol. III, 157
  God's Fighting Forces, Vol. IV, 202
  God-Governed Life, Vol. VII, 340
  God in Christ, Vol. IV, 176
  God's Thought of the King, Vol. VI, 273
  Has Man Anything to do With God? Vol. III, 143
  How Can a Man Walk With God? Vol. X, 49
  How God Has Made Possible What He Requires, Vol. X, 63
  Jehovah of Hosts—The God of Jacob, Vol. IX, 161
  Nearness of God, The (two sermons), Vol. VII, 273, 286
  Rights of God, The, Vol. IV, 332
  What Does God Require of Man? Vol. III, 171

Godliness and Gain, Vol. VI, 234
Good Friday Meditation, A, Vol. VIII, 87
Grace, The All-Sufficient, Vol. II, 191
Grace and Law, Vol. VII, 327
Grace of Giving, The, Vol. IV, 35
Great Apostle, The, Vol. II, 164
Great Commandments, The, Vol. VII, 115
Great Confession, The, Vol. VII, 60

H

Halting, Vol. VII, 208
Hardened, Vol. II, 255
Harvests of the Word of God, The, Vol. IX, 269
Has Man Anything to do With God? Vol. III, 143
Healing of Life, The, Vol. IX, 106
High Purpose, Failing and Fulfilled, Vol. VII, 34
Hindrances (to Holiness), Vol. III, 328
Holy Spirit, The:
    Through Christ, in the Church, for the World, Vol. VI, 127
Hope, Vol. VIII, 75
Horizoned by Resurrection, Vol. IV, 123
How Can a Man Walk With God? Vol. X, 49
How God Has Made Possible What He Requires, Vol. X, 63
How the Wall is Built, Vol. X, 103
How to Succeed in Life, Vol. IV, 136
Holiness:
    Definition, Vol. III, 276
    A Present Possibility, Vol. III, 289
    Conditions, Vol. III, 303
    It's Fruit, Vol. III, 316
    Hindrances, Vol. III, 328
    Worship, Beauty, Holiness, Vol. II, 88
Humanity and Deity, Vol. II, 37

I

If Christ Did Not Rise—What Then? Vol. I, 139
Individuality in Religion, Vol. X, 91

"In the Beginning, God," Vol. V, 312
Is the Religious Life Necessary? Vol. III, 237
Is the Religious Life Possible? Vol. III, 223
Is the Religious Life Worthwhile? Vol. III, 250
It's Fruit (Holiness), Vol. III, 316

J

Jehovah of Hosts—The God of Jacob, Vol. IX, 161
Jesus Christ:
  Christ and Sinners Identified and Separate, Vol. IX, 232
  Christ in You the Hope of Glory, Vol. I, 24
  Christ Jesus the Lord, Vol. IX, 217
  Christ's Call to Courage, Vol. VII, 9
  Christ's Knowledge of Men, Vol. II, 319
  Christ's Next of Kin, Vol. VII, 22
  Christ's Vision of Jerusalem, Vol. II, 177
  Four Mistakes About Christ, Vol. IX, 51
  God in Christ, Vol. IV, 176
  His Workmanship, Vol. I, 242
  If Christ Did Not Rise—What Then? Vol. I, 139
  Jesus and Sinners, Vol. II, 151
  Keep Yourselves in the Love of God, Vol. IV, 243
  Manifestations of the Risen Lord, Vol. X, 175
  Men Looking For Their Lord, Vol. VII, 155
  The Ascension, Vol. IX, 281
  The Atonement, Vol. V, 48
  The Authority of Jesus, Vol. I, 71
  The Deity of Jesus, Vol. II, 243
  The Exalted Christ, Vol. VI, 192
  The First Message of Jesus, Vol. VI, 154
  The Fruit-Bearing Friends of Jesus, Vol. VIII, 270
  The Looking of Jesus, Vol. IX, 328
  The Madness of Jesus, Vol. X, 92
  The Mind of Christ, Vol. IV, 229
  The Name Jesus, Vol. II, 77
  The Secret of the Lord, Vol. IV, 216
  The Shock Which the Spell of Jesus Brings to the Soul, Vol. X, 310

The Son of Man Delivered Up, Vol. VII, 168
The Spell Which Jesus Casts on Men, Vol. X, 298
The Spirit of Christ: The Supreme Test, Vol. IV, 110
The Triumphal Entry, Vol. V, 87
The Unstraitened Christ, Vol. VII, 220
Jubilation in Desolation, Vol. VI, 140
Justification of the Sinner, The, Vol. IX, 189

K

Keep Yourselves in the Love of God, Vol. IV, 243
King, The, Vol. V, 247
King at the Door, The, Vol. VI, 23
Kingdom, The:
    The King, Vol. V, 247
    "Thy Kingdom," Vol. V, 260
    "Of Such is the Kingdom," Vol. V, 274
    The Oath of Allegiance, Vol. V, 287
    Traitors, Vol. V, 299
King's Thought of Man, The, Vol. VI, 287

L

Lack of the Spirit, The, Vol. I, 230
Led Out—Led In, Vol. X, 188
Life: in Flesh, or in Spirit, Vol. IV, 97
Life in the Light, Vol. IX, 293
Life Through Death, Vol. VI, 206
Light and Darkness, Vol. III, 128
Like Gods or Godlike, Vol. VII, 246
Limitations of Liberty, The, Vol. I, 13
Looking of Jesus, The, Vol. IX, 328
Love:
    Amazing Love, Vol. I, 125
    Love's Proof and Prize, Vol. I, 218

M

Madness of Jesus, The, Vol. X, 92
Manifestations of the Risen Lord, Vol. X, 175
Maran Atha, Vol. II, 23

Men Looking for Their Lord, Vol. VII, 155
Mind of Christ, The, Vol. IV, 229
My Friend, Vol. I, 111
My Lambs, My Sheep, Vol. IV, 149

N

Name Jesus, The, Vol. II, 77
Nearness of God, Discovered, The, Vol. VII, 286
Nearness of God, Unrecognized, The, Vol. VII, 273
Nehushtan, Vol. VIII, 194
No Abiding City, Vol. V, 140

O

Oath of Allegiance, The, Vol. V, 287
"Of Such is the Kingdom," Vol. V, 274
One Offering, The, Vol. VIII, 21
Optimism of Faith, The, Vol. IV, 294
Opportunity of Calamity, The, Vol. X, 151
Opposing Forces of the Religious Life, The (three sermons),
    Vol. III, 183, 196, 209
Our Altar, Vol. VIII, 246
Our Hope and Inheritance, Vol. X, 77

P

Pardon by the Cross, Vol. VI, 61
Passion-Baptism, The, Vol. V, 74
Pathway of the Passion, The, Vol. VII, 73
Pathway to Power, The, Vol. VII, 101
Peace, Vol. V, 9
Peace Among Men of God's Pleasure, Vol. VI, 340
Peace by the Cross, Vol. VI, 86
Perils of Procrastination, The, Vol. VII, 300
Peter, Simon:
    The Sifting of Peter, Vol. I, 190
    The Turning Again of Peter, Vol. I, 204
Playing the Fool, Vol. IX, 9

Possibility of Restoration, The, Vol. VIII, 207
Potter's Work on the Wheels, The, Vol. I, 46
Power by the Cross, Vol. VI, 100
Power for Service, Vol. II, 307
Power of the Gospel, The, Vol. VIII, 284
Powers of the Presence, The, Vol. VII, 87
Prayer or Fainting, Vol. III, 49
Preparation for Service, Vol. II, 295
Preparing the Highway, Vol. X, 163
Presence Needed, The, Vol. VIII, 257
Present Possibility, A, Vol. III, 289
Priestly Benediction, The, Vol. VIII, 128
Problem of How to Begin, The, Vol. IX, 78
Problems of the Religious Life, The:
    Has Man Anything to do With God? Vol. III, 143
    Can a Just God Forgive Sins? Vol. III, 157
    What Does God Require of Man? Vol. III, 171
    The Opposing Forces of the Religious Life—The World, Vol. III, 183
    The Opposing Forces of the Religious Life—The Flesh, Vol. III, 196
    The Opposing Forces of the Religious Life—The Devil, Vol. III, 209
    Is the Religious Life Possible? Vol. III, 223
    Is the Religious Life Necessary? Vol. III, 237
    Is the Religious Life Worthwhile? Vol. III, 250
    The All-Sufficient Solution, Vol. III, 264
Profound Question, A, Vol. I, 270
Progressive Revelation, Vol. II, 101
Promise at the Cross, Vol. VI, 113
Purity by the Cross, The, Vol. VI, 75
Purpose of Life, The, Vol. III, 102

R

Regeneration, Vol. X, 115
Responsibilities of Salvation, The, Vol. VIII, 141
Restlessness and its Remedy, Vol. IV, 48
Resurrection, The:

Horizoned by Resurrection, Vol. IV, 123
The Resurrection, Vol. IX, 134
The Teaching of the Resurrection, Vol. V, 113
The Value and Proof of the Resurrection, Vol. III, 89
Righteousness Which Exceeds, The, Vol. VI, 300
Righteousness or Revenue, Vol. IV, 59
Rights of God, The, Vol. IV, 332

S

Saints, Vol. II, 282
Salvation in Zion, Vol. IV, 320
Sanctification, Vol. VIII, 168
Sanctions of Ordinances, The, Vol. VI, 327
Sanctuary, Vol. II, 51
Search for the City, The, Vol. V, 153
Secret and Revealed Things, Vol. III, 22
Secret of the Lord, The, Vol. IV, 216
Secrets of Rest, The, Vol. VI, 248
Service:
   Preparation for Service, Vol. II, 295
   Power for Service, Vol. II, 307
   Clean for Service, Vol. III, 341
Set Time, The, Vol. IV, 188
Shining Faces, Vol. IV, 85
Shock Which the Spell of Jesus Brings to the Soul, The, Vol. X, 310
Short Beds and Narrow Coverings, Vol. X, 9
Sifting of Peter, The, Vol. I, 190
Sin:
   The Beginning of Sin, Vol. V, 338
   Can a Just God Forgive Sins? Vol. III, 157
   Sin, Vol. II, 64
   Sin, Sorrow, and Silence, Vol. VIII, 61
   Unpardonable Sin, Vol. IV, 71
   The Wages of Sin, The Gift of God, Vol. IX, 340
Son of Man Delivered Up, The, Vol. VII, 168
Songs in Prison, Vol. IX, 304
Sour Grapes, Vol. IX, 38
Spare Thyself, Vol. II, 125

Spell Which Jesus Casts on Men, The, Vol. X, 298
Spirit, The:
  The Filling of the Spirit, Vol. VIII, 181
  The Fruit of the Spirit, Vol. I, 166
  The Holy Spirit Through Christ, in the Church, for the World, Vol. VI, 127
  The Lack of the Spirit, Vol. I, 230
  The Spirit of Christ, The Supreme Test, Vol. IV, 110
  The Spirit of Life, Vol. I, 180
  The Spirit's Testimony to the World, Vol. I, 153
Spiritual Leprosy, Vol. VIII, 48
Strength of the Name, The, Vol. IV, 281
Stumbling-Block of the Cross, The, Vol. II, 217
Submission and Responsibility, Vol. III, 35
Suffer the Children, Vol. III, 63
Supreme Inspiration of Faith, The, Vol. IX, 203

T

Teaching of the Resurrection, The, Vol. V, 113
Terms of Discipleship, The, Vol. I, 33
Things New and Old, Vol. V, 23
Things Shaken, Things Not Shaken, Vol. IX, 246
Thomas:
  Was Thomas Mistaken? Vol. V, 126
Thou Shalt Remember, Vol. IV, 9
Thy Kingdom, Vol. V, 260
Tongues Like as of Fire, Vol. VII, 142
Touch of Faith, The, Vol. VIII, 233
Tragedy of Life Without Faith, The, Vol. IX, 175
Training of Our Children, The, Vol. II, 111
Traitors, Vol. V, 299
Tribulation, Kingdom, and Patience, Vol. IX, 257
Triumphal Entry, The, Vol. V, 87
True Focus, The, Vol. III, 9

U

Unchanging One, The, Vol. IX, 65
Understanding; or, Bit and Bridle, Vol. VI, 36

Unpardonable Sin, Vol. IV, 71
Unstraitened Christ, The, Vol. VII, 220
Untrodden Pathway, The, Vol. IV, 22

V

Value and Proof of the Resurrection, The, Vol. III, 89
Value of Vision, The, Vol. VII, 47
Verdict, The, Vol. IV, 307
Victorious Christian Life, The, Vol. III, 76
Vine, The, Vol. VII, 260

W

Wages of Sin, The Gift of God, The, Vol. IX, 340
Waiting for God, Vol. IX, 316
Was Thomas Mistaken? Vol. V, 126
Watching for Souls, Vol. VI, 260
Way of Righteousness, The, Vol. IX, 147
Way to the Altar, The, Vol. VIII, 324
We Have the Mind of Christ, Vol. X, 213
Well-Doing That Brings Harvest, The, Vol. X, 287
What Does God Require of Man? Vol. III, 171
What Is Man? Vol. V, 325
Winning Souls, Vol. VIII, 297
Wisdom: The False and the True, Vol. X, 23
Witnesses, Vol. II, 269
Word Became Flesh, The, Vol. II, 230
Work of Faith, The, VI, 167
Worship, Beauty, Holiness, Vol. II, 88

Y

Young Ruler, The, Vol. II, 138

TEXTUAL INDEX

Gen. 1:1, Vol. V, 312
Gen. 2:15-17, Vol. V, 325
Gen. 13:14, Vol. X, 238
Gen. 28:16 (2 Sermons), Vol. VII, 273, 286
Gen. 32:28, Vol. VII, 313

Ex. 20:20, Vol. VII, 327
Ex. 23:15, Vol. VIII, 257
Ex. 34:9, Vol. IV, 85

Lev. 10:1-3, Vol. VIII, 35
Lev. 14:1, 2, Vol. VIII, 48

Num. 6:22-27, Vol. VIII, 128

Deut. 1:6, Vol. VII, 340
Deut. 4:29, Vol. I, 97
Deut. 4:29, Vol. VIII, 207
Deut. 8:2, Vol. IV, 9
Deut. 29:29, Vol. III, 22
Deut. 32:11-12a, Vol. X, 263
Deut. 33:27, Vol. X, 322

Jos. 3:4, Vol. IV, 22

Judges 7:7, Vol. IV, 202

I Sam. 26:21, Vol. IX, 9

I Kings 18:21, Vol. VII, 208

II Kings 18:4, Vol. VIII, 194

Neh. 6:15, Vol. X, 103

Psalm 4:6, Vol. IV, 48
Psalm 25:14, Vol. IV, 216

Psalm 27:13, Vol. IX, 175
Psalm 32, Vol. VIII, 61
Psalm 32:9, Vol. VI, 36
Psalm 37:7, Vol. VI, 248
Psalm 46:7-11, Vol. IX, 161
Psalm 77:10, Vol. III, 9
Psalm 96:9, Vol. II, 88
Psalm 102:13, 14, Vol. IV, 188
Psalm 112:7, Vol. X, 250
Psalm 115:8, Vol. VII, 246

Prov. 3:6, Vol. IV, 136
Prov. 9:10, Vol. IX, 78
Prov. 11:30, Vol. VIII, 297
Prov. 18:10, Vol. IV, 281
Prov. 18:24, Vol. I, 111
Prov. 22:6, Vol. II, 111
Prov. 29:18, Vol. VII, 47

Song of Sol. 6:10, Vol. X, 201

Isaiah 6:1-9a, Vol. II, 295
Isaiah 9:6, Vol. V, 9
Isaiah 28:20, Vol. X, 9
Isaiah 33:14, Vol. I, 58
Isaiah 40:3, Vol. X, 163
Isaiah 43:7, Vol. III, 102
Isaiah 45:22, Vol. II, 332
Isaiah 46:13, Vol. IV, 320
Isaiah 52:11, Vol. III, 341
Isaiah 55:10-11, Vol. IX, 269
Isaiah 64:4, Vol. IX, 316

Jer. 17:12, Vol. II, 51
Jer. 18:3, Vol. I, 46
Jer. 31:20-30, Vol. IX, 38

Ez. 18:2-4, Vol. IX, 38

Ez. 18:4, Vol. X, 91

Dan. 6:3, Vol. VIII, 221
Hosea 12:3-4, Vol. IX, 106

Amos 3:3, Vol. X, 49
Amos 8:11-13, Vol. II, 206

Hab. 3:17, 18, Vol. VI, 140

Haggai 2:4, Vol. VIII, 310

Zech. 4:6, Vol. VI, 48
Zech. 8:5, Vol. I, 256

Mat. 1:21, Vol. II, 77
Mat. 3:15, Vol. IX, 147
Mat. 3:17, Vol. VI, 273
Mat. 4:4, Vol. VI, 287
Mat. 4:17, Vol. VI, 154
Mat. 5:20, Vol. VI, 300
Mat. 5:23, 24, Vol. VIII, 324
Mat. 5:48, Vol. VI, 314; Vol. X, 127
Mat. 6:10, Vol. V, 260
Mat. 6:24, Vol. IV, 59
Mat. 7:28, 29, Vol. I, 71
Mat. 8:9, Vol. III, 35
Mat. 9:2, Vol. VII, 9
Mat. 9:22, Vol. VII, 9
Mat. 10:34, Vol. V, 9
Mat. 11:27-30, Vol. VII, 233
Mat. 12:50, Vol. VII, 22
Mat. 13:51, 52, Vol. V, 23
Mat. 14:27, Vol. VII, 9
Mat. 14:28-33, Vol. VII, 34
Mat. 16:16, Vol. I, 190
Mat. 16:16-17, Vol. VII, 60
Mat. 16:21, Vol. VII, 73
Mat. 16:21, 22, Vol. I, 204
Mat. 16:21-24, Vol. II, 125
Mat. 16:24, Vol. I, 33

Mat. 18:3, Vol. V, 274
Mat. 18:15-20, Vol. V, 219
Mat. 18:18-20, Vol. VII, 87
Mat. 20:20-23, Vol. VII, 101
Mat. 22:35-40, Vol. VII, 115
Mat. 22:42, Vol. I, 270
Mat. 26:2, Vol. VII, 168
Mat. 26:36, Vol. VII, 182
Mat. 27:22, Vol. IV, 307
Mat. 27:45, Vol. VII, 195

Mark 3:4, Vol. VI, 327
Mark 3:5, Vol. I, 284
Mark 3:21, Vol. IX, 92
Mark 3:28, 29, Vol. IV, 71
Mark 6:3, Vol. IX, 51
Mark 6:14, Vol. IX, 51
Mark 6:49, Vol. IX, 51
Mark 8:34 (2 Sermons), Vol. X, 298, 310
Mark 10:14, Vol. III, 63
Mark 10:21, Vol. II, 138
Mark 11:11, Vol. IX, 328
Mark 14:71, Vol. I, 190

Luke 1:74, 75, Vol. III, 276
Luke 2:7, Vol. VIII, 337
Luke 2:14, Vol. VI, 340
Luke 8:45, Vol. VIII, 233
Luke 9:51, Vol. II, 177
Luke 9:51-62, Vol. IV, 162
Luke 12:35-36, Vol. VII, 155
Luke 12:49, 50, Vol. V, 74
Luke 13:6-9, Vol. IV, 332
Luke 14:15, Vol. V, 287
Luke 14:27, Vol. V, 287
Luke 14:33, Vol. I, 33
Luke 15:2, Vol. II, 151
Luke 18:1, Vol. III, 49
Luke 18:14, Vol. V, 36
Luke 19:10, Vol. X, 127
Luke 22:37, Vol. IX, 232

Luke 24:32, Vol. I, 85
Luke 24:50, Vol. X, 188

John 1:4, Vol. III, 128
John 1:11-13, Vol. VI, 9
John 1:13, Vol. X, 115
John 1:14, Vol. II, 230
John 1:43, Vol. VI, 220
John 2:23-25, Vol. II, 319
John 3:36, Vol. VI, 181
John 6:15, Vol. IX, 51
John 6:29, Vol. VI, 167
John 9:1-5, Vol. VIII, 154
John 10:11, Vol. VI, 206
John 12:12, 13, Vol. V, 87
John 12:36, Vol. IX, 293
John 14:9, Vol. I, 326
John 14:21, Vol. I, 218
John 15:5, Vol. VII, 260
John 15:15, 16, Vol. VIII, 270
John 16:7-11, Vol. I, 153
John 16:12, Vol. II, 101
John 16:33, Vol. VII, 9
John 19:30, Vol. X, 275
John 20:28, Vol. V, 126
John 21:1, Vol. X, 175
John 21:15, 16, 17, Vol. IV, 149
John 21:18, 19, Vol. I, 204

Acts 1:1, Vol. VII, 220
Acts 1:8, Vol. II, 307
Acts 2:3, Vol. VII, 142
Acts 2:4, Vol. VIII, 181
Acts 2:24, Vol. IX, 134
Acts 2:32, Vol. V, 113
Acts 2:33, Vol. VI, 127
Acts 5:32, Vol. II, 269
Acts 10:34, 35, Vol. IV, 256
Acts 16:25-26, Vol. IX, 304
Acts 17:29, Vol. II, 37
Acts 19:2, Vol. I, 230
Acts 20:21, Vol. VIII, 114

Acts 20:24, Vol. VII, 129
Acts 20:28, Vol. V, 191
Acts 23:11, Vol. VII, 9

Rom. 1:4, Vol. IV, 123
Rom. 1:14, Vol. X, 226
Rom. 1:16, 17, Vol. VIII, 284
Rom. 3:26, Vol. IX, 189
Rom. 5:8, Vol. I, 125
Rom. 6:23, Vol. IX, 340
Rom. 8:2, Vol. I, 180
Rom. 8:9, Vol. IV, 97, 110
Rom. 8:24, Vol. VIII, 75
Rom. 8:29, Vol. VIII, 337
Rom. 8:32, Vol. VI, 113

I Cor. 1:18, Vol. VI, 100
I Cor. 1:30, Vol. X, 23
I Cor. 2:9, Vol. IX, 316
I Cor. 2:16, Vol. X, 213
I Cor. 5, Vol. V, 220
I Cor. 6:12, Vol. I, 13
I Cor. 10:23, Vol. I, 13
I Cor. 12:31, Vol. IX, 23
I Cor. 14:1, Vol. IX, 23
I Cor. 15:14, Vol. III, 89
I Cor. 15:14, 17, 19, Vol. I, 139
I Cor. 16:22, Vol. II, 23

II Cor. 4:5, Vol. IX, 217
II Cor. 5:17, 18, Vol. III, 316
II Cor. 5:19, Vol. IV, 176
II Cor. 7:1, Vol. III, 303
II Cor. 8:7, Vol. IV, 35
II Cor. 11:5, Vol. II, 164
II Cor. 12:9, Vol. II, 191

Gal. 5:7, Vol. III, 328
Gal. 5:11, Vol. II, 217
Gal. 5:22-23, Vol. I, 166
Gal. 6:9, Vol. X, 287

Eph. 1:1, Vol. II, 282
Eph. 1:7, Vol. VI, 61
Eph. 1:20-23, Vol. VI, 192
Eph. 2:10, Vol. I, 242
Eph. 4:9-10, Vol. IX, 281
Eph. 5:3, Vol. II, 282
Eph. 5:16, Vol. X, 151
Eph. 5:17, Vol. VI, 36
Eph. 6:13, Vol. III, 76

Phil. 2:5, Vol. IV, 229
Phil. 2:9-11, Vol. VI, 192
Phil. 2:15, Vol. III, 289
Phil. 3:10, Vol. VIII, 87

Col. 1:14, Vol. IX, 120
Col. 1:15, Vol. VIII, 337
Col. 1:18, Vol. V, 205; Vol. VIII, 337
Col. 1:20, Vol. VI, 86
Col. 1:21, 22, Vol. V, 48
Col. 1:27, Vol. I, 24
Col. 2:6, Vol. X, 63
Col. 2:9, Vol. II, 243

I Thess. 1:8, Vol. V, 233

II Thess. 2:13, Vol. VIII, 168

I Tim. 3:15, Vol. VIII, 9
I Tim. 6:5, 6, Vol. VI, 234
I Tim. 6:12, Vol. II, 11

II Tim. 1:10, Vol. V, 100
II Tim. 2:8, Vol. IX, 203
II Tim. 3:2-5, Vol. V, 299
II Tim. 4:22, Vol. IV, 269

Heb. 2:3, Vol. VIII, 141
Heb. 3:7-8, Vol. VII, 300
Heb. 3:13, Vol. II, 255
Heb. 7:26, Vol. IX, 232
Heb. 9:14, Vol. VI, 75
Heb. 9:28, Vol. I, 339
Heb. 10:14, Vol. VIII, 21
Heb. 11:1, Vol. IV, 294
Heb. 11:6, Vol. X, 139
Heb. 11:10, Vol. V, 167
Heb. 12:1, 2, Vol. III, 116
Heb. 12:27, Vol. IX, 246
Heb. 13:8, Vol. IX, 65
Heb. 13:10, Vol. VIII, 246
Heb. 13:13, Vol. V, 179
Heb. 13:14, Vol. V, 153
Heb. 13:17, Vol. VI, 260

James 1:15, Vol. II, 64
James 3:17, Vol. V, 9

I Peter 1:2, Vol. VIII, 168
I Peter 1:3, Vol. VIII, 100
I Peter 1:3-5, Vol. X, 77

II Peter 3:18, Vol. IV, 269

I John 1:3, Vol. V, 60
I John 3:2, Vol. VII, 246
I John 3:4, Vol. II, 64
I John 3:5, Vol. I, 312
I John 3:8, Vol. I, 298

Jude 21, Vol. IV, 243

Rev. 1:9, Vol. IX, 257
Rev. 3:20, Vol. VI, 23
Rev. 19:16, Vol. V, 247
Rev. 22:21, Vol. IV, 269

www.ingramcontent.com/pod-product-compliance
Lightning Source LLC
Chambersburg PA
CBHW052143300426
44115CB00011B/1496